Acknowledgments

To pass on the spirit and essence of aloha, that has been the purpose of this book. We have done our best, at times when only our commitment led us on. Loving Hawaii as we do, we hope to pass the best of it on to you.

Many people contributed their aloha to this project and we wish to thank each and every one for their kokua. We love you all!

A big thanks to Bill Fong and Leo Gonzales for their wonderful designs. Without their expertise, this would not have become such a beautiful book. Thanks, also, to the Bishop Museum for their assistance on the historical portions of the book; and to Mark Bernstein for his invaluable advice; and to Herb Kane, Robert Lyn Nelson and Andrea Smith for allowing the use of their artistic work.

We also wish to thank Allan Cahan, of Columbia Broadcasting Systems and Charles Johnson, Jerri Char, Pua McGuire of Universal Studios, who allowed us to be the first Hawaii publishers on the Magnum P.I. set; and, the wonderful comments for the book made by Tom Selleck, John Hillerman, Larry Manetti and Roger Mosely. Thanks also to Charo for the special interview, and Kjell Rasten for making it possible; and to Don Ho for his willingness to reminisce.

Of course, it couldn't have been done without the help of Teresa Garbe, Julie Zimmerman, Gary Tanimitsu and Christopher DeWinter.

And, a special thanks to those people who helped us with their continued support, not because it was in their interest, but mostly just because they care: Mary Anne and Sandy Flint, Shannon Stewart, Deborah Greene, Paula Mantel, Jeff Reiss, Thomas Fetzek, Ellen DePover and Carla Beachcomber. Our son, Aron Suzuki, deserves a big note of thanks for his patience during the long hours he had to do without us.

Mahalo a nui loa!

ISBN # 0-934997-00-4
Library of Congress # 85-061611
© Copyright 1986 by Pacific Productions Inc.
All rights reserved.

Premier Edition - June, 1986

Pacific Publishing
1750 Kalakaua Avenue, Suite 3901
Honolulu, Hawaii 96826

1

Foreword

It is sometimes difficult to determine just how much the newcomer will like Hawaii. Those of us who have left friends and family to make this our home, can only attempt to explain the feeling we experience by being here. We can only hope that you will share some of this with us, and even take a little of it back home in cherished memories of your visit to paradise. The "magic" of Hawaii, we speak of, cannot be expressed more eloquently than this:

"No . . . land in all the world has any deep strong charm for me but that one; no other land could so longingly and beseechingly haunt me sleeping and waking, through half a life-time, as that one has done. Other things leave me but it abides; other things change but it remains the same. For me its balmy airs are always blowing, its summer seas flashing in the sun; the pulsing of its surf-beat is in my ear; I can see its garlanded crags; its leaping cascades; its plumy palms drowsing by the shore; its remote summits floating like islands above the cloud rack; I can feel the spirit of its woodland solitudes; I can hear the splash of its brooks; in my nostrils still lives the breath of flowers that perished twenty years ago."

—Mark Twain

Contents

THE HAWAIIAN ISLANDS

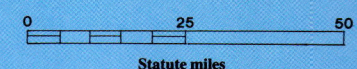

Kaulakahi Channel

KAUAI

NIIHAU

Kauai Channel

OAHU

Kaiwi Channel

MOLOKAI

Pailolo Channel

MAUI

LANAI

KAHOOLAWE

Alenoihaha Channel

HAWAII

Hawaii—A Tropical Paradise

Soft warm breezes, beautiful white sand beaches, exciting coral reefs surrounded by crystal clear, warm waters—just what you would expect in a tropical paradise. That's the one overriding reason over five million visitors choose to spend some of their vacation time in Hawaii each year.

Arriving in Hawaii, you're sure to notice the outstanding beauty and contrast of this small chain of islands almost in the center of the Northern Pacific Ocean. After flying several thousand miles over the water, you'll notice the color of the ocean change from a deep rich blue to the inviting turquoise as you draw near to Hawaii's shores. The natural lush greenery of the hills is a remarkable contrast to the imposing skyline of Honolulu and Waikiki. Though these areas appear to be densely populated, most of the land in the various islands is much more sparsely settled. The hotels that so dramatically punctuate the skyline provide some of the accommodation for many of Hawaii's visitors, with a strong sense of aloha and welcome. The people that live here in Hawaii, with their many different nationalities, truly welcome you to these islands. They hope that you will enjoy your time here and leave with wonderful memories of the best vacation of your life.

Many visitors discover a great deal more than the outstanding natural beauty of the islands. They discover that Hawaii has a rich history, as deep and fascinating as a slice of history from anywhere in the world. From its volcanic origins millions of years ago, to our present day ethnic melting pot, Hawaii has developed in a way that is both romantic and natural; progressive, yet with a respectful eye on tradition.

Unique in their isolation from other landmasses, the Hawaiian islands have fostered the development of many different plants, birds and other species found nowhere else in the world. Human development too, is taking place where Eastern, Western and Polynesian cultures are meeting and adapting to the rapidly changing needs of the world. These islands have a magical quality about them that goes hand in hand with the vital pulse of the waves breaking on Hawaii's shores. Although they may be geologically young, their cultural background spans many centuries of Polynesian history.

Creation Out of Pele's Fire

Wherever you step in Hawaii, you'll be walking on volcanic rock. The chain of islands that we call Hawaii includes 132 scattered islands, shoals and other half submerged land areas. Each of these has its origins in the darkness of the deep Pacific Ocean.

The major continents of the planet were established around several 100 million years ago, so the Hawaiian islands are clearly youngsters in the geologic time frame. When dinosaurs were maintaining their early vigil throughout the major landmasses, these islands were in the process of creation, still unfit for habitation.

As recently as 25 million years ago (a short time in geologic history), magma began to spill out through vents in the earth's thin crust. The surrounding sea water boiled with the heat. Starting at nearly three miles below sea level, shield volcanoes built up, layer by layer, until many of them burst into the sunlight amid clouds of steam, smoke and ash. The vents, or hot spots, have remained in the same place, while due to geological phenomena, the earth's tectonic plates have moved the islands northwest at a rate of about three inches per year, stringing a necklace of magical landforms for 1600 miles, the distance from Los Angeles to Louisiana. Out of the fire and steam were born the major islands that you now see. Some volcanoes, such as Mauna Kea and Mauna Loa, continued to grow skyward until they tower almost 14,000 feet above sea level. From the seafloor just 45 miles away, these huge mountains rise a total of almost six miles, making them the tallest continuous peaks on the planet. The process continues, as the youngest island, called Hawaii or the Big Island, still erupts at the fiery

Kilauea and Mauna Loa volcanoes. And more islands are on the way. Scientists report that a future island, called Loihi, is growing from the ocean floor and may break the surface south of the Big Island in the near future. Don't hold your breath though—the near future in nature's terms is still several thousand years away.

After the volcanoes boomed into sunlight, the islands formed more gently and gradually. Rain, winds and the other surface forces of Mother Nature have eroded and modified the stark volcanic outcroppings. What is left are shallows, more gently sloping areas formed as sand, gravel and soil washed down from the mountains. Even the Ice Age played a significant part. A 28 square mile glacier sat atop Mauna Kea helping to crush the lava into soil, and leaving smoothed slopes that now provide a haven for Hawaii's tropical skiers during the annual white season.

Meanwhile, what comes up can go back down. The older islands, submitting to the intense and continuous forces of weather, tsunamis (tidal waves) and gravity, have tended to subside and

A Different View of Diamond Head

They thought they had struck it rich. Back in the early 1800's, a group of British sailors were exploring Diamond Head crater, when they looked down and spied what they thought were diamonds. "We're rich!," they surely cried and word spread quickly of the diamonds on the crater.

Word spread quickly to King Kamehameha too, who immediately declared the crater kapu (off limits) until his European advisor informed him that the "diamonds" were actually worthless calcite crystals. But the name stuck, and the crater became known as Diamond Head, and is probably the most recognizable

landmark of all Hawaii today.

It's a crater that's 300,000 years old and 760 feet high, commanding a breathtaking view of Honolulu from its summit. Its original Hawaiian name was "Leahi" or "Brow of the Ahi" (Tuna) and at one time was a religious site infamous for human sacrifices.

Today, there are no diamonds on Diamond Head, and of course no human sacrifices either. The only thing remotely close to these tales of old is the ocean front real estate, close to the crater, worth its weight in diamonds, and the people who would literally kill for a Diamond Head address today.

wear away. Awesome valley walls, cliffs falling majestically to the sea and the spectacular waterfalls of Kauai, Oahu, Molokai, Maui and Hawaii were also formed during the erosion process.

Even now, beneath the tremendous weight of these individual mountains sinking into the earth's thin crust, a trench is being formed around the islands. Some of the earlier islands have submerged to about 3,000 feet below the surface of the blue Pacific. Others have been reduced to small atolls and ragged reefbanks inhabited only by birds and sea life.

Oahu was formed about 5 million years ago from two huge volcanoes—the Waianae and Koolau. The tuff cones of Diamond Head, Punchbowl and Koko Head craters represent subsequent, last gasp, eruptions. Only on the big island of Hawaii are volcanoes still active. With time and the

old Hawaiian goddess of fire, Pele, on your side, you could get to experience the birth of new material in one of Kilauea's frequent outbursts.

Located on the Big Island of Hawaii in the Volcanoes National Park are two of the world's most active and impressive volcanoes, Kilauea and Mauna Loa. If you measure these monoliths from the ocean floor to the summit, Mauna Loa, at 32,000 feet is the greatest volcanic mass on the earth. Kilauea emerges only 10,000 feet behind in height.

These two volcanoes are still considered to be young. In the last 200 years since records have been kept of their activities, they have covered jointly some 198,000 acres of land with lava. Huge reservoirs of lava accumulate beneath their surfaces in magma chambers building pressure over months or even years, until the magma finally begins to rise. This upward movement is often heralded by relatively small earthquakes and tremors. Once the pressure has found a means of escape, there are sometimes spectacular eruptions to witness. Fountains of molten lava burst hundreds of feet into the air, cinder cones may emerge, and occasionally a lava dome may rise that is breathtaking to observe. In past years, huge lakes of lava could be witnessed rising and falling inside the crater walls; an awesome sight for those fortunate enough to observe such an event. It is best to keep in mind that Hawaii's active volcanoes are "gentle" when compared with those on the continents and around the Pacific ocean rim. The reason is that they usually erupt before explosive pressure has built up. Three other volcanoes, Haleakala on Maui and Mauna Kea and Hualalai on the Big Island, are down but not out; classified as dormant, but not extinct, since their last eruptions almost 200 years ago.

Distance makes for splendid isolation. The nearest continental landmass is at least 2,100 miles

away; the nearest island grouping is over 700 miles from Hawaii. Such isolation allowed Hawaii to remain untouched, except for early plant and animal life, until the first human settlers arrived.

Life Comes to Hawaii

The Hawaiian *kumulipo,* or creation chant, tells of Hawaii's first travelers. They did not wait until the volcanoes were extinct and the building was complete. They came anyway, by sea and air from Asia, America and other Polynesian Islands just as today's visitors do. Some swam, some floated, and some flew. Some came along for the ride. There were whales, dolphins, fishes, algae, mosses, grasses, and winged creatures. There were seeds, insects, crabs, barnacles, and birds. What they found was a great ecologic diversity— from the dry crater of Haleakala to the drenching rains of Kauai—everything from fire to ice.

As the immigrants adapted, they created even more diversity. Some 1,500 unique plants have developed from an estimated 275 species. Cacti share the islands with orchids; bamboo with bananas. And busily sharing everything are about 7,000 species of insects. Happily for the human population arriving much later, about 98 percent of the native insects are endemic (located in one small geographic area). Of the original birds, most evolved in the dense forest areas, while others adapted in the marshes, tidal areas or coral atolls. An interesting adaptor is the state bird, the nene (nay-nay), or Hawaiian goose. Nenes can exist in desolate lava fields, far from fresh water supplies.

The earliest mammals to settle in or around Hawaii were probably the dolphins, whales and monk seals, who easily adapted to the newly created island environment. Hunting by later human settlers forced the monk seal to leave the main island coastlines to seek refuge on the Northwestern coral atolls of Hawaii's earlier islands.

The process of establishment for both plant and winged life was invariably slow, but once established, species multiplied and developed rapidly. This crucible of evolution would likely have fascinated Charles Darwin more than the Galapagos Islands. Similar dramatic developments have also taken place within the bird and insect world, with hundreds of new species evolving from just a few original settlers. Very few of those early colonists continue to exist in their original form.

Now the stage was set. Some of Hawaii's first mammals had appeared. Others were waiting in the wings. The main act did not follow until much later. Mankind was on its way.

The Golden Plover and Settlement

What prompted the Polynesians to leave the safety of their homes and sail upon the unknown seas? How many canoes were lost? Were the survivors lucky? The Polynesians were skilled navigators, voyaging across distances of over 1,000 miles in their well crafted double canoes. long before Columbus discovered America. Most likely, they made skillful use of passing porpoises and birds, drifting seeds and coconuts, winds and, especially, the stars.

One sign in particular encouraged these adventurous sailors to search for other islands. A small bird common to arctic North America—the

golden plover. In it's migratory travels, the golden plover searches the skies and ocean for warmer climes after completion of nesting in the arctic regions. Intuitively, in its journey through the Marquesas, Tahiti and New Zealand, this small bird made several rest stops at many islands along its path, including Hawaii. Knowledge of its migratory habits probably led the early Polynesians to suspect that their search for new islands was not over. Observing the fragile plover's flight track prompted them to turn north toward Hawaii, first from the Marquesas, and then from Tahiti.

Ancestors of the Polynesians are thought to have originated in S.E. Asia, traveling down the coast of Asia to Indonesia and onward through New Guinea and Tonga toward Tahiti and the Marquesas. Backing this point, the Hawaiian language has its roots in Indonesia, and dialect links between Tahiti and Hawaii cannot be ignored.

The first settlers arrived from the Marquesas about 1500 years ago, landing on the southern tip of the island of Hawaii. After the first voyage to Hawaii, later trips must have been easier, for the Polynesians were excellent navigators, and sure to notice that the star Arcturus, with its noted bright redness, passed over the island of Kauai during that era. The star Sirius, passing directly over Tahiti, was ready to guide them home again. The second major wave of voyagers arrived almost 600 years later from Tahiti, and it was the Tahitians who aptly named the volcanic islands Hawai'ia— "Burning Hawaii." They probably took control over the original islanders by force, driving them north through the island chain until they were either enslaved or destroyed.

Polynesian Cultural Center

Kamehameha Highway
Laie 96762
(808) 293-3333 or 923-2911
(800) 367-7060 (outside Hawaii)

Your family can experience the charm and beauty of seven South Pacific island societies in a single day, just an hour's drive from Waikiki, at the Polynesian Cultural Center on Oahu's beautiful North Shore.

Authentically recreated villages, set against a backdrop of tropical foliage, a peaceful lagoon and a clear blue sky, showcase the ancient lifestyles of Tahiti, Fiji, the Marquesas, Samoa, New Zealand Maoris, and, of course, the unforgettable islands of Hawaii.

Visitors can explore these villages representing the far flung islands of Polynesia by walking at their leisure, aboard the tram shuttle or taking a canoe tour. Walking through the center's beautifully landscaped grounds, you will meet friendly islanders in each village who explain intriguing demonstrations such as the making of *ngatu* or tapa cloth from the inner bark of the mulberry plant in Tonga, climbing a coconut tree and then husking and opening the fruit in Samoa, and pounding boiled taro roots into poi in Hawaii.

The frequent tram shuttle service around the center, with brief narration by knowledgeable guides, is available throughout the day to transport you to and from the entrance and villages.

Canoe tours, leaving from landings near Tonga and Tahiti, will take you on a 15-minute voyage down a winding waterway fed by natural artesian wells. Highlights of these tours include viewing a Maori *waka taua,* or 40-man canoe originally carved for King George V of England, and passing under the unusual *niu kapakahi,* a coconut tree that stretches and winds for 75 feet but is only 15-feet high.

All the villagers at the Polynesian Cultural Center are eager to share the arts and crafts, games, food, music and dances unique to their own islands. They'll also teach the *malahini,* or newcomer, words of greeting and other phrases in their languages, which are quite similar to each other, though not necessarily mutually intelligible.

In fact, there's something to please all the senses at the center, including the Gateway, offering a delicious Polynesian food dinner buffet. Souvenir and gift items can be selected from Shop Polynesia, the curio shop, or browse among the handicrafts in the quaint marketplace, Hale Kuai.

Each day's program at the Center is accented with exciting shows and special programs that highlight the music and dances of the South Pacific. The Polynesian Cultural Center is not only the most popular, paid-admission visitor attraction in the islands, it is also dedicated to helping preserve the cultural heritage of Polynesia.

For further information in Hawaii, contact their office in Waikiki. The Center is open Monday through Saturday (except for Christmas Day).

Perhaps some of the Marquesans or the Tahitians returned in time, for they eventually carried to the islands many of their daily necessities for sustaining life in the new land; pigs, dogs, chickens and plants such as breadfruit, taro and mulberry.

Imagine the first visitors arriving on these totally unspoiled shores, untouched and unvisited by any animals larger than a small bat originally from the Americas or the monk seals. On their arrival, they would have found around 100 species of birds and 1,200 plant varieties that were confined to small areas of Hawaii. This idyllic view was about to end. The winds of change had arrived—with their imported plants and animals, many of Hawaii's own endemic species would become endangered, if not extinct, from this outside competition.

In years to come, the pattern started by these early settlers continued. New varieties and species were introduced, while older varieties and species have become displaced by the newcomers. Hawaii's balmy climate encourages rich growth and invariably, Hawaii's endemic plants have been displaced through lack of resistance to the newcomers. Although it was some time before the worst effects of newly introduced diseases and pests wreaked havoc in Hawaii, the delicately balanced ecosystem had already been upset.

So the next time you eat a banana, mango, pineapple, papaya or any other of the so-called Hawaiian fruits, or stop to admire a plumeria, orchid or anthurium, remember that they are relative newcomers to Hawaii. Welcome newcomers that have added great variety to the "new" Hawaii.

Incredible Island Flowers and Edible Island Fruit

When it comes to fruits and flowers, Hawaii's got the pick of the crop! The fruits you'll find on supermarket shelves, roadside stands or those you see growing beside the road are a good representation of the many ethnic strains that have come together in Hawaii.

Those strange-looking trees that look somewhat prehistoric, with the fruit tightly clustered under the leaves, are probably papaya. And when you see a young man scampering up a coconut tree with machete in hand, chances are he's not going for the fruit, but to remove the danger of dropping coconuts instead!

In stores everywhere you'll find watermelon from Kahuku, pineapple from Lanai, corn from Waimanalo, onions and persimmons from Maui. Then again you might find an exotic selection, depending on the season, of avocados, guava, mountain apples, passion fruit, mangos and of course, bananas in abundance.

And then there are the marvelous flowers that dazzle you with their color and amaze you with their sweet, powerful scent. The first flowers visitors usually see are those presented in that wonderful Hawaii tradition of welcome— the lei. They'll see them on their greeters arms or at the airport lei vendor stalls. One sees ... and smells ... tuberose, pikake, plumeria, rose, ginger and a wealth of other blooming varieties.

Climbing up the hills and spilling over highway embankments, you're going to see the wildly colorful bouganvillea vines, usually accompanied with a pink or white oleander bush. Dotted on hillsides throughout Oahu you'll see a vibrant red flowering tree called the

African Tulip Tree. It's unmistakable vermilion color bursts forth like fireworks among the green hills. But don't mistake the African Tulip for the Royal Poinciana Tree, also deep scarlet color, that blooms for about six months with its most spectacular blooms occurring in the summer.

The Queen Flower Tree, when in bloom, is one of the loveliest flowering trees in the world. It's crowned with beautiful lavender blossoms clustered together at the end of long branches. Of course, one cannot forget the plastic-like anthurium flowers that Hawaii is famous for. They range in color from white, pinkish, to yellow and the familiar red.

The Bird of Paradise is another well-known tropical flower, with tall stalks that look like the neck of a bird topped by a crest. The interesting thing about these flowers is that the older they get the more colorful and lovely they become.

The Red Ginger and Torch Ginger flowers bloom year-round and are quite magnificent to see. They range in size from three to six feet, and look almost unreal with their waxen beauty

One can't forget about the State Flower of Hawaii that's seen everywhere one goes in the Islands, the red Hibiscus. There are all sizes, shapes and colors. You'll see them tucked behind ears (left or right and you'll need to know the difference!), on tables, desks and at luaus and throughout hotels everywhere. They will not wilt for a day after picking, and therein lies their popularity, along with the great variety of color.

There are some 700 species of orchids throughout Hawaii, all amazingly different in color, shape and design. Many grow wild along trails, usually with blooms that are lavender and purple, and occasionally pink, white or yellow. The plumeria is the most common lei flower in the islands. Its fragrant waxy flowers remain fresh for a long time, and range in color from white, yellow and pink to cerise.

Wherever you go in Hawaii, you're going to be surrounded and enthralled with the massive amount of green vegetation sprinkled throughout with a riot of colorful flowers. The fruits will tempt you with their wide, varied selection and succulent sweetness, either eaten raw or in some delightful dessert concoction. And you just won't feel quite right unless you have one of those marvelous flowering leis strung around your neck, competing with your camera for attention.

One last word of advice about the marvelous fruits and flowers you'll find in the islands ... your best bet is to enjoy them while you're here and not try to pack some away for snacking or smelling on the Mainland. Because when passing through agricultural inspection at the airport on your way home, you'll likely find the inspectors have an eye ... and a nose ... for finding those selected flowers and fruits whose export from Hawaii is prohibited!

Both the Marquesans and the Tahitians also brought their cultural values, beliefs and traditions to sustain their natural needs for spiritual and organizational guidance. Almost all of what we know of these early settlers and their descendants was carried from generation to generation by their *mele,* or a tradition of passing knowledge from one generation to the next using tales, chants, music and the *hula.* Using chants and storytelling, the history, skills and knowledge of physical and spiritual life of their *kupuna,* or ancestors, was carefully passed down through unwritten history and mythology. It was only with the appearance of the foreigners many years later that some of this historical and spiritual information was recorded in written form.

Hawaiian life was controlled through the extensive use of the *kapu* system. *Kapu,* meaning taboo or forbidden, was the term used to identify what was not acceptable. Such transgression often resulted in severe penalties, usually death. The *alii* (chiefs or noblemen) divinely ruled over the *makaainana* (commoners), with no crossing of blood lines which was believed to dilute their powers. Often, these tremendous powers were used to single out a specific individual or group to reinforce the power of the *alii* through *kapu.* The breakers of *kapu* were provided with a place of last resort where they could live unmolested, whatever their crime. It was only required that they reach these places of refuge before being caught by the chief's pursuing warriors. Other

Hokule'a Sails the South Seas Like the Polynesian Voyagers of Old

Back in 1976, an organization was formed in Honolulu to show how long inter-island voyages were accomplished by the Polynesians, using only the sun and stars to guide them, centuries before the Europeans came to the Pacific.

It was an ambitious undertaking, made even more demanding by the fact that this organization had to construct an ancient Polynesian canoe and sail it to Tahiti using no modern navigational equipment whatever, not even a compass.

Some historians have long claimed that the Polynesian people traveled throughout the South Pacific "by chance" ... simply by floating from island to island. They also claimed that it simply wasn't possible for these people to actually have sailed from place to place, using only the stars to guide them. This Honolulu-based organization,

called the "Hokule'a" (after the star Arturus, that passes directly over Hawaii) was going to prove these historians and anthropologists incorrect.

The Hokule'a is a 60-foot double-hulled voyaging canoe constructed entirely with the methods of boat-building that have been passed from generation to generation on some of the more remote islands of the South Pacific.

The Hokule'a group extensively investigated construction methods prior to these early voyages, ranging from simple rope construction to how the canoes themselves were carved. Their aim was to construct a canoe that looked and navigated like those of old.

The Hokule'a was to eventually prove their point by making two trips to Tahiti. And then, during 1985 and 1986, to further extend their proof of ancient travel by making a two year voyage from Hawaii to Tahiti, then from Tahiti to

the Cook Islands, and finally from the Cook Islands to New Zealand.

During the first voyage to Tahiti in 1976, the Hokule'a discovered just how difficult the trip could be. Deck space was limited: for such a long voyage to be successful, the crew must get along in crowded quarters. Unfortunately, this did not prove to be true and there was much strife and dissension between the crew members. Tempers often flared, and even though the voyage was a success, another was planned to prove that a crew could cooperate with one another, while accomplishing their mission.

This first journey was an unbelievable 3,000 mile voyage across the Pacific, without the use of navigational equipment. With only the stars above, and the sun and moon to guide them, the feat tested the skills of the navigator to extremes.

Sailing aboard a vessel like this was no fun. There's certainly nothing enjoyable about being tired, cold and wet. However, such a vessel does bring you closer to the elements as sky, wind, waves, sun and stars become your companions.

The second voyage was planned to Tahiti, but disaster struck early on during the trip. This portion of the sail ended prematurely when the canoe became swamped in the Molokai Channel. The entire crew spent nearly 24 hours in the water, clinging to the capsized craft. One of the crew members left on a surfboard to find help and was never heard from again.

The last voyage planned, "The Voyage of Rediscovery," will be a two year sail, beginning in 1985, that will lay to rest preconceived notions of early Polynesian travel. This voyage should prove that the Polynesians did indeed consciously sail from island to island, with the outcome of the voyage serving as a proud symbol to the people of the Pacific, whose ancestors were courageous ocean navigators long before America was discovered.

kapu prevented women from eating pork, bananas, coconuts and shark meat, or eating with the men. Beware if the shadow of a commoner fell upon a chief's house, or that one entered the house prior to changing his loincloth.

It is commonly assumed that the *alii* were the descendants of the gods, ancestors whose bravery and exploits grew in significance through time and *mele.* Each high ranking *alii* would divinely rule over his subjects with the assistance of the *kahuna,* or priest. The *kapu* system, although sometimes abused, served to enforce the spiritual authority of the rulers and often to ensure that the conservation systems for both land and sea were enforced.

In retrospect, it's clear that the Hawaiian culture was more highly developed than many of the early foreign visitors realized. Stepping back in time, you would, at first glance, be impressed by the Hawaiian's highly developed agrarian systems. Immaculate fields existed, with irrigation systems capable of channeling water uphill. The lush taro patches also provided breeding ponds for fish, thus fertilizing and increasing the food source. The commoners diligently worked as tenant farmers for their *alii.*

In each *ohana* (family system), bartering was unnecessary. The *"aloha"* extended to giving freely of goods and services among the *ohana.* Anger, bitterness and jealousy were considered unhealthy and were therefore avoided. Marital disputes and unwanted children were extremely rare. Whenever these did occur, strict rules provided for a solution born of tradition and the needs of the *ohana.*

The *alii,* who possessed the most distinguished lineage to the gods of old, ruled as chiefs. In reality, competing chiefs might settle the issue on the battlefield. The highest ranking *alii,* or paramount chief, ruled over each major island through the appointment of lesser chiefs who governed sections of the land.

Sacrifices were made to many of the hundreds of gods in the Hawaiian tradition. Occasionally these might be of human life, as determined by the *kahuna.* Four gods were more powerful and pervading than all of the others. They were Ku, Kane, Lono and Kanaloa.

The god of war, Ku, also had power to control rain, growth, fishing and sorcery and was often honored by human sacrifices as a prelude to war. Known as the male generating power, his images made of red feathers with mother of pearl eyes and a mouth of jagged dog's teeth (believed to utter cries during combat) were carried into battle by Kamehameha the Great and many other warring chiefs.

Kane was the god of sunlight, fresh water and forests. The leading god among the great gods, Kane was the procreator and ancestor of all the Hawaiian people, chiefs and commoners alike. Unlike Ku, he was not fond of human sacrifices. Kanaloa, the god of healing, lord of the ocean and ocean winds, was also the companion

Cook's Fleet in Kealekekua Bay

of Kane.

Worshipped as the kindly god of fertility, Lono was honored by an annual festival, the *makahiki*, which was held in November, December and January. Lono played a key role during the discovery of Hawaii by Captain James Cook in 1778.

Pele, the goddess of volcanoes, was a lesser diety with more specific responsibilities. Various lesser gods also existed for more specialized worship. Almost all of these gods were worshipped in *heiau,* or temples. All that remains in this 20th century world are several ruined *heiau* that fell into disrepair as the spiritual needs of the native Hawaiians changed in the 19th century.

Thus the culture of centuries was embodied through the *mele* for successive generations of Hawaiians. An unshakable bonding of culture and common sense, that worked successfully for centuries, was called into doubt only by the advent of the decidedly different white man's culture. It would be some time before each opposing culture would recognize and understand the differences that existed. Meanwhile, in a period of changing precepts, each culture would make decisions and take action based on a misunderstanding of the other.

The Foreigners and Their Legacy

The *poe kahiki,* "people of the past," flourished in virtual isolation for several centuries, though early Hawaiian legends tell of *haole,* "strangers of white skin." It is highly probable that, long before Captain James Cook's advent in Hawaiian history, several other European vessels had sailed through the Pacific in search of trade routes, Ptolemy's "Terre Australia," or even gold. Unfortunately, none of the foreigners who came to Hawaii in this early period, or the missionaries who followed soon after, understood or appreciated the native culture or considered any part of it worth preserving. The strange new ideas and practices eventually broke the force of the old *kapu* and weakened the control of the *alii.*

Undoubtedly, the *haole* found Hawaii, although none of them returned to their home country to tell the tale. Legends tell of a number of foreigners that arrived in Hawaii and were treated as supernatural beings. Oral traditions speak of lighter skinned strangers who proved to be great warriors and were accepted as chiefs. As later Western visitors arrived they noted the existence of many lighter skinned natives with distinctly Caucasian features.

The Spanish were making regular voyages across the Pacific between Mexico and the Philippines for over 200 years before Cook's discovery of Hawaii. It is very likely that at least one of their ships might have found Hawaii. A map seized from the Spanish in 1742 indicated the possible existence of islands where no others, except Hawaii, could have existed, though the map did not accurately show their position.

Even more interesting, one account of early visitors was attributed to William Adams in 1580. While searching for the trade routes of the Spanish, his ship found islands where only Hawaii could have existed. Eight seamen abandoned ship and were not heard from again except in the *mele* of the Hawaiians. They told of eight *malihini* or strangers who arrived and made a home on the island. On the advice of the local chief's *kahuna,* the *malihini* were treated as supernatural, and rewarded with gifts and wives. William Adams, an English navigator later landed in Japan, after his ship had been badly battered and his crew weakened. Adams became the favorite of a local Japanese lord, and more recently, the subject of the book and movie called "Shogun."

Cook, with his two ships, the Discovery and the Resolution, was sailing North in search of an artic passage from the Pacific to the Atlantic oceans. In January, 1778 Cook's fleet sighted Oahu and shortly afterwards, Kauai. The appearance of these great ships caused amazement and excitement for the natives of Kauai as the fleet anchored off Waimea. After initial cautions were overcome, trading began earnestly, with a few simple iron nails from Cook's ships buying enough food for the whole fleet for a day. The trade was clearly unequal in modern terms, but iron nails were a commodity that the natives did not possess and were highly valued, making the trade probably quite equal at that time—or even to the advantage of the Hawaiians.

Cook took the opportunity to replenish his fleet's supplies. When ashore, trading parties were always accompanied by armed guards, and the

Bishop Museum
1525 Bernice Street
Honolulu 96817
(808) 847-3511

The Bishop Museum is the cultural and natural history center of the Pacific peoples. It is a treasure house of Hawaii's former Kings and Queens and features world famous collections and exhibits of Hawaii and Oceania. The museum offers three floors of Hawaiian artifacts, including royal thrones, crowns, displays of hand made weapons and mysterious carved gods of early Hawaii. Hawaiian music and dance programs are offered, and craft demonstrations and lessons are given on quilting, lei-making of flowers or feathers and *lauhala* weaving.

Gardens and extensive grounds surround authentic turn-of-the-century architecture. In Hawaii's own Planetarium, at the "Polynesian Skies" show, you can learn how the early Polynesians navigated by the stars.

Be sure to visit the interesting gift and book store, Shop Pacifica, and nearby is the refreshing Lanai Restaurant which offers a pleasant lunch and rest stop.

This unique visitor attraction is open from 9 AM to 5 PM Monday though Saturday except Christmas, and the lst Sunday of the month. You can get there easily from Waikiki by taking the #2 School/Middle Street Bus. For the best experience of Hawaii's past, be sure to visit the Bishop Museum.

Hawaiians were about to experience their first contact with firearms. In an attempt to determinedly remove a boathook from the landing party, one of the natives was shot and killed. Although there was no attempt to cheat the visitors, the Hawaiians did regard many of these new items as very desirable and felt no guilt in openly taking what they desired. In fact, it was expected that Lono, their god of fertility, would want to supply these things. Unknown to Cook, he had arrived during the *makahiki* festival in honor of Lono, and had fulfilled the dreams of the Hawaiians by appearing as Lono was expected to appear, on two legendary islands (ships), bearing wooden crossbars (masts), supporting a white *tapa* cloth banner (sails).

Obvious even to Cook's party, the Hawaiians treated them with absolute reverence, as would be expected for any high ranking chief or god. Not so obvious to Cook and his party was the fact that they were indeed being mistaken for Lono and his retinue. After Cook's departure, word of Lono's visit spread throughout the islands. Upon the fleet's return in November of that year to further explore the islands and rest up for winter, it was not surprising that again, during the *makahiki* festival, Cook should have been honored as Lono. While off the shores of the big island, Cook was visited by Kalaniopuu, the ruling chief of the island of Hawaii, and a retinue of lower chiefs, some of whom stayed overnight on the ship. One of them was the young chief Kamehameha, a fact that was to be very important in later years. His intelligent curiosity about the ways of these foreigners was to serve him well as he later pulled his kingdom together.

The leisurely tour down the Kona coast to Kealakekua Bay may have been suggestive of the movements of Lono reviewing the *makahiki* festivities. By chance, Kealakekua Bay was very significant. Kealakekua—the pathway to God—was a sacred bay where Lono was expected to arrive. Again, Cook was arriving during the *makahiki* festivities, and consequently, was given a ceremonial welcome such as would be expected for a god. Several thousand canoes and over 10,000 people were on hand to welcome the Discovery and the Resolution as they entered Kealakekua Bay. When Cook went ashore, the many natives greeted him with respect, bowing and covering their faces until he had passed by. He was led to the *heiau* of Hikiau, where he underwent a ceremony that acknowledged him as Lono, the religious significance of which Cook was mostly unaware. The next two weeks were spent in celebration with several sacred ceremonies and the presentation of many fine gifts to Cook and his party. Cook and his party then returned these favors with tours of their vessels, other more personal gifts and a fireworks display.

After two weeks of such ceremonies, and with Cook's ships replenished, the Discovery and Resolution set sail on February 4th, 1779. North of the Big Island, they ran into a severe winter storm,

causing damage to the Resolution. Cook returned to Kealakekua Bay, where by now, the *makahiki* festival was over, use of the bay was *kapu* and the area was virtually deserted. Cook's return was a surprise to the Hawaiians, not understanding why Lono would not be able to protect himself in his own element. The incidence of petty thievery increased in frequency until on the night of February 13th, the Discovery's longboat was stolen.

Cook's response was intended to be dramatic in his own cultural fashion. Blockading the bay, he and a party of nine marines went ashore to take the chief Kalaniopuu hostage until the longboat was returned. During a violent scuffle with the Hawaiians, more and more suspicious that Cook was but a mere mortal and not Lono, Cook, several of his marines and several Hawaiians were killed. Anger continued on both sides for some time after the killing, despite the conciliatory policies of the leaders. Several days later, delegations of concerned Hawaiians returned parts of Cook's body to the remaining crew. The crew were horrified by what they saw, viewing such mutilation of the body as sacriligious within their cultural beliefs. Demanding the return of the remaining parts, it became clear that Cook's body had been dismembered in a way that suggested a religious ceremony had been performed. In fact, the chiefs had been so disturbed by the killing of Cook, that he was accorded a honorable burial under Hawaiian culture. Several days later, after burial of Cook's remains in Kealakekua Bay, the squadron left, completing their reprovisioning on Kauai before continuing the voyage.

Cook's squadron, however, had left a legacy that was to have a sad, yet profound impact on the

Hawaiians. Aware that some of his crew were carriers of venereal disease, Cook's orders forbid those who were infected from having any sexual contact with the native women. Despite his declared intention to prevent the passage of these diseases to the native population, Cook was unable to keep the two races apart. It is certain that this disease and other lesser ailments were passed on to the Hawaiians partly from Cook's crew and partly from the many later visitors, with the resulting effect in years to come of decimating the population from an estimated 300,000 in Cook's time, to 60,000 just 30 years later. In future years, the Hawaiians, with their own culture and lack of immunity to outside influences, would again receive new cultural and sometimes lethal health exposure.

It would be five years before more foreigners would arrive and many changes in Hawaii would take place before then. Kamehameha would then be the high chief of Hawaii, and with his experience in dealing with foreigners, he would use their direct or indirect support to unite the islands under one ruler. Hawaii was forever changed. Foreign vessels would visit Hawaii in increasing numbers, not only to reprovision but also in attempts to gain political influence with the Hawaiians. There would be instances of violence; trading would continue and Kamehameha would finally enlist foreign advisors in his quest to unify the islands.

The Unification of Hawaii

Kamehameha was not only a gregarious chief, but also shrewd, and he understood the benefits of the technical expertise of the foreigners. During each meeting he would be very curious and attentive, asking many questions. Very quickly he realized that foreign sailing vessels were superior to the Hawaiian craft and also that firearms could give him superiority over other chiefs. His reputation of being a warrior and a leader grew rapidly, and in fact, the Hawaiians believed that the ancient gods were on his side. He was able to use Western influences and the gods to support his powers.

Kalaniopuu, the high chief of Hawaii, was Kamehameha's uncle. Now an old man, he named his son Kiwalao as successor and Kamehameha as the guardian of the war god. Very quickly, Kiwalao and Kamehameha were in a dispute over a rebel king sacrificed by Kamehameha while Kiwalao was waiting to perform this rite.

Kalaniopuu died in 1782, and Kiwalao succeeded him. Several chiefs asked Kamehameha to lead them against the inequitable practices of Kiwalao. Open war soon broke out and Kiwalao was killed in an early battle, leaving Kamehameha in control of one of three regions. Civil war reigned during the next ten years, while an alliance formed between Kamehameha and one of the other chiefs. While on a campaign against the high chief of Maui, Keoua raided and killed Kamehameha's ally. As Keoua's party returned past the volcano, Kilauea, an eruption killed 400 of his soldiers and their dependents, giving credence to the belief that the fire goddess, Pele, was supporting Kamehameha.

After consulting his *kahuna,* Kamehameha laid a trap and through this trickery, killed Keoua, becoming the high chief of Hawaii in 1791. Kamehameha's success in getting arms, advice and recruits from the foreigners now gave him a large advantage over the other chiefs who were visited less frequently by the traders. Kamehameha now

King Kamehameha's Long Underwear

Long underwear in Hawaii? And worn by King Kamehameha in 1810? Impossible you say. And in one aspect you're correct, but in another, you're wrong. Because, it's true King Kamehameha did not actually wear long underwear, but an actor portraying him did in 1910 during the Centennial reenactment ceremony of Kamehameha's landing on Oahu in 1810.

You see, in 1910 it would have shocked the general populace to have Kamehameha's warriors come ashore for this reenactment ceremony wearing little or no clothes. So the powers that be came up with a simple solution; they dyed long underwear brown and dressed Kamehameha's warriors up in these colored union suits thereby avoiding public censure and scandal.

It must have been quite a dramatic sight to see Kamehameha's invasion fleet approaching Oahu, at the present site of the Outrigger Canoe Club, back in 1910. But drama probably turned to amusement rather quickly as the King's warriors strode from their canoes to the beach clad in their union suit finery.

Today, considering the more relaxed '80's morality, plus the rather chic reenactment site of the Outrigger Club in 1910, and considering today's penchant for designer labels, Kamehameha could only have gotten away with this underwear display in just one way. It would have had to be underwear designed by Calvin Klein.

had two advisers captured from the two American ships involved in a violent incident in February 1790. The Olowalu massacre, in which over 100 natives were slaughtered, was avenged by one of Kamehameha's chiefs who killed all the crew members of the small schooner except for one man, Isaac Davis. The other advisor, John Young, was the boatswain of a companion American ship, and happened to be ashore visiting other white men on the island. Both Davis and Young became loyal chiefs and served Kamehameha faithfully.

The high chief of Maui, who controlled Maui, Molokai, Lanai and Oahu, split his territory between his two sons at his death in 1795. During the ensuing arguments and battles between the new chiefs, resulting in the death of one of them, Kamehameha decided to make his move. Assembling an immense fleet of war canoes, Kamehameha first captured Maui, then Molokai and Lanai. After rest and recuperation, Kamehameha moved on Oahu with his fleet, and in a decisive final battle at the Nuuanu Pali, routed the opposing forces, with many of Kamehameha's enemies being forced over the *pali* (cliffs) to their death.

It was 1795, and Kamehameha was, at last, the master of all of the islands of Hawaii except for Kauai and Niihau. In 1796, and again in 1809, Kamehameha planned to invade Kauai but was unable to complete the attempts because of the dangerous waters in the channel between the islands, and later, disease, which seriously impacted his fighting force. However, the writing was on the wall, and the chief of Kauai and Niihau ceded to Kamehameha, becoming a loyal supporter of the new Kingdom of Hawaii. Kamehameha was the undisputed king of the Hawaiian Islands, and apart from one or two rebellious skirmishes, was able to focus on reinforcing the *kapu* system and the Hawaiian culture.

Dividing his lands between his loyal supporters, and relying on Governors to control each of the islands on his behalf (including John Young as the Governor of Maui), Kamehameha set about restoring the islands to prosperity after the severe neglect during the civil wars. By 1798, the islands were clearly benefiting from his direction, with famine no longer a threat, and his people much more content. Later during his reign, sandalwood became a major trading commodity with the Western ships stopping in Hawaii on their way to China. Kamehameha wisely used his trading knowledge in building up a treasury for his kingdom.

Hawaii was now taking its rightful place as an important trading nation. The Hawaiian cultural system continued to be strictly enforced using the *kapu* customs, and *heiau* were kept well maintained in support of Kamehameha's strong cultural values. Kamehameha died in 1819 at Ahu'ena, near Kailua on the island of Hawaii. His reign complete, Kamehameha would be forever respected for his achievements in uniting the islands, bringing peace to the Hawaiian people, and preparing them for the remainder of the 19th century—a century of many changes.

"Kamehameha at home, in Kailua - Kona" by Herb Kane - Amfac Collection

Commerce and the Caucasian Influence

While the later 18th century could be regarded as the period in which Western influences began to change Hawaii, the 19th century would see the Hawaiian culture turned upside down, forever weakening the hold of traditional Hawaiian values and beliefs. Though Kamehameha strictly enforced old Hawaiian customs and *kapu,* the tide had turned with ever increasing visits of foreigner for the purposes of trading and commercial gain.

The pattern of trading though those years changed frequently, often with disruptive influences on the islands. It was during Cook's visits that the value of trading furs from North America to China was discovered, and the strategic importance of Hawaii as a supply point was recognized. As early as 1785, when the first fur trading vessel arrived for provisioning the Hawaiians began to adapt to those outside influences. No longer were easy bargains made for a few scraps of iron. The Hawaiians began to realize the value of what their islands offered. The chiefs increasingly bartered for firearms to use in their local fighting. Several ships had stopped at the islands by 1787, when one of the Hawaiian chiefs, Kaiana set sail with an early fur trader. He traveled to China, then back to Alaska and Vancouver Island, before returning to be one of Kamehameha's trusted advisors. Kaiana was the first of many Hawaiians who followed that route in later years, many of whom did not return to the islands. As excellent sailors, their skills were often in demand, eventually leading to a significant reduction in the numbers of Hawaiians remaining in the islands.

Captain George Vancouver, who had been a member of Cook's original party in 1778–1779, arrived in Hawaii in 1792 with many new plants and seeds which were given to the Hawaiians. After a trip to California, Vancouver returned to Kealakekua Bay in 1793, and for the first time since Cook's death, met Kamehameha. Vancouver attempted to arrange a permanent peace with the islands. Though he was unsuccessful, he did gain a high regard for the abilities of Kamehameha and his two *haole* advisors, Davis and Young. At the end of Vancouver's third visit in 1794, a party of chiefs led by Kamehameha ceded Hawaii to the English with two conditions—the English would protect Hawaii from foreign enemies, and would not interfere with the native religion, government or customs. Although Vancouver's government did not accept this gift of Hawaii, the English now occupied a favored position with Kamehameha as he set about unifying the islands. Vancouver's visits also provided several cattle from California for the Hawaiians. With customary wisdom, Kamehameha ordered a *kapu* on slaughter of the cattle for a period of 10 years, to allow the animals to become established. The visit of Vancouver and his dealings with Kamehameha were conducted fairly, and the attention given to the high chief of Hawaii increased his stature in the eyes of his people, probably assisting in his efforts toward unification.

The discovery of sandalwood in the islands led to an initial shipment to China in 1790, although the real exploitation of this trade would not occur until the early 19th century. The trade in Hawaii also had some benefits to the Hawaiians. Ships were now frequently arriving in Hawaii on their way to and from China, or for the purpose of wintering in the islands. By 1810, the Sandalwood trade was beginning to boom. Kamehameha shrewdly controlled the cutting of sandalwood and conservatively added the revenues to his kingdom's treasury, kept in a storehouse until his death. Two vessels were purchased by the king in 1816, as his first direct venture into the sandalwood trade. With no knowledge of port and dock operations and dues, the profits from the first voyage were quickly consumed. However, Kamehameha used this new found knowledge to establish his own port and dock charges to be paid by ships visiting Honolulu, which since 1795 had become an important trading center in the islands. By 1805, Honolulu had become the center of inter-island trading also, with almost all goods being transhipped through Honolulu.

Upon Kamehameha's death in 1819, Liholiho became Kamehameha II and ruled in conjunction with Kaahumanu, the old king's powerful queen. The process of change began to accelerate, firstly with the almost immediate relaxation of many of the old customs and *kapu,* then with Liholiho's desire to expand on the sandalwood profits to be distributed around his supporters and chiefs. Liholiho began to extravagantly cut sandalwood, using the proceeds to buy foreign merchandise without thought to the future. When immediate payment was not available for the merchandise, Liholiho was encouraged by the foreign traders to use credit via promissory notes for future deliveries of sandalwood. Debts began to mount without control, to be satisfied only by working his people beyond the point of exhaustion.

By 1825, the sandalwood forests were almost decimated. Even today, all that remains of the huge forests of fragrant wood are a few isolated groves which were inaccessible for exploitation in those early years. The rapid exploitation of sandalwood had very negative effects on the population. Food production had been neglected,

Scrimshaw: The Whaling Man's Art

Ancient scrimshaw, the whaler's art of carving or engraving ivory, bone and related materials, was an inspired product. Coupled with an abundance of materials and the endless boredom of shipboard life, the sailing men of old recorded their passion for the sea and adventure on whale teeth and bones.

Between 1820 and 1860, when whaling was a booming industry in Hawaii, Lahaina (Maui) was a major whaling center, for a while over-shadowing the more populated city of Honolulu. The tall masted ships have long since left and those hearty young sailors are no more, but the memory of whaling lives on in Lahaina. In a simple stroll down Front Street you'll find many beautiful examples, and even though antique items are rare, you may find some potential heir-looms and truly unique pieces at prices far below their East Coast counterparts.

(See Lahaina Scrimshaw on page 41.) Collectors of these engravings come from all walks of life. The late President John F. Kennedy had 34 whale's teeth in his collection.

With the advent of the Endangered Species Act of 1973, which prohibited the importation of whale products into the United States, conservation-minded scrimshanders have discovered many appealing and unusual mediums upon which to pursue their craft. Fossil ivory, which is really the only truly American ivory, is by far the most popular. This material is dug out of the tundra in Alaska in the short summer months by native Eskimos. Of course, like most of the earth's riches, fossil ivory is a non-replaceable commodity and as such the material itself has increased in value considerably over the past few years.

Honolulu Harbor in the late 1800's

and in their weakened state, many health problems served to reduce the population even more.

By 1820, ships from various nations had taken to spending winters in Hawaii as well as provisioning. Although whaling vessels had been in the Pacific before the year 1800, it was 1820 before they finally reached the sperm whale fishing grounds off the coast of Japan. Naturally, Hawaii became a very convenient stepping off point for the whalers going North to Japan, and a favored wintering spot.

Between 1820 and 1880, whalers became regular visitors to the islands. As the number of whalers arriving for replenishment increased, supplies could not be found locally to support the demand. Imports rapidly increased between 1845 and 1848 to meet the needs of several hundred ships arriving each year. The effect of this trade was to dramatically increase the size of the two main centers of trade for the whalers—Honolulu and Lahaina (Maui). New stores and warehouses were built, along with other less reputable buildings that would house the leisure activities of the whaling crews while in Hawaii. Locally grown foodstuffs became very profitable and government revenues increased substantially through duties charged on imported goods and port charges collected from the shipowners. Hawaii became so important to the whaling trade, that whaling products were offloaded in Honolulu for further shipment to America.

With so many sailors in port at one time, disturbances became common. The death of one sailor in jail, in 1852, caused a riot in Honolulu resulting in the organization of a military company to support the police in restoring order.

In the earlier years of the whaler's visits, many Hawaiians left the islands as sailors. The effect was to dramatically reduce the numbers of native Hawaiians in the islands, so much so, that the government imposed restrictions on their recruitment. It was thought that almost 15,000 left, never to return, from the already depleted native population.

The advent of petroleum signalled the end for the whaling industry, providing lighting and lubricants that replaced whale products. In 1871, over 30 whaling ships were lost in the winter ice of the Bering Straits. Hawaii was now in need of new commercial activity.

The earlier influences of the western missionaries in the 1820's were to have a major impact on Hawaiian land systems in 1850. The missions had successfully infiltrated Hawaiian life and government into the 1840's, and persuaded the Hawaiian leaders to adopt a new concept of land management. Through the *Great Mahele,* land was to be divided into three categories, one third for the king, one third for the government and one third for the people of Hawaii. Under the Hawaiian system of communal land ownership, the Hawaiians had no notion of the concepts of deeds and leases. The newly enacted Western system of real estate law allowed foreigners living in Hawaii to buy property, often at ridiculously low bargain prices. Forty years before the 1893 uprising, power was already being transferred through land ownership, to the merchants, missionaries and traders.

As early as 1835, sugar was planted in Kauai, and with the distribution of land rights through the *Great Mahele,* the time was ripe for an agricultural expansion. An immigration board was formed in 1850 to encourage and oversee the import of plantation workers. The very fabric of Hawaiian society changed as several hundred thousand workers were brought to Hawaii from Japan, China, the Philippines, Korea and Portugal during the period from 1850 to well into the 20th century.

The Chinese were the first to arrive and worked hard to successfully establish themselves in Hawaii, which they did—as merchants and businessmen after they had served their required five years in the plantations. Setting a precedent that follows to the present time, there were many marriages between the Chinese and the Hawaiians. In later years, the Portuguese (1878) to be followed

by the Japanese (1886) and then the Filipinos (1910) would come to Hawaii to work the sugar and pineapple plantations. The Japanese, in particular, remained loyal to their own cultural values and developed successfuly within their own culture in Hawaii.

Sugar and pineapples eventually became the commerce to supercede whaling. With sugar being exported mainly to America, a stronger connection formed between Hawaii and the United States. In 1875, the long sought after sugar treaty with America was signed, not only providing preferential sugar tariffs, but also preventing any other foreign nation from gaining access to a strategically important harbor on Oahu—Pearl Harbor.

The 19th century had seen the transition from a native culture to a major trading center that included many different cultures. The old Hawaiian traditions were almost lost in the rapid process of change, as were the Hawaiian people, whose numbers declined dramatically through disease, exodus and interracial marriages. The monarchy had its own problems, but one point remains clear to the outside observer. Very few nations on this earth have experienced such rapid growth from native culture to territorial government in such a short span of time.

The Monarchy

At the end of Kamehameha's reign in 1819, the islands were already a "melting pot," with over 200 foreigners (English, American, Irish, Portuguese and Chinese) living in Hawaii. In a way that would continue throughout the next few decades, many of these resident foreigners were among the king's advisors. So much so, that in 1816 the Hawaiian flag represented the two predominant trading interests—the English and the Americans—a mixture of the Union Jack, and the stripes of America's flag.

Kamehameha was succeeded in 1819 by his son Liholiho as Kamehameha II. The throne held firm, although Liholiho lacked the strength of

character of his father. Kamehameha had recognized this and left his favorite queen, Kaahumanu, as the *kuhina nui*—an office as powerful as that of co-ruler. The old feudal style of government and the strict religious customs and *kapu* changed quickly. Liholiho broke the first customs by eating at a feast with his queens, and subsequently ordered the destruction of all heiau and idols. Liholiho also ordered the breaking of the *kapu* conserving young sandalwood trees and commenced the rapid exploitation of the sandalwood forests, dividing the profits among his chiefs.

At the same time several thousand miles away, the decision was being made to bring Christianity and civilization to Hawaii. Convinced by reports of Hawaii's condition from previous visitors, the Board of Commissioners for Foreign Missions, in Boston, decided to send missionaries to Hawaii. Amongst the first party to arrive was the son of the chief of Kauai, who had spent some time with the missionaries in Boston prior to their departure.

With the spiritual void that now existed, the task of the first missionaries was made very easy. Without understanding the cultural values of the Hawaiians, the missionaries were determined to rescue the "heathens" from their uncivilized existence. The end of 1820 saw schools in place with over 100 pupils from noble families learning of Christian philosophy. Within a few short years, native teachers had been trained along with several thousand students and for the first time ever, the Hawaiian language was reduced to written form. The first Christian house of worship was established in 1822 on the site where the present Kawaiahao Church now stands in Honolulu.

Liholiho revived the old customs of traveling around his kingdom. Like his father, he also considered Hawaii to be under the protection of England. After receiving the gift of a small sailing schooner from King George, he decided to go to England to meet the royal family and negotiate a defense treaty. Kaahumanu remained in Hawaii as ruler in his absence. Sadly, in 1824, with no immunity from many Western diseases, he and many of his party contracted measles and died shortly after their arrival in London, before ever meeting King George IV.

Kaahumanu continued as *kuhina nui* during the early years of Kamehameha III's reign. Only 10 years old at the time of his brother's death, he eventually became the longest reigning Hawaiian monarch (from 1825 to 1854). Kaahumanu had been friendly with the missionaries since their arrival in 1820, however, conversion of the natives was not a hurried process. It was 1824 before an important chiefess, Kapiolani, publicly rejected her old gods and adopted Jehovah. She descended into the volcano, Kilauea, to defy the wrath of Pele, the goddess of fire. Kaahumanu began to actively promote the movement in 1824 and after learning of Liholiho's death in 1825, proclaimed a code of laws based upon missionary teachings. They prohibited murder, theft, fighting and Sabbath-breaking. Other laws were added later, as a result of the influence of the missionaries on the monarchy. The hula was denounced as being lewd and nudity was condemned, giving rise to the form of dress known today as the *"muumuu."*

On Kaahumanu's death in 1832, Kamehameha III proceeded to open the court to a reign of decadence derived from the traits of some of the foreigners—drinking, gambling and horse racing. To the displeasure of the missionaries, even the hula was permitted. During this time, affairs of state were handled by Kaahumanu's successor as *kuhina nui*—Elizabeth Kinau (Kaahumanu II). The missionaries consolidated their political power through Kinau, until, by the time of her death in 1839, many influential advisory and cabinet posts in the Hawaiian administration were occupied by the missionaries and merchant friends.

Hawaii's first Declaration of rights was proclaimed in 1839, followed in 1840 by the first constitution, establishing an upper ruling house (royalty) and a lower representatives house (commoners), and providing the first legal access to the country's power structure for the people of Hawaii. The legislature did not convene until 1845, but the decline in the powers of the *alii* was now official.

The social and political fiber of the kingdom was further tested by European military ultimatums. For a period of 6 months in 1843, the islands were taken over by an overzealous British officer who misunderstood his country's foreign policy. During a ceremony restoring his kingdom, King Kamehameha III spoke the words that later became the State of Hawaii's motto: *"Ua mau ke ea o ka aina i ka pono"*—the life of the land is preserved in righteousness. Again the kingdom endured another assault on its dignity when, in 1849, a French rear admiral demanded concessions from the King. His demands not met, he sacked the fort and the governor's home, and then stole the royal yacht.

At the urging of foreign advisors, the Hawaiian lands were divided into three parts— one third for the king, one third for the government and one third for the Hawaiian people, who until then had no knowledge or interest in land ownership. A seemingly innocuous change in the law, allowed foreigners to buy property outright. Both missionaries and merchants immediately began to purchase land, either for the "gospel" or sugar cane, at bargain basement prices. By 1886, after this series of events called the *Great Mahele,* two thirds of all government land had been purchased by the *haole.* In a very short period of time, the majority of the land was under new ownership and demands for labor to support the cultivation of sugar cane resulted in the formation of a bureau to encourage immigration of outside workers—the beginning of Hawaii's multi-ethnic population.

By 1854 the islands were deeply involved in economic transition. At the death of his uncle in 1854, Kamehameha IV stepped into the limelight, with a dislike for Americans that stemmed in part from his childhood visit to America. These anti-American feelings did not endear him to the merchants and plantation owners, who were still unsure whether their newly acquired land gains would remain in their possession should Hawaii's politics change. Even then, calls for American annexation of the islands were being heard.

His elder brother, Lot Kamehameha V, came to power in 1863, determined to correct the liberalization of Hawaii, return power to the

throne and bring back much of the old culture. Refusing to uphold the old constitution, he set up a convention in 1864 to revise and bring it more into line with his own values. After a month of indecision, the king abrogated the constitution and reduced voting rights, all with the express intention of strengthening the powers of the monarchy. This 1864 constitution abolished the office of *kuhina nui,* established a one chamber legislature and required literacy tests for anyone born after 1849, before they would be allowed voting rights. Two attempts to obtain a reciprocal trade agreement with the United States both failed due to timing. Kamehameha V died without a successor, though his constitution did allow for the election of a native *alii* to be Hawaii's new ruler.

After an election campaign like many others, Prince Lunalilo was chosen as successor, but he died 13 months later. During that short time, some of his advisors suggested that he use the Pearl River (later to be Pearl Harbor) as a bargaining chip in the negotiation of a trade reciprocity agreement with the United States. This strategy was not implemented because of public opposition. At about the same time, the United States sent over two generals, ostensibly on vacation, but secretly to collect information on the defensive capabilities of the Hawaiian islands.

Again, a royal election, with David Kalakaua becoming the new ruler in 1874. Kalakaua chose to live royally in the style of Western Monarchs, spending his taxpayers money just as royally. He built a new palace, became the first monarch to travel around the world and crowned himself and his queen at Hawaii's first coronation in 1883. He did succeed where several previous kings had tried but failed. During his visit to the United States, a reciprocal trade agreement was signed to the joy of the plantation owners. The cost? The Hawaiian government would not allow any port or harbor to be used by any other nation. The United States thus assured itself of the availability of Pearl Harbor at a later date. The treaty, however, rewarded and encouraged the plantation owners who began to excercise more leverage in the control of Hawaii.

After a series of scandals and blunders, the *haole* and Hawaiian community, mainly plantation owners, merchants and businessmen, openly revolted with an armed insurrection and forced a new constitution on the king. The Bayonet Constitution of 1887 substantially reduced his executive powers, and forced the replacement of his prime minister. The constitution that resulted effectively made the king a figurehead. The revolutionary Reform Party renegotiated the reciprocity treaty with the United States, giving away the exclusive right to the use of Pearl Harbor.

The point had been reached where the executive powers of the monarchy had been contained, with that power now resting with the major landowners. The resultant effects of the *Great Mahele* of 1848 were now obvious—power went with land ownership. In the space of just 80 short years, Hawaii had moved from a strictly enforced, feudal, native culture to a vibrant trading nation run by a government of a choice selection of the people. The monarchy was not yet extinct, but despite a few late kicks, it was only a matter of time.

Transition from Monarchy to Territory

The monarchy would not lie down and die, and the revolutionaries did not yet have what they wanted. Between 1887 and 1891, several revolutionary schemes were hatched on both sides, to either restore the full power of the monarchy via the 1864 constitution, or to replace the king with his supposedly more pliant sister, Princess Liliuokalani. Nature took its own course, and during a rest and recuperation visit to San Francisco in 1891, Kalakaua, the king who tied Hawaii inexorably to the United States, died.

Queen. Both artistic and disciplined, she believed Kalakaua had acted weakly during the 1887 revolution, and was opposed to the Pearl Harbor clause in the reciprocal trade agreement with the United States. Although severly hampered by the Bayonet Constitution, Liliuokalani shrewdly used a good sense of timing and careful planning to vote out the Reform Party cabinet and to vote in her own. Once in power, she intended to reinstate a constitution similar to that of 1864. Her plan failed, when the cabinet, although favorable to the Queen, refused to sign the proclamation into being. Their fears of revolution were well founded. The Reform Party was understandably ill disposed to such a plan, and at this point believed that Liliuokalani could no longer be trusted and must be removed.

On January 17th, 1893 the monarchy was proclaimed defunct, as the revolutionaries took possession of the government building and established a provisional government. An annexation treaty was presented to the U.S. Senate in February 1893, but no action was taken until the Presidency changed in March 1893. The new president withdrew the treaty and attempted to support and negotiate a return to the monarchy with Hawaii's provisional government. Possession being a very strong point of power, the provisional government did not accede to the request, and the attempt to reinstate the monarchy failed.

With a new constitution modeled after those in the U.S., France, and England, the provisional government proclaimed the Hawaiian Republic. An armed insurrection planned by Liliuokalani's followers in 1895 was discovered and routed with many participants placed under arrest. While awaiting a military trial, Liliuokalani formally abdicated the throne and pledged her allegiance to the republic. The monarchy was now officially ended.

The Spanish-American War of 1897 provided a new opportunity for the Republic of Hawaii to petition the U.S. government for annexation. By allowing and encouraging the use of the harbors and facilities of Hawaii, in support of the U.S. Navy and troops during the Pacific operations, Hawaii earned the respect of both houses of the U.S. government and annexation was duly approved. Hawaii officially became a United States territory on August 12th, 1898. No radical change in government was involved as a result of annexation. The final step in the annexation process was the implementation of an acceptable constitution for Hawaii. Implemented in April 1900, the Organic Act provided for all citizens of Hawaii to automatically become citizens of the United States. All male citizens over 21, without property restriction, were allowed to vote, as long as they could speak, read or write in English or the Hawaiian language.

As Hawaii took its place as a territory, it settled more or less happily under the American wing (depending on whether you consulted the Hawaiians or nouveau Hawaiians). By 1900, the

the foreigner's diseases, the native population had declined 80% since Captain Cook's visit, and declined further still as a result of mixed marriages and migration.

The Trend Toward Democracy

The relatively recent history of Hawaii is punctuated by incidents that can only serve to highlight Hawaii's development as a strategic outpost and full scale democracy. Few areas in the world can show such a dramatic growth in production, income and employment in such a short period of time.

After annexation in 1898, the military wasted no time in planning and building the necessary military installations to support the needs of both the army and navy. The largest military post in the United States was established at Schofield Barracks. Pearl Harbor was fully operational as a naval base by 1919, complete with full drydocking and repair facilities. Joint army and navy maneuvers in 1925 were designed to test the strength of the island defenses.

The plantations were still king in the field of industry. Employment in the sugar cane industry reached a peak in 1932. Pineapples became Hawaii's second most lucrative industry by the year 1920. Immigration of plantation workers continued through this period, with the Japanese making up the largest number, followed closely by the Caucasian nationalities. The population of Hawaii increased from 140,000 at the turn of the century to over 1,000,000 in the 1980's.

Communications have rapidly changed through this century. The first cable connection to the mainland U.S.A. was brought ashore in 1902. The first non-stop flights from California to Hawaii were made by amphibious aircraft of the U.S. Army in 1927, and the first commercial passenger flight via Pan American Airways' Clipper service arrived in November 1935 after a 20 hour flight. Flights between the Hawaiian islands commenced in 1929 with a company called Inter-Island Airways, still in business today as Hawaiian Air.

Unionization by immigrant workers became more prevalent throughout this century. Reacting to poor working conditions and low wages, two major confrontations between workers and the law enforcement agencies occurred—one in 1924 on Kauai, where Filipino workers rioted in protest against conditions and pay. Several strikers and policemen were killed before the riot was finally subdued. The "Hilo Massacre" of 1938 did not result in death, but over 50 strikers were injured when a group of them were attacked by armed police in Hilo, Hawaii.

December 7, 1941 is a day that shook the United States out of its complacency, with the undeclared entry of Japan into World War II. Pearl Harbor naval and air forces were virtually decimated in the surprise attack from the carrier borne forces of the Japanese. A state of martial law

was declared throughout Hawaii which continued until late 1944. The military coordinated all government functions during this period, including courts, garbage disposal and health facilities. At the time of the Pearl Harbor attack, some 160,000 Japanese immigrants or American-Japanese descendants lived in Hawaii. Unlike the mainland U.S.A., it was not feasible to place Hawaii's Japanese population under guard, as they comprised almost one third of Hawaii's civilian population. Secondly, for many of the "nisei" (American-born) and "issei" (first generation immigrants), America was their country. After fears of "fifth column" sabotage proved unfounded, a special Infantry Battalion, the 100th,

"President Roosevelt … Your Party's on the Line"

Sunday morning, December 7, 1941, seemed like just another day for Charles F. Penhallow, an operator for Hawaiian Telephone Company. His job was to man the radio-telegraph line from Honolulu to the Mainland, placing calls back and forth between interested parties. Technology at the time demanded that the operator monitor all conversations so he could activate the "Talk or Listen" switch so a conversation could flow uninterrupted and make sense.

About 8:30 a.m., this young operator suddenly had a rather strange request. It was Territorial Governor T.G. Poindexter urgently asking for a connection to Washington D.C. to a certain "President

Franklin D. Roosevelt."

Quite efficiently, the operator placed the call. And quite naturally, he also listened in. Because not only was it his job … but he was also an interested, if not curious, party.

That's when this young telephone operator heard the familiar voice of FDR come on the line. But more than that, he also heard the President of the United States receive the news of Pearl Harbor for the very first time.

The conversation was sensitive. The tone was highly animated. And even though the call ran long, there was one thing this greenhorn operator knew better than to do: and that was to not ask the party in Washington to "deposit another dime."

consisting of about 1,300 American-Japanese recruits was formed. This group was to become a part of the 442nd Regimental Combat Team, referred to as the "most decorated unit in United States military history." A total of 16,000 American-Japanese of Hawaii served during World War II.

Throughout World War II, Hawaii was at the forefront of the conflict—the main staging area for the long Pacific War, with hundreds of thousands of service men and women passing through Hawaii in both directions. The episode showed Hawaii's strengths and its close links with America. At the end of the war, Hawaii was an integral part of the United states lacking only the title of "state." That would soon change.

Hawaii Comes of Age

As early as 1849, the idea of statehood for Hawaii was in circulation in the United States and Hawaii. Had the proposal been formally made to the people of Hawaii at that time, it would have been rejected. But times change. By the end of the 19th century, statehood had a greater popularity, and the annexation in the year 1898, followed by the Organic Act, in the year 1900, were the first of many official attempts to have Hawaii admitted as a full State within the United States.

Throughout the period between World War I and II, several attempts to legislate statehood were made in Congress. In almost every case, very little priority was given to the proposal. The year 1935 brought a more interested response, and an investigative sub-committee recommended, by majority vote, that further study would be required before a conclusive recommendation could be made. By 1937, further investigation recommended "sympathetic consideration" of the statehood proposal. World War II intervened, with all considerations put on hold until the war was over in

1945. Hawaii's direct involvement with the United States during the long war years was to have a very positive impact on the acceptability of the statehood proposal, although it would still be 13 long years before statehood was approved by Congress, the Senate and Hawaii.

Political changes were also occurring in a different arena. Although the period prior to World War II did not provide the environment for equitable labor representation, the ILWU succeeded in establishing itself in 1946 with a successful protracted strike against the sugar industry. Combined with the success of many small businesses during the war, a new center of political power was developing, away from the traditional Republican viewpoint. The politics of Hawaii inexorably moved more to the left, with the election of democratic Governor Ariyoshi in 1974, the first American of Japanese descent to hold such a post in the United States.

The various Asian wars involving the United States each used Hawaii as a major staging arena. The importance of Hawaii's defense facilities was second only to the Pentagon in Washington, D.C. To this day, U.S. defense spending in Hawaii represents a substantial segment of the island economy, as well as swelling Hawaii's population with over 127,000 servicemen and their dependents.

Tourism received recognition as a major segment of Hawaii's economy in 1946, with the formation of the Hawaii Visitor Bureau. By 1959, the first jet airliner had arrived from California, reducing the flight time from nine hours to four and a half. By the mid 80's, an average of 5,000,000 visitors were arriving in Hawaii each year, making tourism Hawaii's number one industry. Each year, visitors outnumber the local population by 5 to 1, with over 30% traveling from countries other than the United States.

In more recent years, the trend has been to support tourism, encouraging visitors from around the world to "come feel the Aloha Spirit." The infrastructure of the islands is largely dedicated to visitor needs with many hotels, easy inter-island travel options, excellent services and fun vacation activity options. In tune with Hawaii's past, opportunities abound to discover more about the traditions of Hawaii, its people and their individual ethnic backgrounds. The new multi-ethnic natives of Hawaii want to share the experience of these islands with you, the visitor. Even though their ways may be more technologically up-to-date, the old magic lingers.

Ancient Hawaii Lives On

Beneath picture perfect ambiance—the volcanoes, trade winds, and ocean—beats a unique Hawaiian pulse. It's made of old rhythms and chants in a language laced with vowels. To speak Hawaiian, open your throat; to be Hawaiian, open your heart. The pulse is the spirit of aloha—love and welcome.

The Hawaiian pulse is in the swing of ti-leaf hula skirts, in the rattle of split bamboo and clacking pebbles. It's in the "shaka" sign (pinky and thumb out, fingers to the palm), the local symbol of "I'm ok, you're ok." It's in the lilting pidgin—half music, half feeling—that binds the folks who say, "Hey brah, howzit?" It's in the muscle of outrigger canoe racers, who one-paddle, two-paddle toward evening. It's in a *lei* of vanda orchids, the whiff of plumeria, the shine of anthuriums. It's in a balloon-trimmed, red-crayoned roadside sign marking "baby *luau*." It's in the twang of a ukulele down the beach.

The pulse beats in ancient superstitions (taking pork over the Pali may cause misfortune; picking the lehua blossom brings rain). Knowledgeable people will not enter a *heiau* without first placing a small, round rock at the entrance. And many a ti plant protects the front door of local homes. You hear of local people who summon their *aumakua,* personal gods, and of pigs, lizards, owls, or sharks who respond. Newspapers report on construction workers who flee their worksite when bones are unearthed and who will not return until the place has been ceremoniously blessed.

The ancient pulse lives on in stories passed the ancient way, from mouth to mouth; of the volcano goddess, Pele, who was seen in her flaming red garb in Waikiki the day before an eruption; or of Pele in her white-clad, old hag form, reportedly seen walking down the beach only to vanish. Believers take gin and cigarettes as offerings when they visit Pele's volcanoes on the Big Island. Non-believers take home her rocks (though warned not to) and later return them in air-mailed packages with apologetic notes and tales of misfortune. There are stories of identical dreams of spirit warriors passing through the house. Others tell of hearing the dreaded Night Marchers, of hauntings, enchantments, and visions.

Sometimes you must ask for these things. Sometimes they seek you out. All are part of the beautiful mystery of Hawaii. Come discover it for yourself!

Hawaiians and the Aloha Spirit

Aloha. Synonymous with the beauty and warmth that is Hawaii, the word and spirit captivates the heart in its all encompassing meaning.

Hello … good-bye … love … compassion … aloha. Each means one and the same, yet grows in its expression as the feeling is shared between friend, lover, family or newcomer. Aloha is for everyone.

The aloha spirit comes alive in the eyes that brighten in greeting, striking the chord that instantly creates new friendships. It is in the open exchange of hugs and kisses; the embrace that reaches for the heart and exudes from the soul. It is the essence of giving. Whether extended to long-time friends or strangers, this spirit is the spark of life that makes Hawaii so unique, so enchanting, so ever-inviting.

Many a time, Hawaiian women will present the flower leis off their shoulders, or the haku headbands from their hair, should a passerby comment on the beauty of the blossoms or the handiwork. Each is an example of the aloha spirit, no matter how humble, memorable and touching, because the giving is freely and fully from the heart.

If you're fortunate enough to be invited home by a Hawaiian friend, whether for a simple family dinner or festive *luau* party, chances are that you'll be laden with hearty portions of extra food to take home at the end of the night. Hawaiians believe that the wealth of home and happiness is a gift to be shared with everyone, and never like to let friends or guests go away empty-handed.

To the Hawaiian people, the bond of love and aloha is the pervasive spirit that keeps the family together. So important is the sense of family to the Hawaiians that often-times relationships extend beyond the immediate family of "blood" ties to include distant relatives and long-time friends. This expansive Hawaiian-style structure of family is known as *ohana*.

The *ohana* is derived from *oha,* the rootlet formed by the taro plant. An important staple in the diet of the Hawaiians, taro was one of the many plants and animals that the early Polynesians transplanted as they settled in the Hawaiian Islands. Looking somewhat like a potato or strawberry plant, the taro sends out tiny rootlets *(oha)* to propagate new plants and to perpetuate its growth. This did not go unnoticed by the Hawaiians, who used the visual image to create a word for their concept of the extended, yet closely connected, family or *ohana*.

The *ohana* is where children first learn the meaning of aloha by sharing among family members. The family is the center of all relationships and the core of mutual warmth and support. It is in this loving embrace of family that Hawaiians learn the spirit of love, generosity and aloha.

Children are considered very special blessings to the Hawaiians. It is said that "a house without children is a house without life." The Hawaiians' feeling towards children are clearly exemplified by the open expressions of affection, caressing and embracing of little ones.

One of the special times to witness the closeness of *ohana* and the celebration of children is at the traditional "baby *luau*." A festive party held in honor of baby's first birthday, the *luau* is a greatly anticipated event where members of the *ohana* look forward to working, playing and partying together.

As with any typical Hawaiian-style party, everything is available in abundance including guests, food, drink and laughter. The aloha spirit flows as the many hands of aunties and uncles prepare and serve the traditional Hawaiian dishes. Cousins get up in turn to do an impromptu *hula* or to play a song in honor of baby, family and friends. Hawaiians call this spirit of many hands joining or working together, *laulima.* It is the way of Hawaiian celebration for everyone to participate gladly and generously; an affirmation of the happiness and love that they feel towards life.

It is no wonder, then, that the Hawaiians naturally carry this exuberance and spirit into adulthood. The common greeting among Hawaiians today is a kiss and warm embrace. Visitors will be quick to notice that a *lei* of flowers around the neck, the traditional island greeting, never goes without a friendly peck on the cheek.

Hawaiians like to amuse themselves by saying, "We're all related, one way or another." It is a display of respect and endearment to call elders "Aunty" or "Uncle." Close acquaintances often refer to each other as "calabash cousins." This term probably comes from the fact that not-so-distant relatives shared together in a meal from the *calabash,* or serving bowl, old Hawaiian style. It is readily and casually assumed that anyone sharing in food and drink together can be considered "family."

These loose, yet interwoven, family ties have allowed children, to be freely given over and raised by grandparents or foster parents. This Hawaiian cultural tradition of adoption is known as *hanai.* Because of the Hawaiians' great love for children and the nurturing structure of family, a child does not lose his or her real parents through *hanai,* but rather gains another relationship of love and learning. *Hanai* is a term of fondness and caring, and parents and children of *hanai* feel a deep and ever-growing sense of aloha towards each other.

From this embracing network of family, the Hawaiians share a generosity and warmth of spirit that extends beyond the *ohana* to include strangers and newcomers. Even from the time that Captain Cook first made contact with the people of these islands, the Hawaiians impressed the world with their openness, friendliness and sense of grace. The aloha spirit, the Hawaiians knew, was meant to be shared.

"*Aloha Oe,*" the famous song written by Hawaii's last reigning monarch, Queen Liliuokalani, expresses the many meanings of love and aloha with its gentle words.

> *Aloha 'oe, aloha 'oe*
> *E ke onaona no ho i ka lipo,*
> One fond embrace, *a ho'i a 'e au*
> *A hui hou aku.*
> Farewell to you, farewell to you,
> O fragrance in the blue depths,
> One fond embrace and I leave
> Until we meet again.

First One in the Water Gets a Dime!

Back in the 1920's and 30's, "Boat Day" in Honolulu was an easy and fun way for local boys to earn shiny new dimes. You see, Boat Day was the time when the big Matson Liners would steam into the islands. They'd dock at Honolulu Harbor and the passengers would toss dimes in the harbor for the eager young boys to dive for. But that was only a small part of the Boat Day festivities.

In fact, much of Honolulu's regular activities would virtually come to a standstill when the Hawaiian Electric Company sounded its whistle signifying the arrival of a Matson liner. Canoe paddlers would escort the ship in as the Royal Hawaiian Band played island tunes to greet the excited passengers. Nothing in the islands could match the excitement and electricity in the air of Boat Day. But that was then.

Today Boat Days are no more. The arrival of the Jet Age and the huge increase in tourist traffic has made the excitement and pageantry of Boat Day obsolete, if not impractical. But something else has changed too.

Today the local island boys are pretty much like their Mainland counterparts in every aspect. In fact, in Honolulu today, and from Hartford, Connecticut to Los Angeles, California, there's just one way to get a boy to jump overboard for money. Today, the money would have to float.

The Hawaiians' beloved queen captured much of the essence of aloha in her poignant song. In saying good-bye, Hawaiians never mean forever. They know that the spirit always travels in the heart with aloha.

Queen Liliuokalani wrote *"Aloha Oe"* after witnessing a moment when two lovers shared a tender good-bye, but many Hawaiians have come to know this song as their queen's farewell to her beloved people and the islands which were her destiny to rule.

The aloha spirit lives everyday in the hearts and actions of the Hawaiians. Should you ever be touched by their grace and beauty, you will know how deep and wondrous is this feeling of aloha. You will feel the spirit move within you, too, and understand why Hawaiians say, "Aloooha!"

Melting Pot and Ethnic Groups

Hawaii today is like a tapestry of vibrant and varied cultures. The array of peoples living side-by-side creates a colorful and interesting mix, with each ethnic group borrowing and blending from the others yet remaining distinct in its own traditional uniqueness. This "melting pot" of races has made living in the islands an ongoing experience of cultural enrichment.

Like the early Polynesian voyagers, who traveled the Pacific before calling the islands of Hawaii their home, and like the many species of plant and animal wildlife that have adapted to the island chain, all the different races made their own journey to the islands to settle and become "Hawaiians."

Each of their stories is a legacy of struggle and triumph. And, as is the American story of the search for identity and a golden dream, they all came to call this new land their home, bringing with them the treasures and traditions of the lands from where they journeyed.

Only in Hawaii will you find, concentrated within the geography of an island community, such a wide variety of ethnic names, foods, celebrations, dress, customs, beliefs and more. While the many cultures have all had to adjust to a new way of living, they managed not to lose their ethnic identities, but rather to share their uniqueness with others. The result is a rich and delightful heritage for the world to see and for Hawaii's children to own.

The first group of *haole* to settle in the islands were the missionaries from New England.

Take your Camera to the Supermarket Instead

We're not kidding. A simple trip to a supermarket in Hawaii can reveal more about the culture and tastes of the island people than all the beaches, lectures and gift shops combined. For it's on these supermarket shelves, behind the glass and in the vegetable bins that you'll find the amazing variety of foods that our island people consume.

In the vegetable and fresh produce section, right next to the apples and corn, you'll likely find Gobo (for chop suey), Lichee (a popular fruit), In Choi (Korean Cabbage), Manoa Lettuce, Tofu, Maui Onions, Mangos and Papayas. In the Seafood Section, you'll find Ahi (Tuna), Opakapaka (Red Snapper), Mahi-Mahi, Ono Poke along with Tako (Octopus) and a variety of other fish used for Sushi and Sashimi.

But don't overlook the Seed Section. That's right ... the Cracked Seed Section ... a variety of dried, salted and packaged seeds that's considered a treat among Island children and adults alike. In fact, the story goes that a kindergarten teacher once asked her class what comes from seeds, and intead of hearing "plants," she heard the unanimous response of "Lee Hing Mui" instead. (Lee Hing Mui is a popular seed treat.)

So next time the day's a bit overcast. Or your sunburn could use a little more air conditioning and a little less sun. Or you just can't face another Mai Tai. Do something really daring and different and slip on a pair of Zoris (flip-flops, go-aheads, Japanese slippers) and head for a neighborhood supermarket instead.

The Hawaiians gave the Caucasians the name "*haole*" because they were genuinely amazed that there could exist men and women with such pale-colored skin and fragile looking bodies. *Ha,* in Hawaiian, means breath and *ole* means without; together, the phrase becomes "without breath" or "without life." It is aptly describes the first image of the white men for the dark-skinned, robust Hawaiians.

The missionaries brought a new way of life to Hawaii and marked the beginning of change in the destiny of the Hawaiian people. In spite of the cultural changes they imposed, the missionaries had sincere intentions of improving the lifestyle of the natives while converting them to Christianity. They succeeded in conferring new knowledge to the Hawaiians about family life and child care, religion, cooking, clothing and education.

Today, the homes that the missionaries built for themselves stand as a cultural attraction near downtown Honolulu known as the "Mission Houses Museum." The names of these early pioneers are perpetuated in the businesses their descendants established, in the chapels and schools in the communities they influenced and in the streets that course through upper-class neighborhoods on Oahu. The surnames Judd,

Thurston, Cooke, Bishop, Wilcox, Alexander, Baldwin, Castle and Wilder have come to mean *kamaaina haole*, or a *haole* descended from the first white inhabitants like the missionary families. A *kamaaina haole* is considered a *"keiki o ka aina"* or child of the land—a person who claims the honor of being born and raised in the islands.

In many cases, when *haole* and people of other racial extractions inter-marry, their offspring exhibit physical traits and appearances that are both very striking and quite enviable. These *"hapa-haole,"* or half-*haole*, appear fortunately blessed with a homogenous blending of the best of both cultures. It is not uncommon to find many individuals in Hawaii whose ancestral roots can be traced from all over the world. When you hear, "Yes, I'm Hawaiian, Chinese, Portuguese, Scottish, German and Filipino," it's almost granted that the person making this remark is a cosmopolitan beauty. They make unique and fascinating examples of the wonder in crossing East and West, light and dark, symbols of Hawaii's "melting pot."

Most of the ethnic groups arriving in Hawaii came to supply the early sugar plantations with cheap labor for the plantations. The exceptions were the native Hawaiians, the Samoans who emigrated from the territory of American Samoa, the Southeast Asian refugees and the *haole*, who owned the plantations. The first group to settle on the island shores for this purpose was the Chinese. Those who left China for the promise of wealth in Hawaii were from the villages and farms, and they brought with them an age-old culture steeped in the wealth of tradition.

The sugar plantations could not keep the Chinese for long, however, and they soon left to fulfill their own dreams of wealth in the city. In no time, a Chinatown in downtown Honolulu had been established. The Chinese stores and merchants were important to the Chinese community, serving as a center of activity where people could gather, gossip and hear the news from home. This activity continues in Chinatown today, although

Bon Dancers Dance to a Different Beat

Bon Dances are definitely a sight to behold. In July and August each year, members of Japanese temples and missions gather to host joyous drum dancing festivals to honor their ancestral dead. It's a colorful, lively link to Japan that's now become a part of the Japanese/American culture too. Everyone from grandchild to grandmother looks forward to these Bon Dances with excitement and anticipation.

During these festivals, people dress up in their Japanese finery and the Japanese Buddhists dress in kimono and yukata. They dance under paper lanterns and around a tower support-

ing the drummer and vocalist. It's a fun, non-stop dance lasting from 7:30 to about midnight when most people head, exhausted, for home.

On the North Shore of Oahu, at the Jodo Mission in Haleiwa, another version of the Bon Festival takes place ... only this one is more sedate, yet equally thrilling in it's simplicity: flickering lanterns are floated on a dark sea under a full moon. It's a moving way to honor their ancestral dead.

It's ceremonies like these that make Hawaii such a beautiful, diverse culture ... and such a wonderful place to visit ... and live.

some of the Chinese businesses have been replaced by those of other immigrant populations.

The Chinese are credited with introducing many new plants to the Hawaiians. The vegetable seeds they had brought for their own cooking needs were raised for sale. These included Chinese peas, long beans, water chestnuts, bean sprouts, watercress, mustard cabbage and bitter melon—all familiar items found today on a typical Chinese restaurant menu. Other Chinese plants that have become part of the Hawaiian landscape are the chrysanthemum, narcissus, honeysuckle, lotus, gardenia and jasmine (pikake).

The Chinese love good food and any happy occasion is cause for celebration. The traditional nine course Chinese dinner has become a standard type of celebratory feast for practically every occasion in Hawaii, including graduations, weddings, birthdays and anniversaries. Everybody loves Chinese food. The custom of serving nine courses has great significance as the number nine symbolizes things long, old and ethereal.

27

Working paniolos on the Big Island

Hawaii's gastronomical development are, the Japanese have also given us many other things that are common to the look of Hawaii. Practically everyone in Hawaii wears zoris, the Japanese slippers that are made from a wide assortment of materials, ranging from high-grade rubber to woven grass. In fact, go to any home in Hawaii and you'll find pairs of mixed and matched slippers and shoes just outside the door. Taking off one's footwear before entering a home is a standard practice in Hawaii, another tradition borrowed from the Japanese.

Judo, karate and aikido are some of the Japanese arts that are popular with Hawaii's schoolchildren and adults. Samurai movies have become an interesting diversion from the usual movie night routine for many locals.

From the Portuguese, Hawaii received one of its most distinctive treasures. The *ukulele,* a small four-stringed, guitar-like instrument that's heard in practically every Hawaiian song, was called the cavaghinho or braguinho in Portugal. It got its Hawaiian name from a musician who used to ardently play the instrument and jump around like a flea; hence the name *"ukulele,"* which literally means "jumping flea."

It's also believed that the Portuguese gave us the look for the formal Hawaiian men's attire; a red sash tied around the waist. These bright and colorful sashes were commonly worn by Portuguese men for festive occasions and holiday dances.

At many local carnivals and the annual state fair, the longest line for any attraction is the one to the malasada wagon. A confectionary delight from the Portuguese, malasadas are a deep-fried, sugar-coated dessert that's easily considered the Hawaiian favorite over the doughnut. Sweet bread, or pao doce, is another local favorite and often served as French toast (now that's cosmopolitan!). The Portuguese also gave us the spicy Portuguese sausage, delicious Portuguese bean soup and vinha d'alhos, a tangy marinade for pork, beef and fish dishes.

The Filipinos have left their colorful mark on Hawaii's ethnic blend. Among their many cultural contributions are their good food, chicken fights and a festive attitude towards life.

Cockfighting is illegal in Hawaii, but judging by the number of police raids reported regularly in the media, it is still a widely practiced sport among the Filipinos and incorrigible gamblers. It's a sport that came from the Philippine islands, along with the men who were to work in the pineapple and sugar cane fields. Because the majority of these immigrant laborers were bachelors, or forced to leave their wives at home, cockfighting became a welcome diversion to cure the loneliness and homesickness they felt in a foreign land. Cockfighting arenas are usually situated in an undercover location in a farming or rural area. The sport remains the same, and a surprisingly large size crowd is always present. The crowd of betters gather round to make their

Home, Home on the (Hawaiian) Range

Not all cowboys are found in the great American West. Because some of the most typical, most bowlegged cowboys you'd ever want to find are rounding up cattle right here in Hawaii. That's right; the "Paniolos" of the Big Island.

In 1832, King Kamehameha III imported Spanish-Mexican "vaqueros" from California to round up the feral cattle that Capt. George Vancouver let loose on the Big Island in 1794. The Hawaiians had domesticated their own brand of cattle but these "wild" cattle kept jumping the protective low stone fences and disrupted their herds.

The cowboys were hired to round up the wild cows, and were dubbed "Paniolos" after the Spanish work "Espanol," and the name has stuck to this day.

The Paniolos introduced Spanish dress, music and style to the Big Island, but these traits were quickly absorbed into the local culture and soon blended with the Hawaiian way of life. With their love of string instruments, they made extensive use of the ukelele; the famous slack key guitar of Hawaii—well, it also came from the cowboys!

Today, the Paniolos are still a major influence on lifestyle on the Big Island, with an ethnic blend of Hawaiian, Portuguese, Spanish, American and Oriental ancestry. So next time you see a western movie with the sun sinking slowly into the west, look again! That mountain range there could be the Kohalas, and that's no mirage you're looking at … it could be Hawaii's palm trees and the Pacific Ocean!

The Japanese also brought many cultural influences to the melting pot that is Hawaii. Like the Chinese, they too were brought in great numbers to harvest sugar cane by hand on the Hawaiian plantations. When their dreams of returning home in wealth never materialized, the Japanese adapted themselves to life in Hawaii and shared their ways and beliefs with their new found neighbors.

Today, it is not very easy to separate things Hawaiian from things Japanese, so profound has been the process of assimilation. For example, almost every family in Hawaii cooks outdoors over a hibachi, a Japanese brazier that has become a standard piece of culinary equipment to island homes. Teriyaki meat, shrimp tempura, sushi and sashimi are regular menu items at many local parties and picnics. The Japanese also gave us saimin and shave ice, two more local favorites that have been immortalized in local-style T-shirt designs.

But, as important as their contributions to

choice and lay down money, as the specially groomed gamecocks strut and preen in a circle. The bird handlers then attach razor-sharp blades to the ankles of the birds and the bloody battle begins. It is a fight to the finish, with the losing handler often shedding tears at the loss of his beloved and prized bird.

Popular Filipino dishes include a tasty egg roll called lumpia, a noodle dish called pancit and a stew made with beef, chicken or pork known as adobo. Filipinos also prepare roast pig, or lechon, over coals instead of underground like the Hawaiian-style *imu*. They often flavor their food with bagoong, a fermented fish sauce with a pungent taste and smell, that most non-Filipinos find takes some time getting used to.

Filipinos love to have parties to mark any special occasion. Baptisms, weddings, birthdays and even funerals are celebrated with an elaborate feast and gathering of family and friends. The networking within the Filipino community is remarkable, as they are generally accustomed to extending their hospitality to distant relatives and folks from the villages back home. Music and dancing play an integral part in the Filipino culture. Many "name" entertainers from Hawaii's music scene are of Filipino extraction.

Hawaii's melting pot got its touch of spice from the Koreans. Known for their fiery, passionate natures, they too have added much to Hawaii's total uniqueness. The Koreans have quickly assimilated the American way of life and are proving themselves as successful entrepreneurs and independent business owners.

As far as food is concerned, the Koreans' famous contribution to Hawaii's palate is kim chee. Actually a pickling method for vegetables, kim chee is at its powerful best when loaded with garlic and hot chili peppers. The Koreans also prepare meat and chicken with a distinctive sauce of shoyu, ginger, garlic, sesame seeds and oil. This sauce marinaded over short ribs makes one of the most popular local barbecue dishes called kal bi.

The Samoans, Puerto Ricans and *haole* (Caucasians) have all made their own important and long-lasting contributions to Hawaii's melting pot. Today, immigrants arrive mainly from Southeast Asia and for different reasons than Hawaii's earlier immigrants. They have continued in the tradition of lending their unique touches to the islands' cultural tapestry.

As the crossroads of the Pacific, Hawaii will always attract people from far and exotic places. Each will find many things both familiar and strange here. They may cling to their own way of doing things. Soon, as with the other ethnic groups that came before them, they will find that everything in the islands is for learning and for sharing. And this melting pot called Hawaii will certainly find a way to make them feel right at home.

Japanese Tea Ceremony

For lovers of Oriental culture, experiencing a demonstration of the Japanese tea ceremony is a must. Sponsored by the Urasenke Foundation of Hawaii, whose goal is to "find friendship in a bowl of tea," a ceremony is held every Wednesday and Friday from 10:00 a.m. to 12:00 noon, free. You will be enchanted in a beautiful garden setting, seated in a formal Japanese tatami room, and introduced to the authentic custom of the preparation and partaking of tea; made from sweet green tea and served in exquisite bowls. For more information, call 923-3059.

You Don't Have to Go to Asia to Find a Chinatown!

Back around the turn of the century, Chinatown in downtown Honolulu wasn't exactly a place frequented by the tourists of the day. It got its start back in January, 1852 when 195 Chinese contract laborers arrived in Honolulu and set up shops and living quarters there.

It quickly gained a rather shady reputation back then as an exotic, if sometimes risque, area of town. And it also gained a reputation as a place where fires were very common due to the simple, closely-built wooden structures.

In 1900, a large portion of Honolulu's Chinatown went up in flames when the Board of Health tried to burn several blocks down to quell an infestation of the plague. Unfortunately, the fire got out of control and much of Chinatown was lost.

Today, Chinatown is a fascinating part of Honolulu history and culture with shops filled with Chinese herbs, noodles, charming grocery stores and restaurants catering not only to the Chinese but to the Filipino, Vietnamese, Japanese, and tourist population too. There is still a somewhat "risque" side of Chinatown, but it's been a part of Honolulu for so long that it's become a tourist attraction unto itself.

Nowadays, the only reminder of the flames and fires of yesterday that you'll find in Chinatown, is when you sit down at one of the many little Oriental eateries and wash down a delicious meal with a cup of hot sake.

"Waiter … water, please!"

The Language of Hawaii

The beauty of the original Hawaiian language is hard to explain, but once you have heard a chant, or seen an authentic hula, true to the spirit and form of old Hawaii, it's hard to forget. Historians agree that the roots of the language traveled its course from Asia, traveling through the islands of Melanesia, and finally arriving in Polynesia. Many similarities have been noted between the Tahitian and Hawaiian language.

The early Hawaiians had no need to put their language into written form. Stories and chants combined with the hula, carried the history of Hawaii in a process called *mele*. It was not until the arrival of the missionaries, that the Hawaiian language was first reduced to written form, and it was these early missionaries who established the Hawaiian alphabet, with the purpose of creating a bible for their new converts.

At first glance, the language seems formidable. However, it is one of the most fluid and melodic languages in the world. Composed of only twelve letters; five vowels, A, E, I, O, U; and seven consonants, H, K, L, M, N, W; it's very simple. To pronounce the vowels: A as in father, E as in vein, I as "ee" in beep, O as in own, and U as "oo" in boo. Pronounce the consonants: H as in hale, K as in Kate, L as in laid, M as in moon, N as in noon, P as in peak, and W as in always.

After you've mastered the few rules of pronunciation, you can easily speak the language. Just remember that every word and syllable ends with a vowel, and no two consonants are ever heard without a vowel sound between them. Also, keep in mind that the next to the last syllable receives the accent, and all letters in the Hawaiian language are pronounced. You're on your way! Practice on the many street signs you'll be seeing.

Here are some Hawaiian words that you may find useful during your stay in the islands:

alii: old royalty of Hawaii
aloha: hello, good-bye, love, welcome
aloha nui loa: aloha with lots of love
 or affection

Things Oriental

Hawaii has often been called "The Melting Pot of the Pacific." A casual walk down any Honolulu street quickly reveals why; the people are from many different races and cultures. A great number are of Asian origin, their traditionally fair complexions now a golden bronze from Hawaii's sun. Many first time visitors assume that all here who are not Caucasian in appearance must be Hawaiian. Not so. Japanese and Chinese ancestry residents vastly outnumber the Hawaiians. Add those of

Korean, Thai, Filipino and other southeast Asian roots and it becomes all too evident why so many businesses, festivals, organizations, and places of worship are extensions of purely oriental cultures.

While old Honolulu boasts a colorful Chinatown similar to those in other western cities, it is not purely Chinese. Vietnamese, Laotian, Filipino, Japanese, Thai and Korean restaurants and shops can be found standing alongside the Chinese herb, acupuncture, import, service, and food shops.

Temples, shrines, and missions afford sites of worship for those who are Buddhist, Shinto, or Confucian. Many of these structures are of beautiful, traditional architecture and some dominate authentic and picturesque settings. Statues of Chinese statesman Sun Yat Sen and Filipino leader Jose Rizal stand only a short distance from a theatre of classical Japanese design, a Chinese tong building, and an elaborate Kwan Yen Temple.

Honolulu boasts lovely and tranquil Japanese gardens, charming and authentic tea houses, buildings and pavilions deliberately patterned after those in royal palaces found in Seoul and Bangkok, and shrines recalling Beijing and Kyoto. There are endless varieties of green or blue tiled roofs with flared corners, moon gates, pools teeming with golden carp, soaring pagoda, shoji paper doors, and wide-stanced tori gates.

Purely western institutions in Honolulu often take on oriental overtones. There are both Japanese and Chinese Chambers of Commerce. Several bank buildings embrace elements of Chinese architecture. There is a Korean Methodist Church, a Japanese Christian Church which would be right at home in Kyoto, and a Chinese Christian Church richly decorated with ornate tiles and topped with a pagoda-like belfry.

Shopping in Honolulu can be a delight for curious visitors. Supermarkets boast produce counters laden with fresh ginger root, Chinese cabbage, and fruits found in Singapore, Hong Kong, or Kuala Lumpur. Jars of pungent Korean kimchee and Japanese pickled radishes or plums are as common as barbecue sauce and dill pickles. Oriental household items, clothing, toys, and even confections are extremely popular. There are scores of shops with exquisite examples of oriental art at very attractive prices.

Visitors to Hawaii can and should enjoy this rich gathering of things oriental. Perhaps no where else in the western world can one see and experience so much of the exotic far east so easily, safely, and with no language barriers to deny satisfying information. And, of course, be sure to take your camera. At least one sightseeing company has designed an exciting half-day tour, "The Mysterious Orient," that focuses exclusively on the fascinating and intriguing orient, made available by Polynesian Adventure Tours, see page 66

ewa: in a Westerly direction*
hana: work; as in pau hana
haole: Caucasian
hapa: half, a part
heiau: ancient temple
honi: to kiss
hui: connected group or association
hula: Hawaiian dance
imu: underground oven
kahuna: priest
kai: ocean, seawater
kamaaina: longtime island resident
kane: man
kapu: keep out, forbidden
kaukau: food
keiki: child
kokua: help
kona: an island's leeward side
koolau: an island's windward side
lanai: porch, terrace, balcony
lei: necklace of flowers, seeds, or nuts
mahalo: thank you
makai: toward the sea
malihini: newcomer, stranger
mauka: toward the mountains
mele: song, chant
menehune: mythological little people
muumuu: long, loose dress
nani: beautiful
ohana: family
okole: rear, derriere
oluolu: please
ono: delicious
pali: cliff
pau: finished, done
puka: hole
pupu: hor d'oeuvres
wahine: woman, wife
wikiwiki: quick, in a hurry

*An Easterly direction is often referred to as Koko Head or Diamond Head.

In Hawaii's multi-ethnic society, it's natural that many other languages have survived the test of time and become embedded in their respective communities. Each certainly adds richness to the vocabulary of the islands, even if not original. As time passes, individual words or phrases from a particular language find common usage in general conversation, such is the mixing that takes place in the "melting pot." None of this, of course, is to be confused with the Pidgin dialect, not a true language, but more a collection of local slang.

Pidgin to da Max!

Every area of the United States has its own regional dialect, from the Southern drawl to the Brooklyn twang, and Hawaii is certainly no exception. Here it's called "Pidgin English," and in many cases, it is harder for the mainland tourist to understand than any other dialect they've ever heard. It's actually a combination of many words, phrases and dialects from the diverse ethnic groups residing in Hawaii. However, it has evolved though the years into a language all its own ... one hard to understand ... and even harder for an outsider to speak.

Many locals actually speak two languages. The pidgin they speak among themselves and the "proper" English they reserve for the grammar teacher, or for visitors who would never understand them otherwise.

Here's a few words to help you understand pidgin a little better. We're not suggesting you try to speak it, but this might help you understand what's being said around you—or about you.

"Rubbah Slippah": You will probably want to purchase a pair of these. So don't go into a store and ask for "flip-flops" or "thongs," because the only thing you'll get is a blank stare. Ask for a pair of rubber slippers and you'll get what you're looking for.

"Kapu": This means "forbidden" or "keep out!" Usually when you see this sign, it's best to obey it, or you might have some rather unhappy local pointing it out to you.

"Auwe!": When someone "does you wrong" this is what you say to them. For example, imagine that you've just spied the perfect carved coconut head for your Uncle Henry, and just as you're reaching for it, the lady next to you grabs it. Let loose with an "Auwe!" and she may be so startled that she may drop it, whereby you pick it up

and run to the cashier.

"Bus' um out!" This is the local expression for "Share it." So if you've got some macadamia nuts tucked away that you keep nibbling on and hoping not to get caught, you better hope you don't hear a "Bus' um out!" anywhere around you.

"Double Lunch": Imagine you're at a luau and the rather heavy man in front of you scoops up all the best stuff before you even get a chance. He is doing the "Double Lunch" ... when you go back for seconds the first time.

"Fah-Out": A common enough word, meaning of course, "Far Out." Even though it's not heard too much on the Mainland anymore, the guy who says it in Hawaii is still considered "cool."

"Hala!": Suppose you're sitting on the beach in Waikiki and your best friend from Iowa laying next to you is turning beet-red. If you were to put an ice-cold soda on his back, someone might yell "Hala!" at you ... or in English, "Shame, shame, shame!"

"High Waters": This you might have heard before and it refers, of course, to pants that are too short. So leave your "high waters" in the suitcase: besides, they don't go well with Aloha shirts at all.

"Boy-Flower": You may buy some of these to send home to your great aunt. This is the local word for the lovely anthurium flower ... and if you need an explanation for this, you've been out in the Hawaiian sun for too long.

This is just an introduction to Pidgin English ... There's plenty more to learn, but if you're smart, you won't try to speak it ... Just nod and say "Yeah" or "Fah-Out."

"Un'erstan', Brah?" ("Understand, Brother?")

Business in the Islands

Hawaii's climate: perfect for visitors and businesses alike. The rainbows, beautiful scenery, and the East meets West melting of cultures provide an idyllic backdrop for a thriving, commercial sector. In no other large U.S. city as cosmopolitan as Honolulu can you experience the aura of warmth and relaxation which pervades the business community; and, see men in aloha shirts and women in muumuus as standard business dress! It is a custom which makes Hawaii unique and disproves the "dress for success" theories supported in other metropolitan areas.

Once dominated by an agricultural society where sugar was king and pineapple the queen, the farmer now also nurtures the growth of macadamia nuts, vegetables, papayas, guavas and other tropical fruits; not to mention Kona coffee,

Five's the Lucky Number in Hawaii!

Five is a lucky number here because "The Big Five" means the five leading corporations established here in Hawaii in the 1800's that have practically dictated life and business here for over a century. These five huge corporations are: C. Brewer Co., Theo H. Davies & Co., Amfac (American Factors), Castle & Cooke, and Alexander & Baldwin.

The founders of these companies were descendants of the early missionary families that came to the islands to spread the good word, and through luck, perseverance and foresight, got rich in the process. They were involved in every aspect of business from agriculture to shipping to banking and more.

You were virtually assured of a prominent place in society and business if your surname was one of those mentioned above ... and it remained that way well into the first half of the 20th century.

Today, the Big Five still play a leading role in business, political and social life throughout the Island but to a much lesser degree. Some have even relocated their head offices to the Mainland.

And in modern Hawaii, there's still a lot more to be gained by having a last name of Cooke, Baldwin or Alexander than to have the name of Rockerfeller, Guggenheim or Kennedy. Just ask around and see.

beautiful flowers and foliage for bouqets, leis and lanais.

Hawaii's resident population of approximately 1,050,000 is concentrated mainly on Oahu (Honolulu County) with a population of just over 800,000. The Big Island (Hawaii) is the next largest population center with 105,000 residents, followed by Maui (84,000) and Kauai (45,000). The island business climate is remarkably more entrepreneurial than most other major business areas. Out of over 21,000 private employers, 50% have less than 5 employees, while 75% have less than 10.

The use of the sun-drenched land for farming is no longer the dominant economic sector, having been replaced by tourism with visitors arriving from all over the world to experience our Polynesian playground. The over $4 billion visitor industry is the number one employer in the state, responsible for thousands of service-oriented jobs. One of the key attractions for the visitor industry in Hawaii is the outstanding variety of hotels, restaurants, retail stores and recreational activities, each with a special appeal to the visitors looking for that personal and special vacation. Whether your taste is for food or fashion, you can find a wide range of assorted cultures represented anywhere you look. Shopping centers with everything from boutique-style ambiance to the hustle and bustle of the large department stores, keep visitors happy with bargain buys, designer clothes and islands' artistic works. Restaurants abound from small, ethnic fast-food counters all the way to five-star elegance. It's an education in itself to sample the many foods popularized by the fascinating cultural variety found in Hawaii.

Doing the business of business is the role of the third largest employment sector—finance, insurance, and real estate. Although there are only ten banks in Hawaii, they operate over 180 branch offices and other facilities. Total assets amount to almost $8 billion, with bank clearings totaling well over $40 billion a year. Banking is big business in Hawaii with Hawaii's position at the center or hub of the Pacific Rim, and the industry continues to foster strong economic ties with the foreign investment community, particularly Japan. Hawaii also has eight savings and loan associations and numerous credit unions with assets totalling over $6 billion. Money, Money, Money! Insurance companies number over 700; and, in recent years life insurance in Hawaii amounted to almost $23 billion.

The unique personality of Hawaii, as an island state, is especially brought into focus by the business of real estate. Land use is a delicate issue and one of critical importance to the future of the state. The Government—federal, state and county—owns over one-third of the land available for ownership. The remaining land is privately owned, primarily by nine major landowners, whose combined ownership is almost one half of the private land available. These large estates then lease the land to thousands of homeowners on a long-term basis. No other state in the country has such an arrangement. Although the many homes have a relatively high price tag, it is comforting to know that because of the gentle tradewinds and mild climate, heating and air conditioning are usually not needed. A great way to reduce your monthly utility bills!

Many of the acres owned by the Federal government are dedicated to military use. The second largest economic sector in Hawaii (after tourism), brings almost 130,000 servicemen and dependents to Hawaii through the various bases around the islands. Each branch of the armed forces is represented at this center of the Pacific Hemisphere. Hawaii's position also lends itself to the wholesale trade business. The center of the Pacific Rim is an especially valuable point to securing products from Australia, New Zealand, Micronesia, and the Orient, including Japan,

Entrepreneurs — The Bermans

The concept of Fabrications as a specialty boutique began back in 1972 when Kilohana Square opened as a small shopping center. In 1978, after several years of evolving from a fashion and crafts combination of merchandise, Fabrications became a full fledged fashion salon for women of distinction. What is now a labor of love, and source of profit, was born of commitment, dedication and hard work.

Both Jan and Jeff Berman, owners and originators of their unique concept, used a strong background in fashion, crafts and textiles to create a totally new idea for the fashion world of the islands. Both designers have taught at the University of Illinois and the University of Hawaii. A weaver by trade, Jeff lives and breathes textile design and fashion. Jan, the business mind of the couple, knows what women are looking for and what they really desire to make them look more appealing and feel great. As a husband and wife team, Jan and Jeff are "Fabrications."

Their look is geared to international city dressing and sunbelt climates, and encompasses daytime dresses and separates along with long caftans for lounge or casual evening wear. Jeff believes that, "clothing should only accent the woman, not dominate her personal aura." The fabrics include prints and solids in cotton blends created especially for warm climates, while the price places it in the higher quality stores.

In January of 1972, as part of their expansion plans, the Bermans launched their Jeffrey Barr wholesale

division on the mainland, introducing the line to the local market later that year. The response has been excellent. Not long ago it was thought impossible for a clothing manufacturer to exist in Hawaii unless they could create Hawaiian wear in the traditional sense. Although the company headquarters is in Honolulu, the designs are currently being shown in Miami, Dallas and Los Angeles. In each area, they reflect a contemporary design approach for warm climate living.

In January of 1984, the company moved its facilities to larger premises, to meet additional business growth while keeping strict quality control. The retail store is now at the Kahala Mall where it continues to be a fashion leader in quality, style and, above all, reputation. The company's steady growth to date has been achieved by plowing profits back into the business. The Bermans offer another example of Hawaii's entrepreneurial business basics: persistance, dedication, excellence and above all, creative skills. These qualities are needed in any successful business, and even more so in Hawaii where 75% of private businesses have less than 10 employees.

Entrepreneurs—Nick Nickolas

Excellence and class—the two words that most describe Nick Nickolas. A self-made millionaire restaurateur who built his businesses in keeping with his belief not to accept anything but the best. From the interior design and layout of his latest restaurant to the fine cuisine and its preparation, right down to each and every employee, Nick always gets what he wants, and he wants perfection!

Nick Nickolas is quite a success story. He played football at San Diego State and graduated with a degree in industrial management. Upon leaving college, his vision of balmy island breezes, expanses of blue ocean and blue sky, and the turquoise waves lapping at the shores drew him like the sweet scent of a flower to Hawaii. He arrived with $85 and the clothes on his back, played semi-pro football and picked pineapples for a living until he landed a job as a bouncer at the Merry Monarch in Honolulu, then moving on to La Ronde and Michel's. Nick worked hard in those early days. He watched, listened and learned. It was here in Hawaii, that he developed the philosophy and style that propelled him to the top of his profession.

Nick did return to the mainland to learn from master builder J.O. Kirby, who left a lasting impression on him. Kirby was well known for building some of the best restaurants in America. However, the turning point in Nick's career came after he returned to Hawaii and went to work for Jeff Harmon at Honolulu's Red Vest. Although he started as a waiter, within two years Nick managed to acquire a piece of the pie. Then, in 1968, Nick convinced Harmon to back his lifelong dream—a swank, white tablecloth, fresh seafood restaurant.

Thus, was born, Nick's Fishmarket. It was a winning idea that grossed a million dollars its first year out. To this day, the Nickolas-Harmon partnership is still going strong.

Again, in 1975 they jointly opened Nick's Fishmarket on Sunset Boulevard in Beverly Hills. The Nickolas-Harmon team had arrived. The team is unbeatable, Nick is the front man, he's great with the customers and his personality lends itself to the high profile he needs to represent their image. While on the other hand, Harmon is the quiet partner working hard behind the scenes, and he enjoys the low profile just fine.

From Beverly Hills, they moved on to Houston where Houston's Fishmarket grossed $2 million by its second year. What was left? Well, Chicago beckoned, and Harmon and Nickolas were ready. And today, Nick's Fishmarket is well known as one of the finest restaurants in the "windy city."

Eventually, the call of the islands lured Nick back to Hawaii with their latest venture—Nicholas Nickolas, high atop the Ala Moana Americana Hotel. Aside from having the same superior food and service of Nick's continued reputation, the chic decor was designed by one of Honolulu's best known architects, and the view from high atop the hotel is breathtaking.

Excellence and attention to detail are the principles that all businesses must have if they want to break into the success category, no matter where you are. Nick Nickolas believes in those principles, and as a successful entrepreneur in Hawaii's very competitive economy, this proves the point. Keep your eyes and ears open, you'll be hearing more of Nicholas Nickolas.

China, and Singapore. For the shopper looking for great bargains, many direct importers sell also to the retail market. Look for many of these businesses near the Honolulu International Airport and throughout Waikiki.

Keeping people healthy is big business in America, and the health service industry is also a large employer in Hawaii, growing significantly larger each year. Specialists in every field of medicine practice their trade in modern, up-to-date facilities throughout the state. Preventive medicine is espoused by many physicians; and with Hawaii's perfect outdoor climate, the entire family can keep physically fit by participating in the many outdoor activities available.

After 30 years of major economic activity, construction in the islands has recently been on a downswing. Investments by large hotel groups to build complete resorts and expand existing facilities is presently boosting the prospects for commercial construction. Recent increases can also be seen in the single-family residential market, providing welcome work to many skilled construction workers in an economy that does not provide many related alternatives to construction.

Since Hawaii has a strongly service-oriented economy, many technically trained people leave to pursue a wealth of technical positions outside Hawaii. Therefore, a major thrust is being made toward diversifying the economic base to include high-tech opportunities. Three separate, yet related, entities are involved: the state, the counties, and private businesses. Two programs, the Pacific International Center For High Technology Research and the High Technology Development Corporation, dominate the state's high-tech efforts. Both stress research and development with the idea that these will eventually generate and support high-tech business opportunities. The counties, particularly Hawaii County and Maui County, are moving ahead with plans for commercial high-tech industrial centers.

Energy is one of those sectors that is beginning to benefit from the high-tech influence. Hawaii's energy supplies are moving away from being 90% dependent on imported petroleum toward renewable energy sources such as ocean thermal energy, hydro-electric, solar, wind, geo-thermal and biomass conversion systems. Although it will be many years before reliance on imported petroleum will be substantially reduced, the promise of these new energy alternatives is strong.

Other areas of Hawaii's business are relatively small in impact on economic total. The manufacturing base is small and mostly related to the sugar, pineapple and petroleum industry sectors. The garment manufacturing industry is growing strongly, with many excellent entrepreneurial designers and manufacturers carving their niche not just in Hawaii, but worldwide.

One industry that takes it roots from the old Hawaiian culture continues unabated, although the technology and the product are different. Surrounded by ocean, fishing remains an obvious source of food for island consumption and outside export. Fish farming (aquaculture) continues with a technology that the ancient Hawaiians would have been pleased to use in their conservation efforts. Providing many excellent sporting opportunities, deep sea fishing for tuna and other ocean fish is a growing sector, as the demand to meet new cultural tastes, both here and in California, requires sashimi and other seafood delicacies.

It is fortunate that these islands are blessed with an abundance of natural resources, and even more fortunate that those natural resources are being used conservatively, following the ages old tradition of Hawaii's original settlers. Hawaii is truly blessed with its climate, resources and people, each inviting the visitor to enjoy Hawaii and respect its good fortune.

Local Government

Beautiful flowers, strains of Hawaiian music, and lavish spreads of local food—it must be a *luau*! Guess again—it's the opening day of the state legislature in Hawaii.

Residents and tourists alike descend upon the grounds of the state capitol located near downtown Honolulu. With standing room only, people from all over the world witness the hours of speeches from local politicians, and music and dancing provided by local entertainers and various ethnic groups. It's an appropriate way for any newcomer to the islands to experience the essence of the beauty and deep feelings of the people who lead the government of the State of Hawaii.

The Capitol building itself becomes even more interesting when one is aware of its symbolism. The two legislative chambers are cone-shaped, like volcanoes, symbolic of the geological origin of the Hawaiian Islands which rose upward from the sea floor. The magnificent columns are representative of the graceful palm trees of Hawaii, so important to the early Hawaiians as a source of food and building material. Surrounded by water, it resembles the islands of Hawaii.

The Capitol's airy, open style suits it ideally to the gentle Hawaiian climate. Here is a Capitol where the sun, rain, and tradewinds are free to enter. The great central court, open to the sun and rain, moon and stars, rises to the sky like the throat of one of the volcanoes that helped build these islands. In the deeply carpeted legislative chambers, the visitor galleries are set in close proximity to the deliberative functions, demonstrating the intimate sense of participation that islanders always have with their government.

Since the beginning of statehood in 1959, Hawaii has been rapidly thrust into the modern world. Honolulu is one of the largest cities in the United States, with multi-national corporations, high-rise office buildings and condominiums dominating the skyline. The government system in Hawaii is unique in its simplicity with only two levels and no separate municipal organization. The state government system provides services that are statewide in nature, such as education, transportation networks, public health and welfare, and public works, all requiring a uniformity of standards and regulations. The other part of the government system is the responsibility of the county governments including police and fire protection, refuse collection maintenance of streets and parks, and other functions traditionally assigned to cities or towns on the mainland.

The primary source of revenue for the county operations is the real property tax. Each county sets its own rate. The state's largest source of income is the general excise (sales) tax levied on almost all commercial transactions (except sugar, pineapple, wholesaling, and manufacturing). The next largest source is income taxes, both corporate and personal.

Government—federal, state, and local—is a major employer in the state and includes members of the armed forces stationed in Hawaii. The U.S. Pacific Command is the largest of the United States' five unified commands, and is responsible for all U.S. military bases and forces in the Pacific Ocean area. This includes more than 50 percent of the earth's surface including the Indian Ocean, Southern Asia, the Aleutian Island chain, and portions of the Arctic Ocean.

General Douglas MacArthur said that the history of the world for the next thousand years will be written in the Pacific. Significant growth and development in the Asian-Pacific area make General MacArthur's words prophetic. The Reagan Administration made the Pacific Region one of its highest priorities stressing strong government-to-government relations. An important new government appointment was made by the President to fulfill a new role as Ambassador to the Pacific Basin.

Cooperation among Pacific nations continues to grow, and there is an emerging sense of community developing in the Asia-Pacific region. In Hawaii, many of those different cultures meet, supported by state and local government. Through various linking groups and commercial exchanges, trade between the many Asian-Pacific countries is being encouraged at all levels, state, local and through the multi-ethnic groups that abound in Hawaii—the melting pot.

Opening day at the Legislature

Educational Opportunities

Congress and state legislatures pass laws, school boards make policies and administrators interpret them, but it is the classroom teacher with the individual child, who is the backbone of our educational system.

Formal education first came to Hawaii in 1820 with the missionary schools. Starting with the sons and daughters of high ranking chiefs and other noblemen, schooling was very soon available to all children. By 1825, Hawaiian text books had been written, and the hitherto unwritten language, reduced to written form. Today Hawaii is the only state with a single, unified public school system, employing several thousand teachers both in public and private schools. Opportunities are available for everyone, no matter what course of study they may choose. Vocational education includes basic education with vocational skills and an occupational skills program, specifically designed for the handicapped students.

There are over two hundred public schools with an enrollment of over 160,000 students. Neighborhood schools are conveniently located in populated areas and a state run bus system accommodates students who are not within walking distance of the school.

The private schools number more than 140 and most offer kindergarten through grade 12. Tuition ranges from $1400 a year at some Catholic schools to $500 a year at Kamehameha Schools, where the student must have a percentage of Hawaiian heritage in his ancestry. Tuition may also be as high as $3,500 at Punahou School, founded by the missionaries in 1841; to over $8,000 a year for a boarding student at the Hawaii Preparatory Academy on the island of Hawaii.

Opportunities abound for the student who wants to pursue a college degree in areas such as communications, the arts, humanities, history and computer science, and fields of studies particularly unique to Hawaii including astronomy, oceanography, tropical agriculture, and geophysics.

Four independent, four-year colleges are located on Oahu: Brigham Young University— Hawaii Campus; Hawaii Loa College; Hawaii Pacific College; and Chaminade University. Students find many opportunities to work on a part-time basis in service related jobs throughout the islands. For instance, a favorite attraction for visitors is the Polynesian Cultural Center, which is operated and staffed, for the most part, by the students of Brigham Young University. Students from throughout the Polynesian islands attend Brigham Young and often work in the "island" center of their homeland at the Polynesian Cultural Center.

Cars and Freeways

Things you "auto" know about Hawaii's cars and freeways.

Most visitors to the islands are surprised by the number of vehicles on the streets and roads. The pristine views of Hawaii are sometimes seen from a "caravan" of cars that all seem to be looking for the same secluded beach as you.

It becomes even more obvious, when you find yourself on Hawaii's only freeway between the hours of 7–9 a.m. or from 4–6 p.m. in the afternoon. That's when you'll quickly realize that Honolulu is much like any city, with its own rush hour traffic. Actually, there are about 580,000 licensed drivers in Hawaii, not counting the tourist population, with the greatest concentration of these found on Oahu.

Most visitors are surprised to learn that there are only about 50 miles of freeway in the entire State of Hawaii, with most of it stretching through the middle of Honolulu. There are, however, about 1,300 miles of other roads on Oahu, practically all of which are paved and well maintained. And you'll find speed

limits everywhere intended to maintain that precious commodity—Hawaii's slower pace of life. This slower pace of life sometimes translates into a potentially dangerous situation for visitors, when the car in front occasionally, and very unexpectedly, brakes to a halt on the freeway onramp, one of the most common causes of accidents for visiting drivers.

About 1,700 taxis serve the Islands, with the majority of them plying the streets of Waikiki looking for tourists with too-tired feet from pounding too-much pavement.

Once you reach the open road, be aware that in some areas service stations are very hard to come by. There are less than 400 service stations statewide, and in some of the more remote areas, both the service stations and the gas prices will be at a premium.

So if you find yourself snarled in traffic, feeling like you're back in Chicago or Dallas at rush hour, take a deep breath, relax and look around you. Chances are there's a coconut palm, a gorgeous ocean view or a few tanned smiling faces to remind you that you're still in paradise.

The State of Hawaii University system is extensive and encompasses over nine campuses. The University of Hawaii, Manoa campus is the largest and offers degrees in over 80 programs; masters degrees in over 70 different fields, and doctorates in over 40 disciplines including medicine and law. The state university system includes six community colleges and a four-year college at Hilo on the Big Island. The community colleges offer both academic and vocational programs.

Trade schools and business colleges offer courses in a variety of vocational interests, from bartending to computing and real estate. The larger business colleges include Cannon's International Business College of Honolulu, the Hawaii School of Business, Control Data Institute, and the Japan-America Institute of Management Science.

Established by Congress in 1960 and chartered as a public non-profit corporation in 1975 by the State Legislature, the East-West Center, near the Manoa campus, is a place where senior fellows and career professionals, from more than 40 countries and territories, study and work together. The center concentrates on studies directly related to the many countries in the Asian and Pacific region and their cultural and commercial relationships. The program is supported by a variety of scholarships, government grants, private enterprise and various other grants.

From the early methods of 1820 to Hawaii's present day systems, education has always been an important part of life in Hawaii, a continuing of the old traditions of passing on knowledge to the young ones. The technical depth of our present day educational systems may be different from the *mele,* but the feeling of family knowledge continues.

Honolulu: A City of the Arts

Honolulu has a long and varied tradition of excellence in the performing and visual arts, a tradition carried into the 1980's as the city earns its rightful place among the leading cities of the United States.

The Honolulu Symphony, founded in 1901, is one of the oldest professional orchestras in the country. The orchestra performs statewide for over 100,000 schoolchildren each year and gives an extensive series of programs at its home at the Neal Blaisdell Concert Hall. It has a Classics series, which has presented such acclaimed artists as violinist Isaac Stern, Van Cliburn and Janos Starker; a "Music on the Light Side" series that spotlights top pops performers; and the ever popular Starlight Series in the Waikiki Shell, a special delight when the Symphony teams with top Hawaiian entertainers for an evening of picnics and music under the stars.

Also popular on the musical scene is the Hawaii Opera Theatre, which annually gives three full-length operas. In 1986, for example, the season includes Tales of Hoffman, The Rake's Progress, and Tosca.

Chamber music lovers enjoy a selection of series presented by such groups as Chamber Music Hawaii (made up largely of top players from the Honolulu Symphony) and the Honolulu Chamber Music Series, which brings in major artists from around the globe to perform at the University of Hawaii's Orvis Auditorium.

Drama is an integral part of the cultural scene in Hawaii. The Honolulu Community Theatre, headquartered on Diamond Head, is the oldest drama group west of the Rockies. It has obtained performance rights to Broadway shows, often while they are still on the Great White Way, and has given such productions as A Chorus Line and the Pulitzer Prize-winning, 'Night, Mother, within recent years.

The Hawaii Performing Arts Company, with its smaller theatre in Manoa Valley, presents an exciting season as well, with such shows as Amadeus and others on tap for 1986. Other theatrical arts in Honolulu include its Theatre for Youth, which provides both school and public performances; the highly acclaimed Kennedy Theatre at the University of Hawaii; and a wealth of smaller companies headquartered in Windward Oahu or sponsored through the military.

Honolulu is also the venue for many fine traveling Broadway shows, including productions such as Annie, Hello Dolly, Evita, and Camelot, starring Richard Harris, all of which have played at the Neal Blaisdell Concert Hall in recent seasons.

With its tradition of hula, Hawaii loves dance! There is Ballet Hawaii, which sponsors such annual productions as Nutcracker, Cinderella and others with imported dance stars from the Mainland and Japan, as well as sponsoring such solo talents as Mikhail Baryshnikov and Friends. The Hawaii Ballet Theatre for Youth also is known for its full-length story ballets and its annual Nutcracker. There is modern dance through the Dance Works, outstanding performances by Dances We Dance founded by former Jose Limon company members Betty Jones and Fritz Ludin, and a wealth of dance performances at the University of Hawaii. In addition, in recent years, commercial promoters have brought in such attractions as the Alvin Ailey Dance Company, Merrill Ashley and Dancers from the New York City Ballet, and Alexander Godunov and Friends.

Honolulu can claim many exciting museums and galleries, including the prestigious Bishop Museum with its extensive collection of Pacific artifacts and its planetarium, a popular spot especially during Halley's Comet-watching year. Honolulu Academy of Arts has one of the finest representative art collections in the country, as well as a theatre to present films and live concerts; the Gallery of Contemporary Art, housed at the Honolulu Advertiser/Star-Bulletin Building on Kapiolani Blvd., and a wealth of smaller galleries showcase paintings, sculptures, and other works of art. In addition, Honolulu is in the planning stages for a new Children's Museum of Art, Science and Technology.

Festivals abound in Honolulu, including the annual Hawaii International Film Festival every December, sponsored by the East-West Center, and bringing in top filmmakers from the United States, the Pacific basin and Asia, in an effort to increase international understanding through film.

Whatever your artistic preference, both visitors and residents alike, will find that Honolulu has an excellent selection of cultural opportunities. For complete information, the Arts Council of Hawaii maintains a cultural calendar, which is available to visitors. Call the Arts Council at 524-7120 or consult the weekly entertainment listings in either of the daily newspapers in Honolulu.

Robert Lyn Nelson

Robert Lyn Nelson is internationally renowned as one of Hawaii's foremost artists. His works hang in the Smithsonian, the Metropolitan Museum of Art and the Museum of Natural History. His work is appreciated in numerous private and corporate collections, including those of President Reagan, Clair Boothe Luce, George Benson, John Davidson, John Denver, Willie Nelson, Robert Wagner and John Hillerman.

Robert has had two great fascinations in his life—art and the ocean. Born in Upland, California and the son of California watercolorist William Nelson, his training in art began at a very early age. At age four, he began, through the use of charcoals, to experiment with light, shadow and perspective. At thirteen he began attending classes in Southern California colleges. Then, at fourteen he was awarded a full scholarship to Pomona's Mount Sac College where he studied the great masters, from Michelangelo and Rembrandt to Rockwell and Parrish. By age twenty, Nelson had mastered the techniques of painting in any medium—oil, watercolor and acrylic. He could handle any subject matter from portraiture and still life, to the narrative and dramatic, either abstract or with realism.

Even with an appointment to attend the San Francisco Academy of Arts, he chose Hawaii instead. During those early years in Hawaii, Robert lived in a house on the beach in Laie (Oahu), always on the lookout for the perfect wave. He also spent considerable time sailing and scuba diving. But, art was in his blood and he continued to support himself as a commercial artist with work on murals, signs and graphic design. While on the North Shore, Robert became fascinated with the folklore of Hawaii's many ancient gods, warriors and heroes, and spent many nights studying Polynesian legends and lore. It was during this time that he completed a series of paintings based on the double-hulled voyaging canoe, Hokule'a.

Then, in 1977 Robert followed a friend to Lahaina, Maui, where he fell in love with the island he now calls home. "This is the prettiest place in the world," says Robert. After settling in, Robert became especially interested in the eighteenth century whaling men and their ships, which began to dominate much of his painting. His canvases were alive with the history of Lahaina and the whalers. Robert's interest in the old whaling days led, naturally, to the whales themselves. "Finally, I just got tired of showing whales being killed. I started to paint them as beautiful creatures, swimming free and peaceful in their underwater environment," says the artist. Through his paintings, Robert brings us into a world few of us have ever directly experienced. He creates windows to the sea where underwater landscapes abound in a rare and beautiful display of whales, dolphins, giant sea turtles and rainbow colored reef fish. A member of the National Audubon Society, a Director of the American Cetacean society, and an avid Greenpeace supporter, Robert's works serve us as a constant reminder that the undersea world is endangered unless man begins to cherish the creatures that share this planet.

A world traveler, Robert has painted subjects from around the globe and although his collections show varied influences, his most famous works are the two worlds of the land and sea. Many of these show split views of a scene both from above and below the sea. In these paintings, he shows us just how much we overlook a part of our planet that is deeply fascinating, alive with exciting beauty and awesome mysteries. His paintings open our minds, transforming darkness and silence into startling new vistas of color and life far beyond our wildest imagination.

Robert's success is a direct result of his approach to the world which becomes his paintings. One of his best known works, Honu, gained international acclaim, as the best serigraph of the International Screen Printer's Association competition, when it was chosen from over 2,000 entrants from 20 countries. Robert is truly an artist without limitation, continually searching out new methods of expression with his drive to experiment and push his talent as far as it can go. What else can this be but that rare combination of talent, training and insight that we call genius. To see more of his work, visit the Lahaina Galleries in Maui (see page 42) and enjoy the feeling of being transported to another realm of reality.

"I want the viewer to react emotionally, to feel what I feel as I paint. there is so much life in my art that sometimes I feel like I'm directing a movie" - Robert Lyn Nelson.

A section from "Beacon of Kilauea"
by Robert Lyn Nelson

Lahaina Scrimshaw

1036 Limahana Place
Lahaina, Maui 96761
(808) 661-8820

As old as it is unique, the beauty of scrimshaw is like a visual poem. Created on fossil ivory, it represents not only the hand of the artist, but also the hand of nature itself. Tradition is the scrimshander's teacher. And timeless treasures are the result.

The art of scrimshaw was crafted by ancient mariners to pass their days at sea. In the booming years of the whaling trade, sailors brought it to Maui, introducing what is still today an original American legacy of collectibles. Since the early 1800s, the market for these famous engravings has centered in Lahaina. And now, more than ever, its finest examples can be found at Lahaina Scrimshaw.

To learn more about this fabulous art, call or write for a free color brochure. There has never been a better time to enhance your personal art collection with one of these classic works. And you can count on Lahaina Scrimshaw for the best selection available.

For gifts of just a few dollars to some worth many thousands, discover the inherent and ageless value of history carved into art.

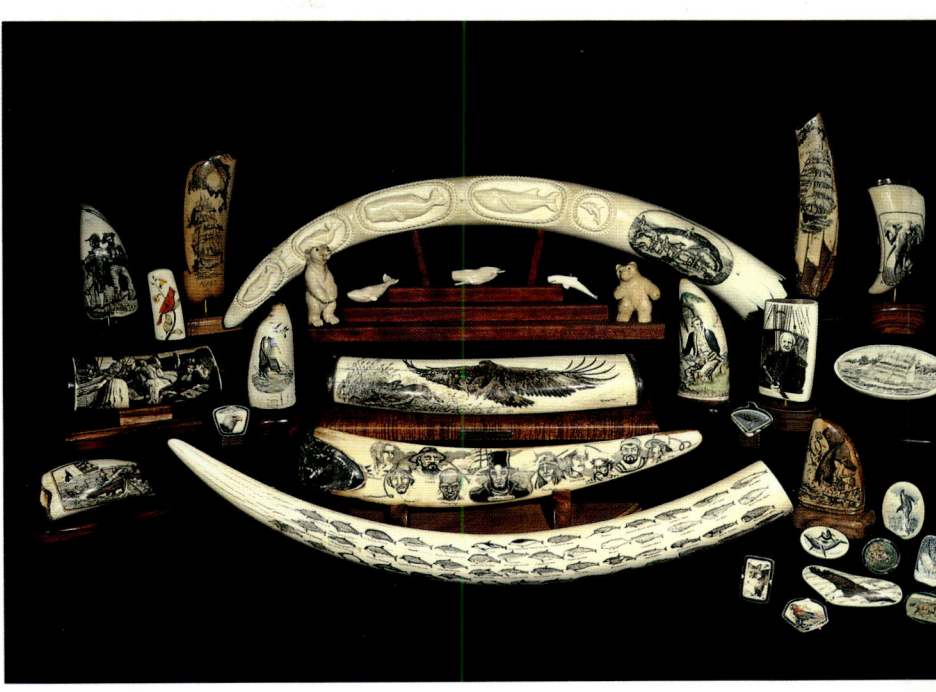

Royal Art Treasures

1716A Kalakaua Avenue
Waikiki 96826
(808) 941-8181

Discover some of the most unique gifts and fine collectibles available in this wonderful hide-a-way shop. Whether you're a serious collector, or just want to browse, this unusual store is literally packed with intriguing gift and fine art items. Choose from intricately carved Japanese miniature ivory netsukes to scintillating, multi-colored rock and crystal sculptures. You are welcome to visit and enjoy the wide variety of treasures on exhibit. For more information call or write.

41

Lahaina Galleries

117 Lahainaluna Road
Lahaina, Maui 96761
(808) 661-0839

Kapalua Gallery

The Kapalua Shops
123 Bay Drive
Kapalua, Maui 96761
(808) 669-5047
(800) 367-8047 Ext. 108
(outside Hawaii)
(800) 423-8733 Ext. 108 Canada

Casay Gallery

The Wharf
658 Front Street, #105
Lahaina, Maui 96761
(808) 667-9023

Gallery Kaanapali

Whalers Village
2435 Kaanapali Parkway
Lahaina, Maui 96761
(808) 661-5571

Lahaina Galleries Maui, one of the foremost art galleries in the islands is pleased to present Andrea Smith, a surrealist and abstract expressionist whose works are exclusively done in water colors and acrylics.

Andrea sees the world in a special way. She is able to paint the way she sees and dreams. "Abstract realism" is the way Andrea refers to her paintings. Her works represent what she believes; the patterns of invisible forces, movements and relationships. Her message is peace with an underlying theme of love and light. She feels that the relationship we have with ourselves is the most important and the act of integrating the self is what she paints about. She celebrates the dignity of all life and seeks through her painting to create a harmony of understanding without the impulse to control.

As did the Twentieth Century Masters, Andrea Smith uses the images, colors, shapes and lines of her paintings to communicate and evoke the whole range of human emotions. You might feel as if you were looking at the works of a woman comparable in talent, new approaches and in the same tradition as Picasso, Miro and Chagall. Her mastery of presentational forms is testimony to an almost intuitive genius and an ability to blend powerfully, mankind's most ancient and unconscious symbols with the textures, tones and movements of the modern world. As did these masters of the abstract and the surreal, she communicates emotions through the images, colors, shapes and lines of her paintings, and she does so with startling impact.

Andrea Smith's professional acceptance was expressed by the United Nations' University for Peace when she was selected as the artist to create the 1987 Art for Peace Calendar and Poster which will bring her international acclaim. Truly, to experience her work is to risk new insights, new attitudes and changed values!

The Lahaina Galleries in Maui specialize in showcasing renowned local artists such as Andrea Smith, Otsuka, and Robert Lyn Nelson (see the feature on page 40). Each of the galleries provide a unique opportunity to view the works of today's living masters, an opportunity not to be missed.

"Love Transforms" by Andrea Smith

Celebrity Tips

Many people come to Hawaii as visitors and within a short time, seduced by the magic of the islands, become residents. That includes many celebrities who came, whether to visit or to work, and have found so much beauty and relaxation that they make it their home, or at least return as frequently as they can.

Hawaii has several important advantages for celebrities. It is not only a paradise, but because it's a part of the United States, all the security, comforts and communication that many celebrities require are available. It's also very easy to commute from Hawaii to the legendary capital of the movie world - Hollywood, and to other major cities on the mainland, as many celebrities have found out. And, it's easier yet to become part of these magical islands.

The film industry is also growing fast here for both T.V. and feature movie productions, bringing many stars to Hawaii to work. Both Jack Lord and James MacArthur of the well-known Hawaii Five-O T.V. series have made Hawaii their home. And, Elvis Presley was so in love with Hawaii, that he performed here with the proceeds going to local charities.

The Magnum P.I. series is presently the largest continuous operation in the islands, using not only the great filming weather and lack of major crowds, but also the spectacular scenic backdrop of Hawaii. Naturally, when the Magnum series is in production, the stars are residing in Hawaii, and often at other times as well.

There are those celebrities who have visited the islands on vacation and became enchanted with the islands such as Sylvester Stallone, Richard Pryor, Carol Burnett, Dolly Parton, Jim Nabors, George Harrison and Billy Jean King, the list could go on, and on . . . all found a spot to call their very own. Some, such as Charo and Roger Moseley, are now active in the business community.

So, there are those celebrities who make Hawaii their home, and there are those who just come to visit, but sooner or later everyone comes here to share in the aloha spirit . . . we hope that you will enjoy the information and tips from some of them.

Everybody comes to Hawaii sooner or later

A "Magnum" of Tips for Visitors

Ask a Hawaii visitor what he or she most wants to see while in the islands and chances are "Magnum" will be right up on the top of their list along with Pearl Harbor and the Banzai Pipeline. For many visitors, catching a glimpse of Tom Selleck and the Magnum cast is as exciting as viewing an eruption of the Big Island's Kilauea volcano.

"Magnum, P.I." isn't on any maps, but some lucky travellers stumble onto location filming. When they do, they are often pleasantly surprised to find Selleck and co-stars John Hillerman, Larry Manetti and Roger Mosely willing to smile and wave in a manner befitting the land of Aloha.

The long-running TV series has made Selleck, Hillerman, Manetti and Mosely, Hawaii's most famous residents. Yet for all of their fame, the four enjoy a higher degree of privacy than they might find on the Mainland, thanks to the low-key attitudes of the local folks. Even autograph-seeking visitors do not bother them too much, although an overzealous fan does occasionally come along.

After more than six years in Hawaii, the "Magnum" stars have become genuine "kamaainas," or longtime residents. The HawaiiGuide visited them on the set at Universal Studios in Honolulu to find out if their perceptions of the islands have changed since they first arrived, and if they had any special tips for visitors.

HG: How has your perception of Hawaii changed since you first came to the islands?

Selleck: My perception hasn't really changed after becoming a resident and feeling part of things here, but my appreciation for the local people has increased because they have such a high regard for an individual's privacy. People let me know they like the show, but generally, they leave me alone and I'm very grateful for that. We work with crowds and I try as hard as I can, without hurting our work, to be friendly to the tourists, but after 14 hours of that, it's nice to be able to go out to a restaurant and enjoy a quiet dinner with a companion. I find that most people here are very respectful and allow me to do that. Even the tourists are pretty considerate, but the local people have been great.

Hillerman: Before "Magnum," I had been over here to guest star in Hawaii Five-O. I thought all of Hawaii was a tourist operation - good restaurants and shows in Waikiki - that sort of thing. When you live here, you discover that the pace is wonderfully low-key compared to Los Angeles or New York. The other big cities. The people are friendly and warm. You really have to live here to get the rhythm of the Islands. It's a less hectic and harried lifestyle than that of any other city I've lived in. I've lived all over the United States - East Coast, West Coast and the Midwest, and this is the best place to live in the States, in my opinion.

Mosely: Initially, I wasn't that turned on to Hawaii. I'd been here quite a few times before the series. I was living a sort of "Waikiki existence," but I finally discovered there was much more to Hawaii than Waikiki. There is a unique sense of community in the other areas of the Islands. On Oahu, I opened TC's Hair Salon in Wahiawa and Reni's

Magnum P.I. Cast
(left to right)
Manetti, Selleck,
Moseley, Hillerman

44

Disco in Pearl City to get more involved with the community. I also work with the Kaimuki Eagles, a small Pop Warner football team. But I had to get through those first tense months in Waikiki to find that "unity feeling."

Manetti: My perception hasn't changed, except that I'm glad I've never gotten "island fever." That's really the only thing. I never thought I'd be here this long.

HG: What do you like and dislike most about living here in Hawaii?

Hillerman: I like the friendliness of the people. And, of course, the clean air. I love living here and I can't think of anything I dislike.

Manetti: The weather is fantastic. So is the food. I was never a fish eater before I moved to Hawaii. Now I love seafood. I enjoy the many ethnic restaurants too. We have all kinds of restaurants, from Hungarian to Filipino to Korean to French. The air is great - no smog. And I never worry about drunk drivers here because people are very conscientious about drinking and driving and they obey the speed limits on the roads. I feel it's a very safe place. I guess I don't have any dislikes about the Islands, either.

Selleck: I like the lifestyle here. It lends itself to sports and recreational activities. So I suppose what I dislike most is my own personal lifestyle. I work too much and don't have enough time to enjoy all the sports and recreational activities that Hawaii affords.

Mosely: I like the ethnic diversity and the variety of people you find here. That's the same thing I dislike because all those people and races don't always get along. Hawaii is the great "melting pot", but sometimes the pot doesn't melt too well.

HG: How do your fans treat you here?

Mosely: They treat me the same here as they do in Africa, Paris, Rome, London and Los Angeles. They all know us and they let me know they like the show. They're great. But sometimes one over-zealous fan can ruin my day. It might be just one person in a crowd of 50, but they can spoil it for the whole crowd.

Selleck: All in all, the fans are great.

Hillerman: Here in Hawaii, my fans wave and smile. The tourists who travel in groups can become very aggressive. But the "kamaainas" leave me alone. In any major city in the United States the fans come up and make a big deal; but in Honolulu I can go shopping or out to a restaurant and enjoy some privacy.

HG: Have you made any exciting discoveries in Hawaii that you haven't found anywhere else?

Manetti: When we were filming on the Big Island, I saw a hummingbird that was as big as a bumblebee. It was so small. That was wonderful. I see things here all the time that I haven't seen anywhere else, like a flock of wild parrots.

Selleck: There's a very unhurried aspect of life here that I enjoy. Of course, it doesn't effect me as much as I'd like it to because of my work. But I partake of it whenever I can.

HG: If you were writing a guidebook for visitors, what important advice would you pass along?

Mosely: Rent a car and drive all over the Islands, especially Oahu. Don't worry about getting lost. Get a road map and remember the ocean is always just a few miles away. If you are driving toward the mountains, turn around and drive back to the ocean and you'll find your way back to where you came from. I always tell my friends not to spend all of their time shopping. The first time I came to Hawaii, all I came away knowing about it was a 50% sale on 14 carat gold chains at a store in Waikiki. A lot of people stay in Waikiki, but they don't realize the beaches are different all around the island.

Hillerman: I would advise visitors to see the Polynesian Cultural Center and learn something about the people and cultures that make up the South Pacific. The Center gives people a better understanding of Hawaii. And of course, the Arizona Memorial is very moving, and an interesting two hours to spend.

Selleck: I agree that visitors should know something about the local customs. I would suggest that they learn as much about Hawaii before they come here and tell them not to do anything at the expense of the local customs. Visitors

45

will enjoy the Islands even more if they learn about them ahead of time. And I always tell anyone who is coming over here to visit friends to remember that their friends are not on vacation and probably have to go about their daily lives, routines and work. Respect that.

Manetti: I tell everyone to have the proper sun block for the sun. I have seen many people wind up in the hospital with sun poisoning because they spent too much time in the sun the first couple of days and didn't use a strong sunscreen. I'd also advise visitors not to blame their friends and companions if the sun doesn't shine. There are lots of things to do here on cloudy days.

Mosely: I'd recommend people take a one-day tour. I always take my friends out towards Hawaii Kai, to the Hawaii Kai lookout. Then we drive on to Hanauma Bay, the Blow Hole, the Rabbit Island lookout, Sea Life Park, through Kailua and back to the Pali Lookout and into town. The next few days they have a choice of places to go back and see and they are no longer afraid to get in a car and drive out to the Polynesian Cultural Center. Of course, at night I would tell them to go to Reni's Disco!

Manetti: I like to let people know that we have everything here in Hawaii, even ice skating! I'd advise them to learn about

the pineapple and sugar industries and maybe even get a taste of sugar cane. Visit the Polynesian Cultural Center and learn about the people. It makes it more fun. A lot of people say they want to go to the outer islands to rest and have quiet, but I've found places right here that are very tranquil, then you have the nightclubbing and the cosmopolitan lifestyle. You can really have your cake and eat it too.

Mosely: When I came to Hawaii the first time, I didn't know what I'd find. I discovered all the conveniences of the mainland, like television and air-conditioning, are right here on this tropical island in the middle of the Pacific. So remember, Hawaii is still a part of the United States!

Each of the stars has their own special loves in Hawaii, as well as their work, of course. John Hillerman's favorite place is the Big Island (that old Texas boy). And, his heart is also very big in the local arts sector. His private collection include pieces by local artists Robert Lyn Nelson and George Sumner, and he was instrumental in getting the support for Wyland's Whaling Wall near the Ala Wai Yacht Harbor in Waikiki.

Roger Mosely is quite happy to have become a resident of Hawaii. So much so that he has become a part of the business community and still finds time to donate to local youth groups.

There always seems to be something for Larry Manetti to become involved in, and he takes a great interest in local civic issues, especially education.

As for Tom Selleck, working so much hardly allows him more free time than for lounging on the beach and playing volleyball. We should all be so lucky!

Charo's Fantasy Island

What would attract an international T.V. and variety star to settle and live in tropical Hawaii? For many people, the opportunity to live in these islands would be very exciting, although not very practical. Finding the right place to live is just the first problem, finding the right income producing job is another. However, that does not deter many people. Judging by the number of small businesses operating here, Hawaii must be the entrepreneur's dream.

For many, those idyllic hours on the beach are often spent with thoughts wondering just what it would be like to take up residence here. For Charo, one romantic honeymoon set the stage and shortly afterwards, she and her new husband, Kjell, decided to make their home in Kauai. HawaiiGuide interviewed the effervescent and lively Charo while between shows, "vacationing" at her home on the beautiful North Shore of Kauai, the Garden Isle. Amid some of the world's most beautiful, tropical scenery, gorgeous beaches, warm waters and gentle breezes, Charo relaxes between shows—or does she?

Charo recently opened a new restaurant in Haena, at the Hanalei Colony Resort. Prior to the interview, she had just spent four hours in the kitchen of the restaurant, aptly called Charo's. "The restaurant is very important to me. It's part of me that I want to give to Kauai, and to the many people that visit Hawaii. Some of these people save their money for several years, so that they can take the vacation of a lifetime here in Hawaii, so I want their experience of Kauai and my restaurant to be perfect. My favorite dish is Paella, from my home country of Spain, and to make this dish perfect you must begin very early in the morning, and use only the freshest ingredients."

What made Charo decide to settle in Kauai? "It was recommended to me by some of my friends in show business. They told me what a beautiful place this was and said that I wouldn't be disappointed. I came here on my honeymoon, and fell in love with the island. We decided to live here right then, seven years ago. There is so much of this island that is still so natural, and that is not going to change in the next 30 years. We have all the things that you want to have when you live in America, and yet, it is all so unspoiled. The local people here are so friendly and so helpful. They have such good religious beliefs and are always such good neighbors, always willing to help if you need it. You're always a part of their family."

What do you recommend that friends and visitors do when they come to Kauai? "I tell them to do everything—there is so much to do here during the day. They should take a helicopter around the island and see the island from the air—the Waimea Canyon, the Na Pali cliffs, the valleys and the mountains, and the ocean. Then, they should go hiking along the Na Pali cliffs—its such a beautiful walk, I have been several times. Then see the cliffs from the sea, they're so marvellous! Snorkeling is so good too. In many places the snorkeling is so safe and enjoyable, with such beautiful fish to see under the water. But, I tell people to always ask someone local if the beach is safe before they go in the water—the waves here are sometimes dangerous if you are not a good swimmer. I am a good swimmer and sometimes I will not go in the ocean because it is too dangerous. You know, the North Shore of Kauai has so much to enjoy during the day, but at night there is not enough. I want to have cabaret in my restaurant so people can enjoy some nightlife—maybe I will even spend some time each night when I am here to play for the people in my restaurant."

What do you most like and dislike about the islands? "I love the quiet and the natural life that you can have here. It gives me time to relax and get away from the pressures of showbusiness. It gives me the time to be with my husband and my children, to be in tune with nature. I like very much to be natural, to enjoy the unspoiled adventure of the island. What I dislike is when I have to leave; I hate to leave. You know, even though I have to spend time here with the restaurant, I don't mind. It is something that I want to give to the visitors that come to Kauai, and to my restaurant—something that makes it worth the trip. When visitors come to my restaurant, I hope if they see me that they will tell me how they like it. I want them to enjoy being by the beach, relaxing and enjoying wonderful food."

Experiencing the beauty of Hawaii does make it more difficult to leave. In Charo's case, her time in Kauai may not be total relaxation, but it certainly does provide an ideal opportunity for regenerating her vitality between shows. And for Charo, leaving Hawaii comes under the category of aloha—until next time. Hawaii offers refreshment and regeneration to visitors and residents alike, and each time they leave, it will always be the same in aloha; come back soon.

Entertainment

When the sun sets, the fun begins, and the cultural smorgasbord of Hawaii's entertainment scene adds a unique seasoning to nightlife in the islands. In lounges and showrooms, large and small, Honolulu is alive with entertainment, mirroring Hawaii's diverse ethnic background.

Selecting your ticket is the big question. The decision is akin to ordering a Blue Hawaii, a Mai Tai or a Chi-Chi. If you can't settle on one, enjoy all three! You'll find most every brand of entertainment here, from unique Hawaiian slack-key guitar music or local comedy revues that specialize in ethnic humor, to the current rock sounds. Hawaii has a strong musical tradition, so if you spend any time in Honolulu, be sure to treat yourself to these authentic sounds.

You'll enjoy the big, professional headliner shows or many of the lesser known, but accomplished entertainers; each will delight you with the latest trends in contemporary Hawaiian music and entertainment. Many of these include exciting Polynesian extravaganzas, with native dances and songs from Hawaii and other parts of the South Pacific, and an accent on beautiful island women and some of the best fire dancers in the Pacific. These shows can usually be seen with a choice of dinner show (around 6:00 p.m.), the show only (maybe 8:00 or 9:00 p.m.) or the cocktail show (between 10:00 and 11:00 p.m.). Starting times, cover charges and drink minimums change regularly, so always try to reserve shows by calling ahead.

Alas, some acts are hard to find. They disappear as quickly as they appear on the circuit. Your tour desk or favorite bartender is often a good source of "the latest." Ask, for instance, about the whereabouts of Herb Ohta, Hawaii's foremost ukulele artist; Sonny Chillingsworth, the foremost slack-key guitarist; Andy Bumatai,

Don Ho - Still A Big Favorite

The name Don Ho is as synonymous with Hawaii as swaying palms and the hula. And Tiny Bubbles is synonymous with Don Ho. As he says in his nightly shows at the Hilton Hawaiian Village, "I've been doing that song every night for over 15 years and I hate that song."

Visitors still flock to see Don Ho and to hear him sing his trademark song. He has mellowed since the hectic, crazy days of the 60's when he and his group, the Aliis, entertained packed houses at Duke Kahanamoku's in the International Market Place. Night after night, the lines would stretch from Duke's entrance in the back of the Market Place out to the street. The crowds were young and often rowdy, but everybody had fun, including Ho.

"We went on tour the same time the Beatles toured the U.S.," Ho said. "We did concerts all over the country and sold out everywhere we went. Of course we didn't have as many fans as the Beatles or the Rolling Stones, but we had our own little gang. And we were just having a good time. We didn't know we were popular. We figured everybody on the Mainland just went to concerts, so everyplace we played would be full," he said.

In those days, fans would follow Ho and the Aliis from city to city which helped ease their homesickness. "We missed Hawaiian food more than anything," Ho laughs. "The kids who came to see us made it fun."

Ho prefers to stay in Hawaii now and it's the grandmas in his audience that make performing enjoyable. He calls the grandmothers onstage to flirt with him and perhaps enjoy a dance or a kiss. "I think I'm going to outlive all my fans," he jokes.

Sometimes Ho joins his old musician friends at local clubs outside Waikiki. "I always remember real quick why I'm happy doing what I'm doing," he said. "It feels good to go to a club and remember what I did in the past at Honey's in Kaneohe, but it also brings flashbacks of the unpleasant stuff like brawls. We joke about it now, but the brawls were bad."

In spite of his international stardom, Ho has always been a "local boy" at heart. He wears faded swim trunks, a Hawaiian shirt and rubber slippers most of the time and would rather be with his family than anywhere, including the stage.

Religion and Grass Skirts - The Hula

Unlike the lovely maidens we see today, in ancient days the first hula dancers were men. Because the roots of the hula were steeped in religion and discipline, it was a religious ritual believed to be too sacred for women to perform.

The early missionaries suppressed the hula, considering it vile and obscene. However, David Kalakaua encouraged a revival in the 1870's and a modern hula emerged. Hula skirts at that time were at least knee length, and the grass skirt was only recently brought to Hawaii from the Gilbert Islands. By this time, most men had dropped out of the dance, leaving it to the women, who gradually adapted it into the graceful performance you see today.

Hula is taught by a kumu hula, or dance master. Dedication of body, mind and spirit is very important to every hula dancer and is taught in their halau, or schools, which forms classes for children as young as 3 years old. Serious students study much more than the dance movements, acquiring a complete understanding of the traditional cultural influences expressed through poetry. The spirit and background of the dance is learned even before the first hip sways. The hand motions have become almost a musical sign language that now flourishes in the schools of hula dance. Each dance composition has a theme ranging from such topics as love, food and weather to battles, kings and gods.

Family traditions and respect for the land and culture support every hula, both old and new, no matter the age or number of participants. Often brothers and sisters will practice in the halau even before formal schooling begins. For most children in a hula program, "R"eading, "R"iting and "R"ithmatic are followed by "R"ehearsal, for hula is as practical to the Hawaiian child as any of the formal education skills.

Annual festivals are held on every island, and statewide events are closely followed by residents and visitors alike. Men and women, boys and girls combine tradition and fun as they retell the tales of the Hawaiian people and their centuries-old history. The most significant event is the Merry Monarch Festival on the Big Island held each year. Local dancers from all islands compete for the best performed dance, music and costumes. All the dancers who participate are not only highly skilled in the techniques, but deeply moving in their graceful expressions of love and appreciation for their culture.

Another very popular event, especially for tourists, is the Kodak Hula Show, performed most mornings in the Kapiolani Park, adjacent to the Waikiki Shell. The show brings together beautiful local dancers and a variety of dances originating from several South Pacific islands. There are several different types of hulas, ranging from the traditional and classical to a graceful grind of fun, vamps, and rolls. One of the all time favorites is the fast-hipped version danced in Tahiti, which is often mistaken for a genuine Hawaiian hula.

Remember "Sweet Leilani," the best song of the year in 1937? The hula became a household word when Bing Crosby, and Hollywood, brought it into every home town in America. Grass skirts were shipped world-wide, and every young maiden was encouraged to "move her hips up to her fingertips." Although visitors can conveniently take home cassette taped music, as well as skirts, leis and ukuleles, the hula remains a very strong Hawaiian tradition, with the old and new hula being practiced side by side with much of the same spirit.

Al Harrington—
The South Pacific Man

The Polynesian Palace
Reef Towers Hotel
227 Lewers Street
Waikiki 96815
(808) 923-9861
(800) 367-2345

Deep in the heart of Waikiki, there is a treasure you must discover. The man with the Irish name, the Polynesian heritage, and the international talent. He's the man you've known as "Ben Kokua" on "Hawaii Five-O," and the man with the most popular show in Hawaii; Al Harrington—The South Pacific Man.

With his entourage of exotic singers and dancers, Al Harrington will guide you on a musical journey through the South Pacific. He'll introduce you to the tales and heritage of these enchanting islands and help you unlock their mystery and beauty. He'll share with you the thoughts and wisdom of the people who make this precious little corner of the world their home.

Al Harrington. Discover the treasure, and you've discovered Hawaii.

Trappers

Hyatt Regency
Waikiki
(808) 922-9292

Trappers is Waikiki's premier Jazz Club and Cabaret. It is "the" place in town where you might spot a famous star or two who just happen to stop in for their own night out. Trappers offers cocktails, appetizers and dancing to continuous live upbeat jazz and contemporary musical entertainment. Be with friends for a special visit and listen to the melodic sounds of top male and female vocalists from the islands. Located in the spectacular Hyatt Regency's Diamond Head Tower, off the porte cochere, Trappers is richly decorated in an art-deco motif with etched glass and mirrors, comfortable couches and cozy booths.

The bar is also Waikiki's largest with an area of more than 336 square feet and a spacious dance floor that allows you to dance to the contemporary beat all evening long. Trappers is open from 4:30 p.m. to 2:00 a.m., Sunday through Thursday, and to 4:00 a.m. Friday and Saturday. Happy Hours are every day from 4:30 p.m. to 9:00 p.m. with specially priced drinks and hors d'oeuvres, including a tempting seafood bar. Casual dress is just fine until 9:00 p.m., when a dress code of no sandals or shorts is required. Reservations are unnecessary.

Dance the night away in Trappers at the Hyatt, Waikiki's premiere Jazz Club and Cabaret.

the most popular and talented stand-up comedian in Hawaii; or, Melveen Leed, Hawaii's hottest female down-home-style singer.

If rock and roll is your forte, you will find it centers around the large hotels. Almost all of them have their own version of local rock talent or a D.J. spinning the current sounds. Some of them are as sophisticated as their mainland cousins; you can easily feel that you're in a rock club on a par with the best of them. Lighted dance floors that flash a rainbow of colors, strobe lights, smoke machines, professional dancers will delight and entertain you. Whatever your idea of a wild, rock and roll evening, it can be easily found with just a little checking around.

It doesn't matter which island you are on, if you want to enjoy the night life while you're here. As you might expect, Honolulu offers the broadest selection, and virtually everything that's available there, is also available on the outer-islands, perhaps with fewer choices and lesser-known artists, but close to the same in quality.

Ah, but what about romance? Of course, in paradise you can expect to find the best that soft lighting, warm breezes, the sounds of the surf and the splendor of a beautiful sunset can provide. And because there's an abundance of beauty everywhere you look, even a romantic stroll on the beach during the evening can be an entertainment in itself.

Hawaii at night. It waits to entertain you.

Magical Places

Wailea Beach, Maui

Once you've made the easy decision to vacation in Hawaii, you'll need to make the difficult choice of which island and where. Each of the islands has its own characteristic beauty, offering a wide variety of scenery and lifestyle to make your vacation special and personally satisfying.

There are many flights in and out of Hawaii every day from most major cities within the Continental U.S.A., and those originating in Singapore, Hong Kong, Australia, New Zealand, Guam, Japan, Taiwan and Korea. Several flights originating within the U.S. now make their arrival directly on the "outer-islands" (outwards from the business and government center on Oahu) of Kauai, Maui and the Big Island.

So the choice is yours - from the visitor high life (day and night) of Waikiki, to the tropical lush greenery of Kauai; the sophisticated resort areas of Maui, the openness and geologic fascination of the Big Island. Each has its own selection of excellent beaches, spectacular sightseeing, historical perspectives, sophisticated visitor facilities and a wide range of other vacation activities.

Every island has a choice of climates ranging from the drier, sunnier leeward sides, to the wetter (but more tropically lush) windward shores. Even in summer, very little rain falls on the windward sections of the islands, and during those very short showers it's still a comfortable 75 degrees. However, the best surf tends to be on the windward, north facing shores. Now you can see how difficult your choice can be.

To avoid that rapid change from the hustle and bustle of city life to Hawaii's very relaxed outer-island pace, many people spend a couple of days on Oahu first, then proceed to the island of their choice for the final "winding down." It is exceptionally easy to travel between the islands by air, some flights taking as little as 20 minutes, with the longest only 40 minutes in length. Three major inter-island carriers with frequent jet and propeller services are supported by a variety of smaller, more personal airlines that offer a combination of inter-island travel and exciting flightseeing on the way, all very competitively and reasonably priced.

Wherever you go, you'll always find something interesting to see or do. For many people, there's so much to do in Waikiki that they could remain there for their entire stay! Even for the local residents (kamaainas), the alternatives are endless. After years of living in Hawaii, there are always new options, new places and new things to do. And it's quite likely that this will always be the case. Driven by Hawaii's number one economic sector, the visitor industry, and combined with the commercial talents of many small entrepre-neurial businesses, new experiences will always be available.

There are two most common pieces of advice given to visitors: First, as Tom Selleck, the star of Magnum P.I., said in the HawaiiGuide interview, "I would suggest they learn about Hawaii before they come here and tell them not to do anything at the expense of the local customs. Visitors will enjoy the islands even more if they learn about them ahead of time." Second, don't stay in one place, when you've had enough of the local beach scene, move around by whatever means you choose. You'll be fascinated and thoroughly enchanted by what can be found out there.

How to move around? The alternatives are virtually endless, from pedicab to private helicopter; from windjammer to luxury tourbus; from Beechcraft to Zodiac; the choice is yours. The most commonly used form of transportation is the rental vehicle, and there are as many options even here; from a basic stickshift compact, through luxury sedans and exotic sports cars to your own private limousine. With any choice, your excursion around the islands can be enjoyable and interesting.

You can easily see all, or a large part of any island in just one day. With the exception of the Big Island, two or three hours driving, without stops, can usually take you from one end to the other! Guided tours can provide many additional insights into a particular area or scenic point. Personal exploration can be enjoyable with it's freedom from time restrictions, and the ability to stay longer when you find something more interesting. Either way, for a relaxed enjoyable view of beautiful islands - drive; get out into the more sparsely populated areas and enjoy the scenic refreshment that Hawaii offers.

Often, some of the most exciting and unusual scenic views can only be seen by being

Paradise Adventures
Travel & Tours

Waikiki Market Place
2310 Kuhio Avenue
Waikiki 96815
(808) 924-9922
(800) 327-7766 (outside Hawaii)

Whether you're a seasoned traveller or a first time visitor to Hawaii, there is only one way to ensure that you get the best possible travel and tour services. Contact Paradise Adventures Travel and Tours. Their local knowledge is unsurpassed. Combined with the service and experience they offer, you can be sure that you'll get the best available selection of local travel and tour opportunities.

Owner, Ellen DePover, and her staff are the perfect people to help you with those special travel arrangements. A seasoned kaamaina, Ellen spent several years as personal assistant to John Hillerman, one of the stars of the Magnum P.I. series. Ellen has also handled the travel arrangements for several of the movie industry's major production companies such as Lorimar, Columbia and Universal, and is experienced with group requirements as well as individual needs. And, if you have a special request - something difficult to do or find in Hawaii, Paradise Adventures can fill it - or it doesn't exist.

Their office is convenient and centrally located, situated in the Waikiki Market Place, just a short walk from nearly all the hotels in Waikiki. Their friendly and experienced staff, will be happy to assist you before you leave home or while you're in Hawaii. Any travel and tour needs can be completed quickly and courteously. And with their fully computerized service this can be done instantly!

The spirit of aloha finds its way to you with personal attention to your travel plans. In fact, that's their specialty; itineraries that are created to precisely match your interests, budget, time frame and personal preferences. Choose what suits you best from a selection of excellent outer-island tour packages to Molokai, Maui, Hawaii and Kauai (included round trip air fare, deluxe room and car). And, for the nautically inclined, cruises on ships that ply the Hawaiian waters, such as the luxurious S.S. Independence, S.S. Constitution, Princess Cruises, or even the Queen Elizabeth II, can easily be arranged. Whatever the scope of your visit, Paradise Adventures Travel has a well organized, reasonably priced program to suit your needs.

Whether you choose to island-hop a little or a lot, no Hawaiian vacation is complete without a traditional luau (Hawaiian feast), shopping trips for aloha shirts and muumuus to take home to loved ones, narrated tours of historical sights such as the Arizona Memorial, Nuuanu Pali, and the Polynesian Cultural Center. There is so much to see, do, taste and experience in Hawaii. Paradise Adventures Travel can help you organize a sightseeing and entertainment schedule to perfectly match your timetable.

Business travelers will appreciate their assistance with a host of services such as frequent flyer programs, visa and passport services, worldwide hotel and car rentals, one day outer-island excursion packages as well as access to 100,000 airlines throughout the world. For the busy executive, all this information is only a telephone call away. So, if you're looking for those secret places in Hawaii, known only to a select few, call Ellen at Paradise Adventures Travel & Tours. Go ahead - make your day!

American Educational Institute

24700 Northwestern Highway, Suite 400
Southfield, Michigan 48075
Oahu (808) 261-6263,
Kauai (808) 742-7244,
Maui (808) 879-6523
(800) 354-3507 (Toll free)

Does mixing business with pleasure in the form of a tax-deductible seminar in Hawaii interest you? American Educational Institute, the country's largest resort seminar operator, has recently added seminar locations in Honolulu, Maui and Kauai to its 29-site menu. Now, qualified Hawaii travelers and their spouses may take advantage of an exceptional educational opportunity and deduct the cost of their trip, including seminar tuition, round trip airfare, lodging and meals.

A five-day lecture series on Investment Strategies and Financial Planning shows professionals, business persons and their spouses how to maximize the return on their investment portfolio. For physicians attorneys and dentists there is an intriguing five-day seminar on Medical/Dental/Legal Malpractice.

Participants may start either or both seminars on any island, any day of the week, and even "island hop" while completing the five-day program. Classroom time is approximately two hours per day per seminar. Tax deductible tuition is $225 for one or $295 for both seminars, plus $100 for an accompanying spouse.

Other American Educational Institute locations include eight Florida resorts, two Club Med villages, eleven Western Ski areas; San Diego and Palm Springs, Scottsdale, and St. Thomas, U.S. Virgin Islands. Call for more information.

---

off the islands; from the surface of the blue Pacific ocean, looking back at the beauty of your chosen tropical island; or flying and soaring gracefully through the tropical tradewinds, looking down on vistas of unbelievable beauty. Ideally, you'll try both!

Many of the ocean borne sightseeing opportunities concentrate on providing more than just a sampling of beautiful scenery, with easy accessibility to some form of water recreation, whether it's sailing, snorkeling, diving, fishing or just plain swimming in Hawaii's gorgeous clear, warm waters. With many different options on each island, the only problem you'll have is one of making a selection. The views from the ocean are magnificent, with beautiful shades of tropical greenery, mixing with the many blues of sea and sky and the varying reds and browns, and sometimes pinks and purples of Hawaii's coastlines. Only in this way, will you come close to seeing the islands of Hawaii as the early discoverers did, although you'll have an added advantage; you already know what it's like on shore!

A flightseeing journey by plane, between and around the islands, is probably the most efficient and economical way to get a real feeling for Hawaii's geography and experience the varied qualities of several islands in just one outstanding day. Another version of flightseeing is the helicopter tour. Usually limited to one island,

these tours offer unbelievable panoramic and close-up views of valleys, waterfalls, and beaches, many of which can only be reached by helicopter. There are a variety of individual tours available, some with drop-offs at isolated points, others intended to be the photographers' dream, with spectacular scenic views, undoubtedly some of the best in the world. Make sure that your camera batteries are working and that you have plenty of film, or videotape!

Seeing the sights is only one of the many interesting visitor activities. When you combine this with learning about some of Hawaii's rich historical past through the Bishop Museum, or visitor attractions like the Polynesian Cultural Center, you'll realize that Hawaii is much more than a sun-seeker's paradise. There's a diversity in cultures, ethnic traditions, entertainment, foods and dining that blend together in a way that just cannot be found anywhere else in the world. From the aloha spirit to the many other cultural influences, Hawaii is still a paradise all its own.

There is no shortage of information either. On each island, there is a selection of free pocket size magazines giving a week-by-week update on what's available in each area, and details of many special offerings. Everything to make the visitor feel comfortable and at home. Whatever the result of your thoughtful decision, you'll be welcome in Hawaii, and every effort will be made to help you enjoy your stay. Aloha!

Video Vacation Camera Rental

Waikiki Trade Center
2255 Kuhio Avenue (at Seaside)
Waikiki 96815
(808) 924-4003
(800) 367-5134 (outside Hawaii)

Rent a video camera from Video Vacation Camera Rental and take your Hawaiian adventure home on videotape! Write your own script, choreograph the scenes, cast yourself and loved ones as the stars of a Hawaiian epic, then produce your very own show. Or just have fun and let the good times roll onto the videotape. Your memories will be relived in full action packed color and sound.

The friendly staff will explain the pleasures of operating the Magnavox video camera that's as easy to use as 1-2-3. It weighs only seven pounds and comes as an easy to carry one-piece unit. Cameras are easily carried on any tour, plane or helicopter ride, either here or on the neighbor islands.

It's fun, easy and most of all inexpensive. Far better than still pictures, it's also more economical when you consider the cost of purchasing and developing two rolls of 35mm prints. Finally, video requires no developing. It is instantly viewable through the camera's built-in electronic viewfinder, and can be watched later on the TV in your hotel room.

Video Vacation Camera Rental will help you recall how great your vacation was in full, action packed, color and sound.

Dollar Rent A Car Hawaii

(800) 367-7006 (outside Hawaii)
Kauai (808) 245-3653
Maui (808) 877-2731
Hilo (808) 961-2101
Kona (808) 329-2744

People who have visited Hawaii more than once will tell you that the most exciting scenery and relaxing feel of "Old Hawaii" is on the neighbor islands of Maui, Kauai and the Big Island of Hawaii. They'll also tell you that to really see these beautiful neighbor islands you must have a car, with the freedom to see it all at your own speed!

Dollar Rent A Car Hawaii has one of the largest neighbor island fleets of rental cars in the State, with convenient locations at all major airports. They maintain thousands of cars to provide you with the make and model of your choice. And, of course, they have all the same cars offered on Oahu, plus some of the more popular Jeep CJ-7s and Renegades, lots of convertibles, and even 8 passenger vans and station wagons.

All Dollar cars are available at excellent rates and come with unlimited free mileage. And to make your island exploring even easier, ask for their free tour maps.

When a visit to the neighbor islands is on your itinerary, enjoy touring Maui, Kauai or the Big Island with the car that fits your personality. You'll find it at Dollar Rent A Car!

First Interstate Bank

18 locations State-wide
Honolulu
(808) 525-8200

Wherever you go throughout Hawaii and much of the mainland, chances are there's a First Interstate Bank nearby to serve you. With over 1,100 offices in 15 states, you can cash a personal check up to $500 a day at any First Interstate location. And with over 1,000 Day & Night Teller machines, you know there's instant cash waiting for you 24 hours a day. First Interstate is also a part of the CIRRUS system, where you have access to your money through over 7,000 telephone machines all across the Mainland, Hawaii and Alaska too.

In Hawaii, there are 18 First Interstate offices on Oahu, Maui, Kauai and the Big Island, most with Day and Night Teller machines. It's always reassuring to spot a familiar First Interstate Bank to remind you of home, while sightseeing or exploring the Hawaiian Isles. So, if you suddenly find yourself short of cash late at night in Lihue, Kauai . . . or if you need gas money to see the sunrise on Haleakala . . . or if you need cash for a sunset Mai-Tai in Waikiki, relax. There's a First Insterstate Bank nearby with cash waiting for you.

First Interstate Bank vacations in Hawaii with you.

Ten Best Lookouts

There are many different ways to sightsee in Hawaii—from the air via helicopter or small aircraft; from the ocean by sail, power boat or zodiac; or from the land. Each has its merits and breathtaking beauty, but in this feature we choose to examine the last of those options.

Hawaii is appreciated for its beautiful beaches, lush tropical greenery, pristine wilderness, and of course, for its views from the mountains, the most spectacular views you'll see anywhere in the world. There are ten lookouts that visitors and locals recommend the most. All of those presented here can be reached by road, as long as you're on the right island! Enjoy them, but remember to keep an eye out for the many other special views, around almost every bend in the road!

Diamond Head

On Oahu, probably the most famous view by far is at the Diamond Head lookout. You'll spot the lookout right past the Diamond Head Lighthouse, built in 1917, which is a beautiful sight in itself. At Diamond Head, you'll look down to the sparkling waters far below and see the windsurfers jumping from wave to wave, like tiny toy people, in the distance.

Above you stands Diamond Head, actually an extinct volcanic cone. It got its name from the early British sailors who landed here and thought they had found diamonds on its slopes. There are no diamonds to be found here, but the view is a jewel in itself. For a really outstanding view of Honolulu, there is a path that will take you to the top ridge of the crater. The entrance is from Diamond Head road on the mauka side of the crater.

The Pali Lookout

Next, the Pali Lookout or the Nuuanu Pali, is probably the most spectacular in Hawaii, if not the world. Tour guides, used to the "Ooohs-and-Aaahs" of people seeing Hawaii for the first time, rate the Pali Lookout high on their lists of the most awe-inspiring sights.

The Pali overlooks a myriad of landscapes. In the cool uplands, there are tropical rain forests, and sharp-edged mountains with cliffs dropping spectacularly toward the ocean. All the colors of the rainbow seem to play here, from orange, to greens, blues and reds, reflecting the diverse land formations, vegetation and the distant ocean below.

Hanauma Bay

Another of the most popular lookouts on Oahu is, of course, Hanauma Bay. It's known as one of the most popular spots in the islands for snorkeling and watching the tropical fish, but the view itself is also worth the trip. Actually a volcanic crater with one side washed away and exposed to the sea, its shallows are inviting. As you sit high above on the lookout, you'll see turquoise waters below, with snorkelers everywhere feeding the fish, or people just relaxing in the tropical sun.

Some people claim that the best view is the short hike up to Koko Head, which is marked at the Hanauma Bay lookout, and others claim that the best way to see this beautiful spot is to hike around the waters to the left of the park along a rocky ledge for a deep water perspective. Either way, it's a real treat. Only be sure to bring your snorkeling equipment and don't forget to bring along frozen green peas, a favorite snack food of the local fish that inhabit the waters!

Haleakala

Next stop is the Island of Maui, where one of the most breathtaking wonders of nature awaits you: Haleakala or "House of the Sun." This dormant, but not extinct volcano, over 10,000 feet at its summit, is so large that the entire Island of Manhattan could fit within its 21-mile crater, with the tallest skyscraper dwarfed by the crater's edge.

The drive up to the summit of Haleakala is also a treat. You'll see the vegetation change from tropical rain forest, to fragrant Eucalyptus trees, to brushland at the rocky volcanic summit. Here, if you're lucky, you may find the famous Silversword plant. It's a brilliant silvery-colored spiked plant that blooms only once in its lifetime. You may spot one of the brilliantly colored 6-foot stalks that are actually the blossoms. It's as thrilling as the view around you. Once you arrive at the top, you're more than 2 miles high. There are a total of nine cinder cones in the crater, each one over 60-stories tall. Whether you see the crater at sunrise (along with many other people), or later, you'll see a rainbow of beautiful colors ranging from the most vivid imaginable volcanic reds to subtle rocky blues and greys, depending on the time of day.

Waimea Canyon

Kauai, the Garden Isle, is an emerald-green island sparkling in the midst of the blue Pacific. Many claim it to be the most beautiful of all. One of the most dramatic lookout points is the incomparable Waimea Canyon, the "Grand Canyon of the Pacific." Actually a part of the Koke'e State Park, the canyon is one mile wide, ten miles long and 3,657 feet deep. One of the most popular pastimes in this lovely spot is to sit at the lookout and gaze at the clouds' shadows as they float by, creating patterns on the canyon walls below you. After millions of years of erosion, many different strata levels can be seen. You'll see every conceivable color, and as the clouds drift by, it really is a sight to behold.

59

Kalalau Lookout

The Kalalau Lookout is another very popular spot on Kauai. Quite different from the Waimea Canyon lookout, yet just as spectacular in its own right. From this vantage point, the Kalalau Valley stretches for more than 4,000 feet down! It's no wonder that Kauai is called the Garden Isle when you see the lush greenery surrounding you. In the distance and far below, you'll see a sparkling rib-bon of sand that separates the tropical greenery from the blue waters of the Pacific. Beside this stretch of green, you'll see the mountains rise from the sea, with cascades of water forming glittering waterfalls in the distance, especially after a large rainfall. It's truly one of the most beautiful spots on earth and one of the most visited on Kauai.

Hanalei Bay

Not far from Princeville, is the last of our lookouts on Kauai: Hanalei Bay. Whereas the Waimea Canyon can be considered dramatic and awe-inspiring, Hanalei Bay can be considered dreamy and peaceful, yet uniquely memorable. Hanalei is what everyone imagines the perfect beach setting in paradise to be. Below you, a long half-moon of sandy beach stretches for several miles, surrounded by lush green vegetation reaching back through the Hanalei Valley to the mountains.

During certain seasons, the waves coming onto shore can be immense and dangerous, some measuring over 30 feet. At the distant point, after travelling for thousands of miles, the waves meet Kauai's rocks in a frenzied release of power. During the summer, when the waves are smaller, brightly colored boats anchor where the Hanalei Stream meets Hanalei Bay, creating a pastoral setting of gently moving boats on a turquoise sea. It's definitely a lookout not to be missed.

Kalaupapa Lookout

On the island of Molokai, the world's largest cliffs rise over 3,000 feet, from the sea. From the air, one gets a bird's eye view of these sheer cliffs, but there's an equally dramatic view to be seen from land: the Kalaupapa Lookout. Looking down from Kalaupapa, you'll see the old leper colony of Kalawao below you. The site of the colony was selected for its remoteness and inaccessibility. These cliffs form a geological barrier that isolates the penin-sula from the rest of Molokai. In 1886, however, an immi-grant from Madeira carved a narrow trail into the cliffs for mules to carry supplies to the community below. Today, tourists can travel down this 1,600-foot precipice on the famous Molokai Mule Ride.

Kilauea

Finally, on to the Big Island of Hawaii, where some of the most varied scenery on Earth waits for you. Throughout the Big Island, you'll see dramatic lookout points, but none more dramatic than Kilauea Volcano. This is a wonderland where lava deserts meet tropical rainforests. You're up around 4,000 feet when you enter Kilauea National Park, and the most dramatic view you'll find is directly behind the Volcano House right inside the park.

Before you stretches a scene that resembles a moonscape. In the distance, you'll see steam vents releasing puffs of smoke, as they have for centuries on end. Far away and above you, stretches one of the highest points in Hawaii, Mauna Loa, sloping 13,680 feet into the sky. Crater Rim road circles the Crater of Kilauea and is worth the drive to visit all the fascinating points along the way. You'll see many other lookouts that rival the view from back of the Volcano House, all of them special in their own right. And, if you're fortunate, Kilauea will honor your presence with an eruption, and you'll see the continuing process of creation in action.

Waipio Valley

The last stop on our lookout tour of the Hawaiian Islands, is one of the most serene and beautiful in all of Hawaii. It's the Waipio Valley, at road's end, on the east side towards the northern tip of the island. Once at the lookout, many people simply sit and stare for hours at the scenery that stretches below them. Here is a place that combines all that is the best in Hawaii—sheer cliffs dropping sharply to the sea, a coastline gently curving in the distance with crashing waves, forming a frosting of white foam on the turquoise waters that surround it.

The Valley itself has a rich history. One mile wide at the shoreline and six miles long, the valley was once the home of kings, including Kamehameha. It's also a scenic treasure that can be visited with four wheel drive vehicles, with 1200-foot waterfalls and a few farmers still living in the valley. It's paradise as you always knew it could be.

Wherever you go in Hawaii, there's always a sight to take your breath away. If you manage to see all these ten lookout points on your tour of the Hawaiian Islands, you'll have seen enough dramatic vistas to last you a lifetime ... and more.

Oahu - The Gathering Place

Oahu, nicknamed "the gathering place," is the third largest in size among the island chain, yet it contains more than three-fourths of the state's population, most of whom reside in the capital city, Honolulu. Oahu is approximately 40 miles long and 26 miles wide, with two major mountain ranges, the Koolau and the Waianae.

Honolulu, meaning "sheltered bay," has

The Elephant who Vacationed in Waikiki

Over the years, people have had many mistaken ideas about the animals native to the Hawaiian Islands. For example, many people arrive expecting to see monkeys swinging from the palm trees. Others half expect to find gorillas hiding out in the Hawaii uplands waiting to pounce on unsuspecting tourists. But back around 1915, there arrived an animal to the islands that would delight people for almost two decades, until her rather unfortunate and ignominious death.

It was an African elephant named Daisy, who arrived in 1916 on a ship bound for the Mainland, but was such a novelty here in Hawaii, that she was purchased by money raised by the city's school children. Through the

years, Daisy became a favorite at the Honolulu Zoo. But slowly, Daisy began to make a rather startling personality change. From the sweet, docile elephant the school children adored, she became quite the temperamental beast. So much so, that on March 3, 1933, Daisy ran amok and trampled her keeper to death. Daisy was immediately shot by the Honolulu police. A rather sad end to such an illustrious zoo career.

So today, as you stroll through Honolulu and hear something big and powerful behind you, move quickly out of the way. It could be the spirit of Daisy breathing down your back, or maybe another animal recently introduced to the islands ... a big, white and yellow one called The Bus.

Waikiki - the most famous beach in the World

been an economic center of the islands since the early 1800's when Honolulu Harbor was the only protected port of call of its size within 2,000 miles of Hawaii. Honolulu Harbor hosted countless sailing vessels, from sandalwood traders to whalers, during its 19th century heyday. Early this century, Pearl Harbor was made navigable and subsequently became the home of the U.S. Pacific Fleet. Today, Honolulu Harbor remains a shelter for the world's largest freighters and luxury liners.

Kamehameha III moved the royal court from Lahaina, Maui to Honolulu in the mid-19th century. Since then, Honolulu has been the seat of the islands' government, from the monarchy through to statehood. Hawaii's last king, David Kalakaua built the Iolani Palace that now stands in regal splendor near downtown Honolulu. The palace served as Hawaii's center of government well into the 20th Century. The much more recent (1968) State Capitol Building, just mauka (mountain side) of Iolani Palace now serves that function.

Although agriculture is no longer Oahu's most important industry, pineapple and sugar plantations still cover much of the island's land, especially the fertile Schofield Plateau at the center of the island.

Several major airlines have initiated direct flights from the U.S. mainland to Maui, Kauai and the Big Island of Hawaii, but most of Hawaii's nearly five million visitors each year pass through Honolulu International Airport and spend at least one night in one of the more than 33,000 hotel rooms in Waikiki.

The trip from the airport to Waikiki is about 9 miles. A taxi ride costs about $13. There are many car rental agencies located at the airport, many of which operate desks in the larger Waikiki hotels. Many hotels have shuttle buses to pick-up and return guests to the airport, and there are also several airport to Waikiki buses specifically for arriving, and departing, visitors. Whatever mode of transportation you choose, you'll be treated almost immediately to the scenery on Nimitz Highway between the airport and the downtown Honolulu business district. It is by far the worst anywhere in the islands. You will see everything from unfinished freeway overpasses and huge piles of dirt and debris to used car lots, and neon-lit roadside bars. But don't be put off; in a way it's fortunate that you see this side first. You'll have more appreciation for the outstanding island scenery elsewhere!

Once you pass the Dole pineapple cannery and Hilo Hattie's Fashion Center, you'll wind your way past Honolulu Harbor and some colorful glimpses into Hawaii's past. On your right, you'll see the Aloha Tower, a waterfront landmark only 10 stories high. Built in 1926, the tower's four clock faces and harbor traffic signals greeted visitors on "Boat Days," in the 1940's and 1950's, when luxury Matson liners arrived and departed at Piers 10 and 11. The "Boat Day" tradition of

Circle Rainbow Air

Honolulu International Airport
Commuter Terminal
(808) 833-3507

For those of you who want to see and experience the majestic beauty of Hawaii in one adventurous day, while enjoying many of the sights that can only be seen from the air, take a round the islands trip with Circle Rainbow Air. Started in 1979 with one Beechcraft, Circle Rainbow Air now has several planes and a staff of 15. Enjoy taking a one day personalized tour you'll be sure to remember. Circle Rainbow Air offers an exciting and comprehensive sky/ground tour that includes hotel pick-up at 6:00 a.m., complimentary continental breakfast prior to departure, and return at approximately 6:00 p.m.

Their adventure takes you to the second largest island in the Hawaiian chain, Maui. Each of the excellent pilots is very knowledgeable about the Hawaiian Islands and provides full narration during their flight tours. So, imagine the excitement of viewing and learning about the magnificent islands from a twin engine Beechcraft with your own wide view window seat. Outstanding coastal and mountain vistas will open up before you as you travel out of Oahu, to Maui via Molokai, Lanai and Kahoolawe. If you're flying during the months of December through May, it's an excellent time to see the world's largest aquatic mammals, the whales, diving up and out of the deep blue Pacific waters in the channels around the islands.

Once on the ground in Maui, you will travel in air conditioned vans or buses on a 160-mile, fully narrated tour to see many of the island's outstanding views and sights. At the top of the world's largest dormant volcano, Haleakala, the air is bracing and the views are magnificent. At the peak, you'll be looking at a scene closely resembling a lunar landscape, the inside of Haleakala, now dormant but not extinct!

Lunch will be hosted at the delightful Maui Plantation, located in central Maui. They offer an excellent buffet (price not included), as well as shopping. After lunch you will be escorted through lush tropical scenery to the Iao Needle, the second rainiest peak in Hawaii, and the famous JFK profile carved by nature in the rocks. Then on to the west end of Maui to see one of Hawaii's major agricultural industries at the Puunene Sugar Plantation. A special stop in Lahaina, an old whaling port, will give you insight into an interesting part of Hawaii's past as well as time for shopping. Your ground tour's final feature will tour along the hotels, golf courses and beaches at the Kaanapali Resort area, one of the most famous in the world.

Circle Rainbow Air provides a superb, no hassle service that will give you a wealth of information and many exciting memories. Call their 24-hour reservation service and begin the adventure of a lifetime; flightseeing with one of the most complete tours designed for your comfort and enjoyment.

OAHU

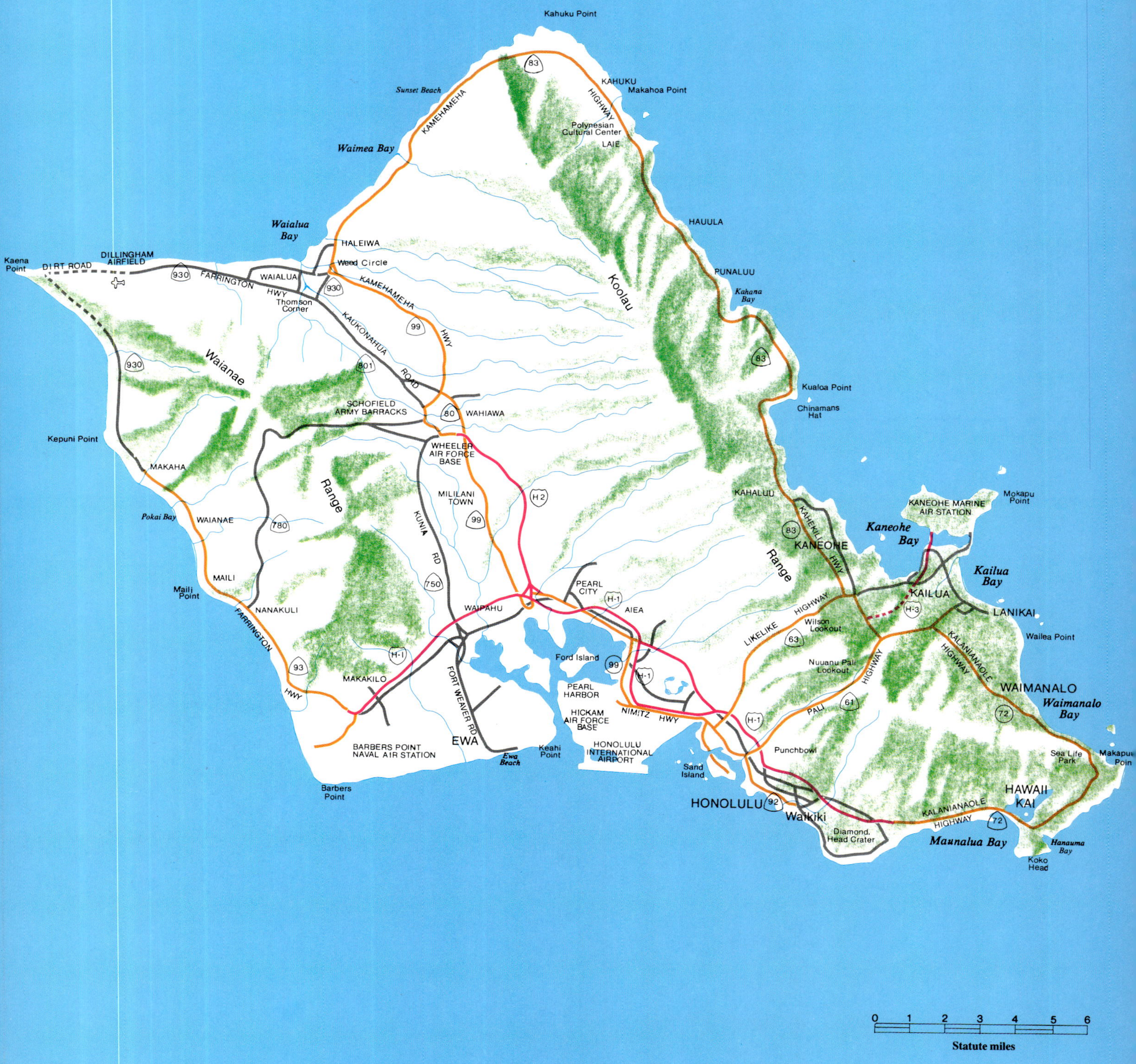

Kahuku Point

83

KAHUKU

Sunset Beach

Makahoa Point

Waimea Bay

KAMEHAMEHA

Polynesian
Cultural Center

LAIE

*Waialua
Bay*

HALEIWA

HIGHWAY

HAUULA

Weed Circle

Koolau

PUNALUU

930

DILLINGHAM
AIRFIELD

FARRINGTON

WAIALUA

930

KAMEHAMEHA

*Kahana
Bay*

Kaena
Point

DIRT ROAD

HWY

Thomson
Corner

KAUKONAHUA

99

HWY

83

Waianae

801

ROAD

Kualoa Point

Chinamans
Hat

Kepuni Point

SCHOFIELD
ARMY BARRACKS

80

WAHIAWA

WHEELER
AIR FORCE
BASE

MAKAHA

Range

MILILANI
TOWN

KAHALUU

KANEOHE MARINE
AIR STATION

Mokapu
Point

Pokai Bay

WAIANAE

780

KUNIA

H2

99

83

KANEOHE

*Kaneohe
Bay*

*Kailua
Bay*

*Maili
Point*

MAILI

750

RD

Range

KANEOHE
HWY

KAILUA

LANIKAI

NANAKULI

WAIPAHU

PEARL
CITY

H-1

AIEA

LIKELIKE

Wilson
Lookout

63

H-3

Wailea Point

FARRINGTON

H-1

Ford Island

99

Nuuanu Pali
Lookout

HIGHWAY

KALANIANAOLE

WAIMANALO

MAKAKILO

93

FORT WEAVER RD.

PEARL
HARBOR

H-1

61

PALI

HIGHWAY

72

*Waimanalo
Bay*

HICKAM
AIR FORCE
BASE

NIMITZ

HWY

HIGHWAY

H-1

Punchbowl

HAWAII
KAI

BARBERS POINT
NAVAL AIR STATION

EWA

Keahi
Point

HONOLULU
INTERNATIONAL
AIRPORT

Sand
Island

KALANIANAOLE

*Ewa
Beach*

Sea Life
Park

Makapuu
Poin

Barbers
Point

HONOLULU

92

Waikiki

Diamond
Head Crater

KALANIANAOLE

HIGHWAY

72

Koko
Head

Maunalua Bay

*Hanauma
Bay*

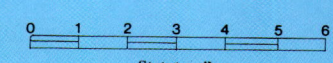

0 1 2 3 4 5 6

Statute miles

64

Glider Rides

Dillingham Airfield
Mokuleia 96791
(808) 677-3404

Come to the North Shore and rise above it all. Airborne in a bubble-topped sailplane, the North Shore panorama unfolds with its unique capsule of island life. It's an idyllic picture with the Pacific Ocean lapping at the shore fringed with coral reefs, Haleiwa harbor dotted with fishing boats, and the once fiery volcanic mountain range now topped off with a satellite tracking station.

Once on the North Shore, follow the signs at the Haleiwa traffic circle to Thomson Corner. A right turn leads to the rustic plantation town of Waialua. Continue on to the gliderport at Dillingham Airfield, just ten minutes away at the northwest end of the island. (See Oahu Map, page 64.) Take your camera along for some spectacular shots; the pilots will indicate points of interest along the way. Open daily from 10:00 a.m. to 5:30 p.m. and you don't need reservations. Enjoy the beauty and profound serenity of soaring in a glider high above some of Oahu's most breathtaking scenery.

meeting visiting cruise ships with leis, hula dancers and the music of the Royal Hawaiian Band has been recently revived.

Just past the Aloha Tower is the "Falls of Clyde," the world's only surviving completely rigged, four-masted sailing ship. It is proudly maintained as a maritime museum and is still undergoing reconstruction. Visitors are welcomed onboard daily for a small admission fee.

Continuing along Ala Moana Boulevard, you will reach Kewalo Basin, next to Fisherman's Wharf where numerous "dinner cruise" boats and fishing vessels are berthed. Just a block farther on the right is Ala Moana Beach Park, one of the most popular recreation sites in Honolulu.

Directly across the street from Ala Moana Beach Park is the Ala Moana Shopping Center, Hawaii's largest shopping center housing over 150 stores, restaurants and amusement areas. It is well known as one of the best people-watching spots anywhere in the state because of the blend of visitors and residents shopping seven days a week.

As you pass the end of Ala Moana Beach Park, you will drive onto the bridge over the Ala Wai Canal which serves as the gateway to Waikiki. On your right, you'll see the Ala Wai Harbor and yacht basin, which serves as home to the TransPac yachts that visit every other year, following the Transpacific Yacht Race from Los Angeles to Honolulu.

Exclusive Limousine Service

2020 Algaroba Street
Honolulu 96826
(808) 946-7905

For your personalized tour of Hawaii, Exclusive Limousine Service is the ultimate in limousine service. Choose from options such as special charters and tours, VIP airport ramp service, all with Japanese/English speaking drivers. Exclusive Limousine Service provides the maximum in comfort and travel luxury for a few hours, a day or for your entire stay. In addition, the Exclusive wedding planner will attend to all wedding details from minister, to flowers, music and site to make your wedding picture perfect.

Polynesian Adventure Tours

2250 Kalakaua Avenue, Suite 501E
Waikiki 96815
(808) 923-8687

Pearl Harbor! Arizona Memorial! The exciting Polynesian Cultural Center! The fun and beauty of Hawaii is yours, from a simple beach picnic to exploring the "Mysterious Orient," when you sightsee with Polynesian Adventure Tours. Choose from a complete list of full and half-day tours and let Hawaii's leader in mini-bus sightseeing do the rest to insure your Hawaii vacation is as relaxed and memorable as you want it to be.

See your travel agent, any Waikiki hotel tour desk, or write for a free full-color brochure.

Odyssey Rentals

P.O. Box 22985
Honolulu 96822
(808) 947-8036
(800) 826-8601 (outside Hawaii)

Becoming the trend setter in Hawaii for its car rentals, Odyssey Rentals has exotic cars that would please any of the rich and famous. If you would like to feel like a Prince in a Ferrari, Maserati, convertible Porsche or Mercedes, try Odyssey Rentals. Soak up the warm Hawaiian sun and really enjoy Hawaii from a different vantage point.

The very nicest thing about Odyssey Rentals is that you don't have to be rich or famous to afford an exotic car while in Hawaii. Not only do they provide a wide selection of cars but they also rent jeeps, mopeds, bicycles, and great snorkel equipment! They have convenient locations on Oahu and Maui, providing free maps, mileage, pick-up in Waikiki and, above all, excellent service. So whatever your rental needs are while in Hawaii, Odyssey Rentals will be happy to serve you, or to work with your travel agent.

Waikiki

Waikiki, is truly the world's most famous beach resort. The weather is almost always beautiful, the water and sky are clear, the sand is warm and white, and the night life is sensational. No matter how many episodes of "Hawaii Five-O" and "Magnum, P.I." first-time visitors have seen, they are often surprised by the inner city, concrete world. Folks who enjoy city life, crowds, shopping, great food and dancing the night away come back to Waikiki year after year.

Kalakaua Avenue is Waikiki's main street. Ala Moana Boulevard dead-ends at Kalakaua just past Fort DeRussy. A right turn onto Kalakaua will send you through a maze of shops, street stands, tour buses, taxis and pedicabs. In the midst of the mass of cars, people and shops are the hotels, many of which are located on the streets running perpendicular to Kalakaua, as well as lining the beach.

The oldest hotels in Waikiki are still the most charming. The Royal Hawaiian Hotel, affectionately known as the "pink palace," opened in 1927 on the site of the former summer home of the Kamehameha monarchs. The Royal was the "in" spot of the 30's for the Hollywood elite such as Mary Pickford and Douglas Fairbanks, as well as Fords and Rockefellers, presidents, kings and queens.

Honolulu Sailing Co.

P.O. Box 1500
Kaneohe 96744
(808) 235-8264

Honolulu Sailing offers the ultimate in ocean adventures aboard private passenger yachts carrying from four to eight people; or catering to private parties of up to 50 people. Sunset dinner cruises, day cruises and outer-island cruises are all available. Licensed skippers will see that your trip is fun and exciting, while instructors help you with snorkel equipment and underwater cameras to assure you great times while you enjoy the colorful coral reefs. Refreshments will be provided while warm trade winds whisk your cares away. For more information call or write Honolulu Sailing.

Dollar Rent A Car Hawaii

1600 Kapiolani Blvd., Suite #825
Waikiki 96814
(800) 367-7006 (outside Hawaii)
(808) 926-4200

One of the most important things a visitor wants when renting a car is the right kind for their personal taste. It used to be that you took what was available, within the price category you requested. But today, at Dollar Rent A Car Hawaii, the customer gets to make the choice.

And what a choice you have! Dollar, one of Hawaii's largest car rental fleets, offers more than 35 makes and models of vehicles that come in 8 price categories. Customers can select from compact Toyotas and Nissans, to mid-sized Chevrolets, Fords and Dodges. They also offer full-sized sedans, luxury sports coupes like the Oldsmobile Cutlass and Buick Regal, and a large selection of the popular Chrysler Fifth Avenue luxury four-door sedans.

And for those wanting sportier transportation, Dollar has Pontiac Fieros and Chevy Z-28's, and the very popular convertibles, including Dodge 600s, Ford Mustangs and Chevy Cavaliers.

The best part of renting from Dollar is the great value you'll get on the latest model cars, carefully maintained and cleaned, and available at

20 locations throughout the State. In Hawaii, you'll find Dollar Rent A Car on all major islands, at all airports, and convenient Waikiki and hotel locations. When you need a car in Hawaii, remember: Dollar has it all!

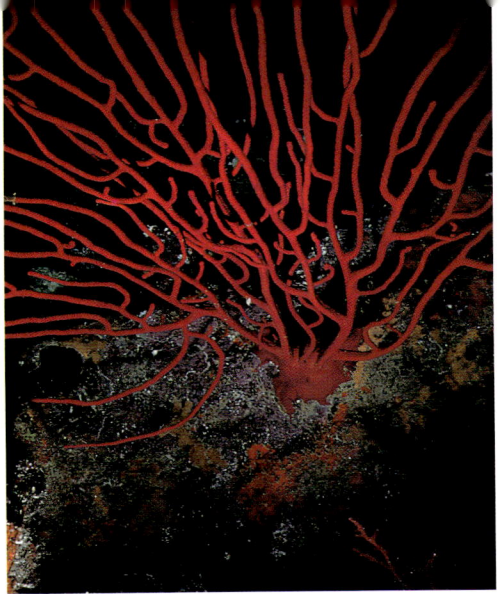

Hawaiian Divers

4510 Salt Lake Blvd., Suite D7
Honolulu 96818
(808) 487-8969

Experience the beauty of Hawaii's underwater sea life. Hawaiian Divers will take you there with a wide variety of charter dives or classes to qualify you for openwater certificates. Their classes or charters suit the beginner and professional; and their facilities and equipment are all first class, as the PADI 5 star and NAUI Pro Facility ratings show. So, to assure your diving adventure will be fun and hassle-free, contact the professionals at Hawaiian Divers.

Tropical Water Sports

P.O. Box 1604
Kaneohe 96744
(808) 235-2888

This sensational superstar tour offers you the widest variety of oceansports experiences all in one tour, designed specifically for your ultimate in enjoyment and safety. Beginning with a scenic catamaran ride around dramatic Kaneohe Bay, then anchoring at their private launching platform.

From here the fun begins as you can take advantage of any or all of the many things to do, with the jet skis launching the fun. Qualified instructors will help you with windsurfing or HobieCat sailing, or you can experience canoeing, Polynesian style in an outrigger. The finest snorkeling equipment will be provided so you may enjoy watching our abundant coral reefs. Whether you wish to view squid, sea urchins or schools of colorful island fish, or try your hand at catching a "big one," they'll see that your fancy is filled. To top it off try the "tire tube tow," an exhilarating experience full of laughs. The first class tour from Tropical Water Sports provides you with a first class barbecue for lunch. Call or write for more information.

Offshore Sports Hawaii

Koko Marina Shopping Center
Hawaii Kai, 96825
(808) 395-3434

Discover the most exciting sport that ever hit the water by joining the crew of Offshore Sports Hawaii, located in the Koko Marina Shopping Center. Just 15 minutes from Waikiki, on the way to Hanauma Bay, Sandy Beach, and Sea Life Park, thrills and excitement can be yours as you jet ski the waters of beautiful Maunalua Bay.

Offshore Sports Hawaii offers everything you need to enjoy an action-packed day of sunning and skiing with the latest and best jet skis and equipment. Lessons and boogie boards are also available, as well as a fully-equipped accessories and sportswear shop for your convenience.

Offshore Sports Hawaii offers the best in jet ski rentals with new 550 and 650 jet skis. After check-in and orientation, guests board one of the islands's largest Zodiacs (Boston Whaler) and are taken to the spacious pontoon boat, anchored in scenic Maunalua Bay. Once there, professional instructors issue you a life vest and assist with your jet ski to assure a safe and exciting day.

Regardless of age or experience, everyone can enjoy the thrill and excitement of jet skiing.

The whole family is invited to watch the fun and picnic on the pontoon boat, and of course, don't forget your camera. It just may be your biggest adventure in Hawaii!

You'll find shopping galore in Waikiki. One of the most visited is the Royal Hawaiian Shopping Center, located on the makai (seaward) side of Kalakaua; three 4-story buildings connected by bridges. Inside you will find department stores, handicraft shops, Hawaiian wear, restaurants, displays and demonstrations.

There is also the International Market Place, across the street on the mauka (mountain) side. This two-level bazaar is spread under a roof of enormous banyan trees. It's jammed with kiosks, shops and carts carrying everything from apparel and jewelry to handicrafts and flowers.

Waikiki Beach is actually a series of beaches, each with its own flavor and fans. The biggest crowds can be found in front of the Royal Hawaiian Hotel and Kuhio Beach Park. In many areas you'll find concessions offering everything from shave ice and pretzels to surfboards and outrigger canoe rides. Even when the ocean is rough, the swimming is easy because of the lack of dangerous currents. If you dislike crowds, try visiting the beach early in the morning or late in the afternoon. At night, the hotel lights cast a romantic shimmer on the sand and the music enhances the atmosphere for a stroll along the beach.

Kapiolani Park, between Kapahulu Avenue and Diamond Head, is a 170-acre park given to the people by King Kalakaua in 1877 and named after his queen. It is a favorite spot for picnics and Sunday sports outings. It is also the home of the

Paradise Snorkel Adventures

Holiday Isle Hotel
270 Lewers Street
Waikiki 96815
(808) 923-7766

Paradise Snorkel offers a variety of tours to this area all reasonably priced. The crystal clear water and colorful coral reefs of Hanauma Bay are teeming with fish. They offer free round trip transportation from your Waikiki condominium or hotel, providing you with the best of equipment and expert instructors. There's the half day or the full day tour, which includes a hot lunch. One of their finest trips is the escorted half day outing which takes a maximum of five people and provides the use of underwater camera during a fish feeding session. You won't want to miss this fun, safe, snorkeling experience.

Real Estate Showcase

Royal Hawaiian Shopping Center
Waikiki 96815
(808) 926-5677

Have you ever thought of owning Real Estate in Hawaii? Thousands of people purchase real estate in Hawaii each year because Hawaii has more to offer than just vacationing; live, retire and invest surrounded by the most beautiful weather, scenery and people in the world.

Real Estate Showcase is one of Hasegawa Komuten Co., Ltd.'s unique concepts in the sale and purchase of real estate, a real estate department store located on the ground floor level of the world famous Royal Hawaiian Shopping Center. Here is an opportunity to look at over $500 million worth of real estate in over 130 different displays on multi-level floors. They provide a vast selection of properties ranging from beach front homes, ranches, and luxury condominiums to commercial properties. Real Estate Showcase Hawaii devotes the walls of two floors to colorful displays offering you, at a glance, an exciting collection of quality properties.

Their real estate professionals are some of the most experienced and knowledgeable in Hawaii, with integrity and innovation as the hallmarks of this constantly expanding corporation. They offer total Real Estate Investment Services, and will be glad to assist you in all levels of acquisition.

Now, if you're looking for maximum exposure for real estate that you want to sell, then Real Estate Showcase Hawaii is ideal because of its location at the Royal Hawaiian Shopping Center. Of the 5 million visitors who come to Hawaii each year, most will stay in Waikiki. Real Estate Showcase Hawaii has established itself at the crossroads of the visitor activity in Hawaii. It is within walking distance of more than 22,000 hotel rooms and condos. Over ten thousand people walk by each day. Every day they host 250 groups of visitors, negotiating millions of dollars each week. The properties are exposed 13 hours a day, seven days a week. Each property is placed strategically in the proper category, price range, and location to be quickly identified to meet buyers preferences.

Real Estate Showcase Hawaii back their property sales with full color ads in Waikiki's leading publications, as well as television, constantly attracting thousands of prospects each week to see their multi-media displays and unobstructed showcase areas. Why not see what you might be missing?

Paul Brown

1347 Kapiolani Boulevard
Honolulu 96814
(808) 947-3971

Since 1972, the name Paul Brown has become synonymous with progressive, contemporary and professional hairstyling. Boasting a list of clients that include top fashion-makers such as Hawaii's First Lady, Jean Ariyoshi, Paul Brown offers a range of beauty services for both men and women that always make you look and feel your absolute best.

Trained in the leading cosmetology centers of San Francisco and New York, Paul began his career as style director for the Liberty House Beauty Salon. The successful professional training program that he developed there is the same program he now uses to train his own staff of 40 at his Kapiolani Boulevard salon, directly behind Ala Moana Center.

Although known primarily for the pacemaking hairstyling it offers, Paul Brown also provides shampooing, coloring, permanent waving and straightening. Come by for relaxing manicures, pedicures and facials. Waxing is also available. Their specialist will be happy to give make-up application lessons. And for the truly ultimate in relaxation, Paul Brown gives professional full body massages, using a jacuzzi for the final step adding to your completely refreshing experience.

Honolulu Zoo, Waikiki Aquarium, tennis courts, archery, driving ranges, free concerts at the bandstand, beaches, a jogging path and the Waikiki Shell - a large outdoor amphitheater where top name Hawaiian and mainland entertainers perform concerts under the stars in the shadow of Diamond Head.

There is so much to do and enjoy in Waikiki that it's impossible to give a full description in a few short pages. When you're here, you'll find plenty of free pocket size magazines that will give you all the current information you'll ever need.

Around the Island

When you're in need of a change from the hustle and bustle of the visitor city, take a tour or rent a car and drive. There are as many beautiful places to visit on this island as there are on Hawaii's outer-islands. It is possible to make the round-the-island trip in one day, although you may not be able to spend as much time at some of the more interesting areas, so it's recommended that you break your tour into two days if possible.

From Diamond Head traveling toward Kokohead, you'll pass several suburban areas before Hawaii Kai and Maunalua Bay, a favorite place for jet skiers. Just beyond Maunalua Bay is Hanauma Bay, a submerged volcanic crater, with large expanses of colorful coral and sealife in

Kino Nani

P.O. Box 10412
Honolulu 96816   (808) 923-6737

Kino Nani means "body beautiful" in Hawaiian, and that's the experience of Sabrina Stevens' high tech body sculpting. Sabrina is well known throughout the movie industry for her exclusive beauty treatments. Whether you're interested in facial sculpting and lifting, body rejuvenation relief from jet lag, a sport injury or pain, her electrotherapy equipment can help make that special difference. Everything from total beauty needs to physical therapy, Kino Nani will make you look and feel beautiful from the inside out.

crystal clear, shallow water. It's the place to experience snorkeling at it's best, but go early to avoid the crowds.

Then continue past the rocky coastline with the blowhole, the "toilet bowl," and where, on a clear day, you'll be able to see Molokai, over 30 miles away. Sandy Beach and Makapuu beach, just around the end of the island, are the "in" beaches for bodysurfing, or bodywhomping if you're not experienced!

At Makapuu, you'll find SeaLife Park, with many marine life exhibits, set amidst the beautiful scenery of the cliffs and beaches at Waimanalo. As you move onward through Kailua to the Pali Highway, and head back toward Honolulu, be sure to stop at the Pali Lookout for one of the most spectacular views anywhere in the world. As you look along precipitous cliffs out toward sandy beaches and blue ocean, the view is one of lush tropical valleys, and large curving bays. Then back to Honolulu past several churches, consulates and Queen Emma's Summer Palace, all located on the Pali Highway closer to the city.

The next full day tour will take you back over the Pali and westward past Kaneohe Bay along the beautiful scenic coastal road. You'll find various areas to stop and picnic or swim; places for snacks, and interesting sites to tour, including the Polynesian Cultural Center and Waimea Falls Park (both of these places require two or more hours to gain a full appreciation). After you pass the northernmost point of the island at Kuilima Point, the beaches are subject to heavy surf during certain seasons. Carefully check conditions before approaching the water, since waves are often up to 30 feet high, and sometimes up to 50 feet. You'll understand why these beaches are favorites with surfers, and absolutely a no-no for inexperienced swimmers.

Past Waimea Bay to Haleiwa there are quaint, artsy little shopping centers and restaurants. An excellent place to try a shave ice cone! Your choice is now either to head back toward Honolulu through Wahiawa, or continue further along the coast to Dillingham Airfield, where you'll be able to take a flight in a glider, should you wish. The experience of soaring gracefully like a bird is exciting and enlivening, and the views are incredible. The Mokuleia polo fields are also situated here, right next to the beach; games are played most Sundays in the summer, providing for an excellent picnic outing.

Back toward Honolulu, you'll pass over the Schofield Plateau, home of the largest Army base in the U.S.A., amidst acres and acres of sugar cane and pineapples. The panoramic view before you, as you drop down toward Pearl Harbor, shows the whole of the leeward side of the island laid out, Pearl Harbor to Diamond Head.

Pearl Harbor's history goes back to the early 1900's, although most people remember December 7th, 1941 as the key historical date. There are a variety of cruises and other tours available to visitors, from viewing the Arizona Memorial, to touring a World War II submarine and submarine museum, although you'll probably want to leave these tours to a different day. After your drive around the island it is usually preferable to sit by the beach, relaxing with your Mai Tai or Blue Hawaii, and recounting you memories of the day's sightseeing.

The island of Oahu is still the most visited island in the chain. What many people don't realize is that, even though 75% of Hawaii's residents live on Oahu, there are still beautiful and secluded areas to be found. You can have both untouched beaches and exciting Waikiki nightlife in one reasonable package. What could be better?

Maui - The Valley Isle

Maui, holds a special place in the hearts of many visitors and residents alike. This island combines the sights, sounds, colors and softness of all Hawaii and offers it generously night and day. Every minute here will permeate your memory for years to come.

If you'd like, challenge yourself to a daybreak trip up Haleakala to greet the sun from high atop the world's largest dormant volcano. Your rental car or one of many bus tours will take you up the Haleakala Highway route, where you can just follow the road signs.

Pack a light lunch, beverages and plenty of film as the spectacular visual effects startle even the most jaded photographic buffs. Just two miles up, along the edge of the crater, is the Haleakala Observatory Visitors Center, where you'll be able to see several cinder cones; one of them as tall as the Empire State Building. Manhattan Island could easily fit inside this crater. Dark shadows play hide and seek within this dormant, but not extinct volcano. Just 200 years ago, it erupted reminding the world that the demi-god Maui was still awake and powerful.

The great summit lies a few minutes beyond the observatory at Red Hill. Atop a 10,023 foot high volcanic cone it dares you to brave the cold morning air to scan the horizon, over one hundred miles away. Other adventures await you on the trip down. Several lookouts offer magnificent vistas in every direction and you might even venture to descend with one of the downhill bicycle tours. "Cruising" down from the summit requires skill, good physical condition and sometimes more than a fair share of courage.

Also deserving of an early morning start is the spectacular eastbound trip to heavenly Hana, via ancient bridges and narrow hairpin turns; a popular one or two day visit to yesteryear. Try to allow 3 to 4 hours each way and stop often, for the turnouts are a destination in and of themselves. Cascading waterfalls by the dozen flow from Haleakala's foothills, rushing past your bridge or roadside rest, falling thousands of feet to be welcomed by the lush forests and azure seas.

There are no facilities to rescue the forgetful driver, so fill your gas tank before you go, and take lots of film. Your adventure continues past taro fields, through pastures filled with horses and contented cows. Be prepared to slow for

Come and Get It at the Hasegawa General Store

A visit to Hana just isn't complete without a stop at the famous Hasegawa General Store. Get ready for a treat because this isn't your usual convenience store, or your typical supermarket, or your run-of-the-mill five & dime store ... it's totally unique unto itself. It's so unique, in fact, that a song "Hasegawa General Store" was created about the establishment and has become an island favorite!

Upon entering the store, you'll get the feeling of an old-time general store that's "got it all." And you better believe they do. A fun game to play with the owner Harry Hasegawa is to try and stump him with a request for

merchandise. Ask for a yo-yo for junior, or a spool of hot-pink thread for yourself or a particular fishing lure for your husband. Chances are good that Harry can find it for you.

Only one word of advice, don't expect instant service because the old-fashioned inventory control only adds to the store's charms and it may take a (ahem) minute or two to fill your order. Besides remember this is Hana, with a much slower, more tranquil way of life. So slow down, stop a minute (or more) and enjoy a cold soda at the Hasegawa General Store. It could only happen in "Heavenly Hana."

MAUI

Honokohau Bay
Lipoa Point
Nakalele Point
Napili Bay
HONOARAILANI HWY
HONOKAHUA
30
KAHAKULOA
Kahakuloa Point
KAANAPALI
PUU KUKUI
KAPALUA HWY
WAIHEE
340
Waihee Point
Pauwela Point
Uaoa Bay
PAUWELA
360
Waipio Bay
Kahului Bay
SPRECKLELSVILLE
HAIKU
HANA HWY
LAHAINA
MILL ST
WAILUKU
IAO VALLEY RD
KAHULUI
KAHULUI AIRPORT
PAIA
32
WAIKAPU
KUIHELANI HWY
PUUNENE
HALEAKALA HWY
HALIIMAILE
MAKAWAO AVE
Pukaulua Point
WAILUA
Wailua Bay
Papiha Point
HONOAPIILANI
380
WAIKO RD
MOKUELE RD
PUKALANI
HALEAKALA HWY
377
378
HALEAKALA CRATER RD
Kalahu Point
HANA HWY
HANA AIRPORT
OLOWALU
MOPUA
MAALAE
KIHEI
KIHEI
KEKAULIKE AVE
360
HANA
Hana Bay
Maalaea Bay
KIHEI RD
HALEAKALA NAT. PARK
WAILEA
31
37
KULA
KEOKEA
KIPAHULU
Wailua Cove
Kukui Bay
MAKENA
Molokini Island
ULUPALAKUA
HANA HWY
Makaalae Point
Ahihi Bay
31
PIILANI HWY
Huakini Bay
Apole Point
Mamalu Bay
Waiaha Bay
La Perouse Bay
Cape Hanamanioa

Kuikui Point

KAHOOLAWE
Ule Point
Kanapau Bay
Kamohio Bay
Kaka Point

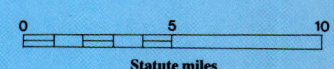

0   5   10
Statute miles

74

oncoming traffic and be alert for interesting flowers and patches of lush tropical plants.

Toward the end of the road, your reward can be found at the Seven Sacred Pools. If you are not staying overnight at one of the small colorful hotels then make the Hasegawa General Store your most important stop. Besides gas, you can get anything and everything your heart desires. Roadside stands will tempt you on the way back, so treat yourself to an ice-cold pineapple, mango crisps, coconut meat and milk, assorted seeds, drinks and Hana-style souvenirs. They'll even offer to mail a big souvenir to your hometown - a complete coconut, husk and all, right off the tree in their own backyard! Do be sure to plan the return trip during daylight hours as the winding road doubles in difficulty after sunset.

Shopping and sunning, cruising or just playing all apply to the Lahaina-Kaanapali area. Plan carefully your mix of watersports, eating and sightseeing, for this world famous whaling port has it all - and has over 100 years of proof! Outdoor dining and shopping are side by side overlooking the harbor, home of charter and private vessels that dot the oceans from sunrise to glorious sunset.

If you feel inclined to barefoot for a while, Kaanapali, just a few minutes drive past Lahaina Town, has many miles of sugar-fine, white sand beaches and world famous hotels, all sharing the

Hooray for the Nene!

The Nene Goose of Hawaii has made a dramatic comeback in recent years from virtual extinction. Back in the 18th century, there were an estimated 25,000 Nene Geese populating the Hawaiian Islands. But by the 1940's, there were less than 50 left.

The reason for their decline was manifold; ranging from the encroachment of man through ranching, hunting and the building of beach resorts on their breeding grounds, to the introduction of feral animals. These feral (wild) goat, sheep, cattle and pigs trampled and ate the grasses that protected the bird and served as their

breeding ground. The rats and the mongoose, also introduced by man, ate many of their eggs and nestlings.

Finally in the 1940's, a massive campaign was begun to protect and regenerate this rapidly dwindling species. Today, there are over 2,000 Nene Geese surviving in captivity and over 1,000 surviving in the wild. So through this diligent conservation effort, the Nene's goose wasn't cooked

... and with the continued effort of visitors and locals, they'll continue to breed and thrive as the State Bird of Hawaii.

Scuba Schools of Maui
1000 Limahana Place, #A
Lahaina, Maui 96761
(308) 661-8036 or 667-7500

Scuba Schools of Maui, located in the old whaling port of Lahaina, has everything an experienced or beginner diver could want to enjoy while scuba diving in Hawaii. They offer free Scuba lessons for beginners, a selection of specially tailored diving adventures, underwater photography equipment, full service equipment rental and all their certifications are recognized internationally. Their inter-island dives take you on half-day trips to the famous Molokini Island or Lanai, for some of the best diving in Hawaii.

It's never been so easy. On your vacation this year, you can become a certified scuba diver with their 4-day Scuba Course. So, now is the time! Experience Hawaii's beautiful underwater world with all equipment available, while safe instructors and knowledgable guides show you the sights!

beds of La Perouse Bay, two of the best diving and snorkeling areas in Maui. Ocean Activities Center has experienced instructors who'll guide you safely into the water for many unforgettable adventures in snorkeling or diving (if you're certified). Molokini is a marine life preserve, so you can expect to see many brightly colored reef fish, live coral formations, spiny sea urchins, lobster and octopus. A delicious lunch buffet is provided on the cruising excursions, with complimentary Mai Tais for the celebration on the way home!

Ocean Activities Center has a full range of cruising and water activities, including "divine diving," taking visitors to the best diving on Maui, Molokini, Kahoolawe or Lanai. Top quality scuba gear is provided, along with support by a highly trained crew for one of the best diving adventures you'll ever experience.

The sunset dinner cruise is an ideal way of completing your active Maui day with the brilliant, dynamic colors of the typical Hawaiian sunset. With great entertainment and the beautiful Maui vistas in the background, you'll have another unforgettable experience in paradise. Call Ocean Activities for reservations and more information on the full range of what is available; you'll experience the sea, a part of the real Hawaii. Let it become a part of you.

Ocean Activities Center

Wailea Shopping Village
714 Front Street
Kihei, Maui 96753
(808) 879-4485

Lahaina, Maui 96761
(808) 667-7794

There are worlds upon and beneath the sea that are never known on land. That's even more true in Hawaii, surrounded by the crystal clear, warm Pacific Ocean. You can discover the spectacular undersea life of Hawaii on one of several ocean cruises available with the Ocean Activities Center out of Maalea Harbor in Maui. So if you want to cruise, snorkel, dive, dine in the sunset or discover virtually untouched islands, the place to start is Ocean Activities Center. Try a discovery cruise to Lanai on board their catamaran, Maka Kai. You'll cruise the channel between Maui and Lanai, watching Maui's famed humpback whales in season, December through April, and arrive at Lanai ready for their special tour with lunch at the historic Hotel Lanai. After lunch is the time to head for one of Lanai's undiscovered coves for an afternoon of swimming, snorkeling and underwater video exploration before the cruise celebration heading back to Maui.

Or you can thrill to the freedom of the sea and the play of the porpoise, sea birds, whales or flying fish on the way to Molokini or the coral

Maui Helicopter Adventures

Wailea Shopping Village
Kihei, Maui 96753
(808) 879-1601
(800) 367-8003 (outside Hawaii)

Paradise is truly a reality when you are among the privileged few to see Maui's most exquisite and breathtaking beauty aboard the luxury of a jet helicopter.

Fly in private comfort and experience the single most luxurious way to see the exotic and rare beauty of Maui. There is more to Maui than you can imagine! Let Maui Helicopters show you the magical areas accessible only by air as you glide past exotic lush rain forests, cascading waterfalls, towering cliffs, secluded and untouched beaches, giant volcanic craters, and a hidden Hawaiian village.

Experience one of the most uplifting experiences in paradise. The visual spectacle of the panoramic views immediately opens your eyes to the reality of the beauty and highlights of Maui's natural wonders. Just when you thought you'd seen all of the beautiful sights, you soar to the summit of Haleakala Crater and hover above the world's most famous, dormant volcano. Haleakala means "House of the Sun" and some of the most beautiful sunrises and sunsets are viewed here.

From the slopes of Haleakala, escape to the ancient Hawaiian village of Hana, where you will see lush tropical jungles, inaccessible rain forests, cascading and unforgettable waterfalls and the beautiful unspoiled jagged coastline. "Heavenly Hana" is nestled on the remote eastern shore of Maui and is home to not only local residents but also to the rich and famous. They are offered anonymity unavailable elsewhere and they are also offered the serene beauty and privacy of Maui. A picturesque journey to "Heavenly Hana" is priceless!

An all-around island adventure will take you to the scenic coastline of West Maui to discover historic Lahaina and Maui's western coastline. The resorts of Kaanapali and Kapalua will also give you the opportunity to view the biggest gentle underwater creatures, the humpback whales. Viewing the humpback whales is an added treat, during the whalewatching season, December through April. Next, enter remote Waihee Valley and view spectacular cliffs and breathtaking waterfalls. Also explore Iao Valley where King Kamehameha conquered Maui in the bloody battle of 1790 and soar past Iao Needle, a lava monolith rising 1,200 feet from the valley floor.

Maui Helicopters even offers a memorable journey to the friendly isle of Molokai. Your inter-island flight will take you across Pailolo Channel to the majestic valleys and sea cliffs of Molokai. Tour the Kalaupapa Peninsula, the Halawa Valley, and hover over cascading waterfalls and the remains of an ancient Polynesian village. Enjoy a rest stop on one of Molokai's inaccessible beaches before returning to Maui's western shore.

Also ask about the sunrise/sunset flights and the popular honeymoon package. The honeymoon highlight is truly an unsurpassed adventure offering a private air tour of Maui and a gourmet picnic in a remote meadow with complete privacy. The pilot drops off the couple and they are left alone in the tall grass and wild flowers overlooking the entire island and the Pacific Ocean. The helicopter returns at a pre-scheduled time (whenever the couple wishes) and returns the honeymooners to reality after a day above the world.

Maui Helicopters has been flying individuals and large groups on Maui for years. Their experience and reputation of being the best has made them the helicopter company on Maui. Let Maui Helicopters show you the wonders of Maui in the luxury of a jet helicopter, and experience the ultimate. Live a piece of your paradise dream to carry home with you forever. Intimate and incredible!

Hilo Hattie's

744 Front Street
Lahaina, Maui 96761
(808) 667-2577

3252 Kuhio Highway
Lihue, Kauai 96766
(808) 245-3404

75-5597-A Palani
Kona, Hawaii 96740
(808) 329-7200

An exclusive collection of Hawaiian fashions.
Available at over 50 stores throughout the islands.
Call for the location nearest you.

same soft tradewinds. Nowhere else do the old
and new come together as gently and as elegantly
as this. The Hyatt Regency Maui is a world class
hotel complex with its own swim-up bar inside a
lava cavern, tropical birds, a suspension bridge,
an acre wide swimming pool, water slide, snorkeling and a multi-million dollar art collection. Take
the free guided tour of the grounds or just browse
on your own.

Most agree that Kaanapali has the safest
beaches around, and while you dry off, you can
watch the activities of sailboats, windsurfers and
para-sailers on the bay. Fascinating shapes and
designs abound with the myriad sails of boats and
private yachts. There are many fishing and sailing
charters, snorkeling or diving trips, whale watch
cruises and, to finish the day, romantic sunset
cruises available. And, if you just want to rest your
mind, sip a cool Mai Tai or Chi Chi and ponder
living here in paradise.

As the sun changes into its evening attire,
the colors coalesce into silver and gold, with sails
becoming silhouettes and the palms hush to a
mysterious whisper. What magical treat is in store
for you tonight? Dining outdoor perhaps; or the
beach? Just relax with some pupus during happy
hour and soon your thoughts will drift to dinner
and maybe some dancing. Every major hotel
offers music, entertainment, piano bars and even
more shopping and strolling.

Crossing the island once again allows you to

Genesis Yacht Charters

P.O. Box 10697
Lahaina, Maui 96761
(808) 669-7557 or 667-5667

Be the skipper or just a relaxed sailor aboard the luxurious and spacious Genesis. Comfort and safety abound aboard this 44′ cruising ketch with a fully equipped galley, a large salon for dining and a spacious cockpit for viewing and sunbathing; and for your personal comfort, two double state rooms, each with a private head and shower. Professional USCG-certified captains take you on romantic and exciting sunset, half day and full day sails, each with refreshments and lunch or dinner on board. Personalized snorkeling tours are also available with all equipment and instruction provided, and private charters can be arranged by the hour, day or week.

Let yourself experience the spectacular view of the island Maui from the same vantage point the early explorers did when they first arrived centuries ago. Take time to sit in the cockpit or lay on the deck with cool refreshments and converse with friends. If excitement is your thing, take the helm and experience the exhilaration of piloting a sailing ship in the brisk trade winds of the blue Pacific Ocean. In Hawaii, this is one of the most exciting ways of seeing the islands—from the ocean!

Maui Physicians

Maui Marriott
100 Nohea Kai Drive
Lahaina, Maui 96761
(808) 667-7001
After hours: 244-5939

Lahaina Physicians

Lahaina Square
840 Wainee Street
Lahaina, Maui 96761
(808) 667-2534

Offering a convenient health care center to the visitors of the West Maui area, Maui Physicians and Lahaina Physicians serve the medical needs in the areas of Family Practice, Pediatrics, Industrial Medicine and Internal Medicine. Patients have available, personalized primary medical services for adults and children at extended office hours, laboratory, support services, and the convenience of after-hour, House Calls within the West Maui area.

Maui Physicians is located at the Maui Marriott Resort on Kaanapali Beach; Lahaina Physicians is located in Lahaina Square. Office hours are Monday through Friday, 8:00 a.m. to 6:00 p.m. Saturday, 8:00 a.m. to 12 noon. Sunday by appointment. Hotel Room calls are available 24 hours a day, 7 days a week.

Spats Restaurant and Nightclub

Hyatt Regency Maui
200 Nohea Kai Drive
Lahaina, Maui
(808) 667-7474
Dinner: 6:00 to 9:30 p.m.
Valet Parking

Located in the magnificence of the Hyatt Regency Maui you'll find a Travel-Holiday award winning restaurant that is also Maui's hottest nightclub. Spats is well known for exquisite Northern Italian Cuisine, an extensive selection of quality Italian wines and the excitement of dancing the night away to the latest sounds on a spectacular lighted dance floor.

Begin your Italian experience at dinner with appetizers that include calamaretti fritti, succulent fried squid with lemon marinara, or antipasto Casa Spats, a delicious variety of Italian meats. Super light salads include a spinach salad, insalata di pomodoro con cipolla, tomatoes and onions with caper and basil vinaigrette and a curly endive; or insalata Enrico Caruso, a radiccio lettuce, purple onions, garlic, cheese and vinaigrette salad.

For "Pasta with Passion," choose from spaghetti al pesto; angel hair pasta with clam sauce—the most delicate pasta served with a light, creamy sauce of fresh butter clams; or fettucine with mushrooms and prosciutto in a cream sauce. Each dish is guaranteed to satisfy your desire for homemade Italian style pasta.

Naturally, the entrees at Spats are as romantically Italian and befitting of the reputation as the fountainhead of Western cuisine as any you'll experience in Italy. Choose from a succulent breaded veal chop with olive butter, a delicate thinly sliced veal scallopine sauteed in a Marsala wine sauce, chicken breast stuffed with shrimp, or chicken braised in marsala and mushrooms.

Brush up on your Italian and order gamberri con aglio e burro, large prawns with garlic and lemon butter, or the chef's seafood creation, pesce fantasia del giorno. Fresh vegetables and a choice of gnocchi, pollenta or risotti are served with all entrees.

For a delightful way to complete your dining experience try the specialty dessert, Bella Casa Spats, a light chocolate mousse prepared at your table. In very typical Italian style, of course, freshly made gelato, sherbet or a choice selection from the pastry cart are available as alternatives.

Spats has fifty varieties of especially selected wines featuring bianco wines like Valenti and J Brigl and rosso wines like Prunotto and Mastroberardino. If you prefer to stay local, choose from a selection of California wines that include Chardonnays and Cabernet Sauvignon from several quality vineyards.

Then, relax awhile until the beat of the music awakens your pulse. Time to dance away those newly acquired calories to the latest popular sounds played by an energetic D.J. to arouse your senses, passions and circulation. Spats is easy to find at the Hyatt, and evening attire will support you in enjoying a stylish evening on the town.

Swan Court

Hyatt Regency Maui
200 Nohea Kai Drive
Lahaina, Maui
(808) 667-7474
Breakfast: 6:30 a.m. to 11:30 a.m.
Sundays to 1:30 p.m.
Dinner: 6:00 p.m. to 10:30 p.m.

Swan Court is the Hyatt Regency Maui's fine dining restaurant. Open to the peaceful influence of Japanese gardens, this Travel-Holiday award winning restaurant provides just the ambiance for a sophisticated and romantic evening that you'll always cherish. The sound of waterfalls and the ever present beauty of swans gliding gracefully by, are reflected in an atmosphere of elegant high ceilings, mirrors and dramatic spaciousness. The exquisite quality of the cuisine at Swan Court is perfectly complemented by the attentive service.

Swan Court's cuisine is decidedly International, with a strong continental influence. Heinrich Wiegmann, food and beverage director

says, "We have a blend of the traditional American dishes and the wonderful cuisine brought to this country by immigrants from around the world. If it isn't fresh, we won't serve it. Fresh fish, meat and poultry as well as vegetables and fruits not only taste and look better, they're healthier."

Naturally, there's a well designed selection of hot and cold appetizers, with a delicious smoked salmon and sturgeon on a potato pancake, a sophisticated Beluga caviar, escargots Swan Court and an excellent choice of soups or salads. Be tempted by the fresh Kauai shrimp bisque or the salad of the court; an array of leafy green and fresh vegetables with shrimp and seasonal specialties, topped with a choice of house dressings, including a tangy peppercream.

A selection of enticing entrees offer your palate a variety of sophisticated taste experiences, with seafood, poultry and meats, all fresh, tasteful and beautifully presented. You will always have the choice of local fish dishes, as well as a captivating fresh Maine lobster fricassee in a natural sauce flavored with vanilla beans. Poultry is very well represented by the baby chicken Noilly Prat, sauteed and topped with wild mushrooms and served with a tantalizing creamy vermouth sauce. Prefer beef or lamb? As well as excellently prepared steaks and prime rib, your choice includes tournedos of beef with lobster sausage, served with a red wine sauce, or the chef's carving board—a special roast of the evening carved to order.

As in any classic restaurant, Swan Court has it's specialties. Veal cutlet aux morilles, grenadine of veal, Chinese steamed fish, tiger prawns "black coral" and medallions of beef and fish, all especially created dishes capturing a variety of continental and oriental cuisines for your gourmet dining pleasure.

The dessert selection is exquisitely prepared to complete your repast, with delicate continental offerings and other very tempting choices, displayed buffet style for your enjoyment and ease of selection. Swan Court's connoisseur wine list is extensive and carries an obvious Hyatt quality, with many European and Californian vintages especially chosen to complement your dining adventure. The piano lounge is an ideal place to await your table, giving you a sampling of the Swan Court atmosphere and the soft musical background to entertain you while you dine.

Swan Court also has a fabulous breakfast buffet every day. At dinner, evening attire is suggested. Take the opportunity—Swan Court is a dining adventure you should not miss.

take a trip back into time to the Iao Needle; over 2,000 feet of lava rock, jutting straight up to the sky. Set in the lush green Iao Valley just 3 miles out of Kahului, the battle for control of Maui was fought here with King Kamehameha emerging as the victor. It is said the fighting was so fierce that the waters of the Iao Stream were dammed up by the bodies of both armies; the waters red and ominous. Today it's a favorite spot for picnicking. Throughout your time here you can hear the interplay between trickling stream, the rushing of the wind through the canyon and maybe even the crack of thunder from a storm high atop Haleakala in the distance.

The most relaxing tour is the comfortable drive to the coastal road and waters edge in the Kihei-Wailea area. Just 15 minutes from Kahului and a little over 40 minutes from Kaanapali, the drive presents many opportunities to stop for a quick swim, just a few feet from the road. Kalama Park offers nice facilities with a good public beach. Further on are other beautiful parks with outstanding snorkeling (except when afternoon winds pick up). Near the road's end is the world famous Makena Beach. Soon to be developed and become even more popular, it is considered by most well traveled visitors to be the most beautiful beach on Maui.

Take your own snorkeling equipment or rent right at the beach and experience the less traveled sights of this undersea wonderland. Hundreds of varieties of fish, of as many colors, swim here. Oblivious to the curious snorkelers or scuba divers, life below the suface remains unchanged and is as fascinating as ever. Reef fish play within inches of the shoreline. A drier approach are the glass-bottom boats who will feed them an underwater lunch while you watch. Scuba introduction dives are available from many harbors taking you to a world of utter silence save for the sound of your own breath and bubbles.

Kihei and Lahaina offers various sailing cruises to Lanai, with picnics, sightseeing and even whale watching along the way. Increasingly more popular are the entire tour packages including transportation, food, entertainment, history, activities, narration and time to meet the person next to you.

While in Maui experience all it can offer; land, sea and air. Among the newest developments are breathtaking helicopter rides into the very heart of Haleakala, through verdant valleys and over ancient lava flows. Seen from the air, Maui's tropical wonder becomes larger than life and more real than mere words can describe.

The Spirit of St. Louis
... and Charles Lindbergh too

Many visitors to Hawaii are unaware of the special connection the islands have with Charles Lindbergh. For it's in Hana, Maui that you'll find the grave of this famous aviator. One of the most beautiful spots in the world, Hana, is appropriately enough the final resting place for the man who first crossed the Atlantic aboard "The Spirit of St. Louis."

Lindbergh died in 1974 at his nearby cottage. His body was placed in a rough-hewn eucalyptus casket and buried in a simple, unpretentious grave here, covered with native Hawaiian stones. It's a grave-site that's visited by hundreds of travelers each year. To

find it, look for a tiny cemetery next to the Kipahulu Hawaiian church on the sea-side of the Hana Road. It's in this picturesque spot that you'll find the grave of one of the world's greatest heroes.

However, remember that this is "Heavenly Hana," and the grave of a very special man. Please accord the respect due this man ... and remember the equally special place, Hana, where he is buried.

What a nice thought to ponder ... that even though the "Spirit of St. Louis" is found today in Washington, D.C., the spirit of Charles Lindbergh remains forever in the Hawaiian Isles.

83

MOLOKAI AND LANAI

Llio Point

Kahiu Point
Makanalua
Peninsula
KALAUPAPA
Mokapu
Island
KALAE
Kikipua
Point
Lamaloa Head
Haupu
Bay
Pelekunu
Bay
Halawa
Bay
MOLOKAI
AIRPORT
470
HALAWA
460
KUALAPU
Hipuapua
Falls
MAUNALOA RD
480
Moaula
Falls
MAUNA LOA
460
Laau
Point
Kaunakakai
Harbor
KAUNAKAKAI
KAMILOLOA
WAIALUA
HALENA
KOLO
MOKU
KAMEHAMEHA
KALUAAHA
HWY
PAUWALU
450
PUKOO
UALAPUE
KAMALO

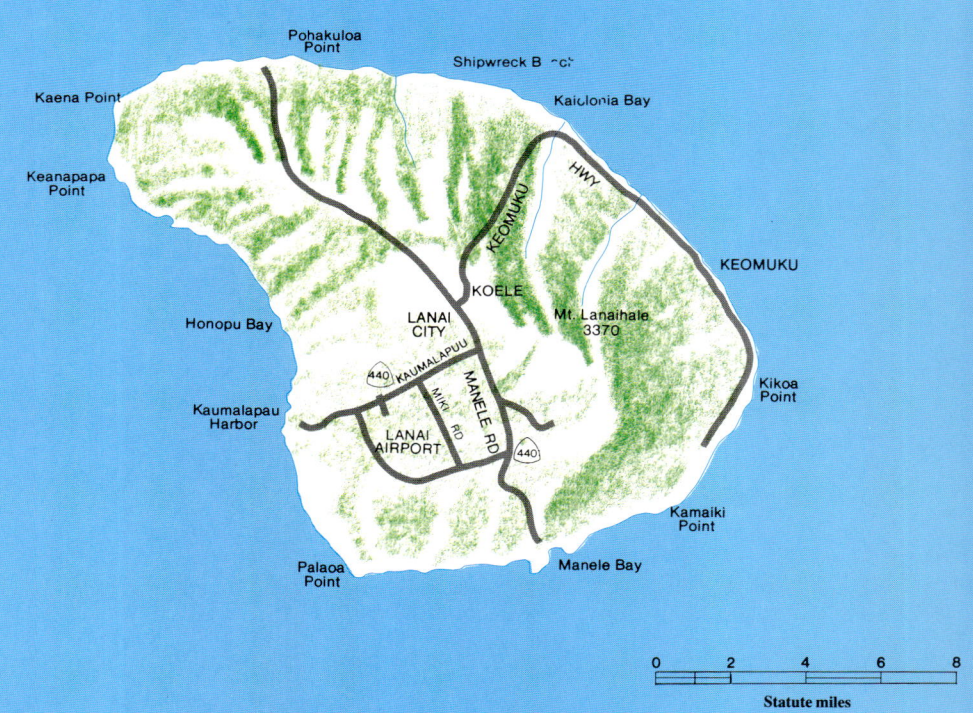

Pohakuloa
Point
Shipwreck Beach
Kaena Point
Kaiolohia Bay
Keanapapa
Point
KEOMUKU
HWY
KEOMUKU
KOELE
Honopu Bay
LANAI
CITY
Mt. Lanaihale
3370
KAUMALAPUU
440
Kikoa
Point
Kaumalapau
Harbor
LANAI
AIRPORT
MANELE RD
440
Kamaiki
Point
Palaoa
Point
Manele Bay

0   2   4   6   8
Statute miles

Molokai and Lanai

Molokai, The Friendly Island, and Lanai, The Pineapple Island are the 5th and 6th largest islands in the Hawaiian chain. Both islands are relatively untouched by tourism, and offer superb insights into old Hawaii.

Only 37 miles long and 10 miles wide, Molokai has three distinct geographical areas, starting with the mountains rising up to nearly 5,000 feet in the East, an adjoining section leading to the lower, dry Mauna Loa tableland, and a small, flat area seemingly added on to the North Shore, forming the Makanalua Peninsula (often called the Kalaupapa Peninsula). The island has a very high proportion of native Hawaiians, stemming from the heavy local settlement in 1921 under the Hawaiian Homes Act. With them came their aloha spirit, giving the island it's present reputation of friendliness. Today, Molokai is the place for untouched island scenery and a quiet relaxing vacation free from many of the often found commercial influences.

Kaunakakai, the main town on the island, is situated centrally on the south facing coast. Travelling east along the coastal route will bring you to many interesting and unusual features, including several heiau and a large number of fishponds dating back to the 15th century. Many of the heiau are fenced and locked, and others require permission and keys for entry. Some of the fishponds, originally built to provide seafood for local chiefs and their followers, are still in use with modern day aquaculture.

At the end of the road to the east, you'll find Halawa Valley and Bay. A truly outstanding scenic area, the difficult drive over the last few miles, as the road becomes narrow and twisting, is well worth the effort. At some time in the past, several hundred people lived in the deep valley, making the virtually deserted, present-day scene seem especially poignant.

A popular sightseeing area, to the north of Kaunakakai, is the Kalaupapa Settlement, settled and developed by Father Damien in the later 1800s. It is located on the Kalaupapa Peninsula on the northern shore. A 1 600 foot high cliff divides the peninsula from the rest of the island and

Father Damien: Hawaii's Resident Saint

Father Damien was truly a man loved by the people of Hawaii ... and especially by the lepers he lived with at Kalawao on the Island of Molokai.

During the 1880's, leprosy was a dreaded disease that was thought to be very communicable. Therefore, lepers were sent to the lonely community of Kalawao, cut off from civilization and the taunts and fears of the human race. When Father Damien first arrived there to help the lepers, he was a handsome man untouched by the disease. But through the years, the martyr-priest contracted the disease himself and began to waste away into one of the so-called "untouchables." But this did nothing to deter Father Damien. He continued to work for the good of the people of Kalawao and to advance their cause.

Today, in front of the state capitol stands a modern sculpture of Father Damien, sculpted in the last stages of his bout with leprosy. It's a very controversial statue, because it shows the pain and suffering this man went through. Many felt he should have been depicted as he first arrived in Hawaii; a handsome, strong, healthy man.

But today, this is one of the island's most touching historical monuments, ironically enough, to a man people were afraid to touch. He's truly Hawaii's resident saint ... a loving symbol of our island spirit today.

North Coast of Molokai

there is no road connection. However, you can ride a mule, hike, or travel by plane or helicopter to this scenic and quaint town.

Kalaupapa was founded by people who suffered from Hansen's disease. Commonly called Leprosy, it was discovered in Hawaii in the 1830s. In 1866, the victims were roughly dumped at the peninsula and left in isolation to exist in whatever form they could fashion for themselves. In 1873, they were joined by Father Damien who selflessly assisted them in carving out a life for themselves, regardless of their condition. Father Damien brought them acceptance, trust and dignity. He eventually contracted the disease himself, dying in 1889. In 1946 Sulfone drugs were discovered and the disease was brought under control. Residents of Kalaupapa were then free to leave, but most remained to live their lives out in the privacy and beauty of the little town.

The mule ride down the cliffs, from the Kalaupapa Lookout area, is an exciting way to visit Kalaupapa. You'll see spectacular panoramas of the ocean, with the small harbor, the church and houses in the foreground and the incredible cliffs along the North shore of Molokai stretching in either direction.

Westwards from Kaunakakai, you'll head through the drier areas of Molokai, with relatively few interesting landmarks. There are few hotels and most are located on this side of Kaunakakai, as well as the Molokai Ranch Wildlife Park

The Lanai Landing

P.O. Box 10758
Lahaina, Maui 96761
(808) 667-7798

The Lanai Landing is a most unique adventure and exclusive visitor attraction. Located on the east side of Lanai and only seven miles directly across from the whaling port of Lahaina, the Lanai Landing offers an experience we have all dreamed about. Swaying palms, covered shelters and a white sand beach that travels for miles, void of any footprints except one's own, make this remote and private estate a rare discovery even in Hawaii.

Virtually inaccessible by land, visitors can only journey to this remote site by way of one of Sea Sail's sailing fleet, leaving from the beachfront at Kaanapali. A short 45-minute sail away lies the Lanai Landing. On the way, there's time for snorkeling off the clear reefs fronting the island, or even viewing whales frolicking in the waters during the months of December to May. Because of the natural setting, only a limited number of people can be permitted to experience a day in this romantic backdrop.

Awaiting those fortunate few is a tropical oasis, right out of Melville or Michener. As the sailing boats arrive at the 270-foot private pier, a small village, lagoons and over eight acres of natural landscaping fronting a deserted beach seem to leap from the rugged and untamed land that surround it. At docking visitors are welcomed and briefed about the landing and its rich histori-

cal past. After that it's for them to select one of the many activities offered or just savor the solitude.

Those so inclined can enjoy a wide variety of recreation, including a historical walking tour of the area surrounding the landing. There, one can discover long forsaken churches and village sites, stonework and several major *heiau,* serving as silent reminders of the original settlers of the island, dating as far back as 1400 B.C.

The more active can enjoy an abundance of water activities including outrigger canoes, wave skis, snorkeling and regularly scheduled underwater instruction and tours. Then there's the beach. A beach for playing. A beach for sunning. A beach just to call your own. Whether lying in the sand, under your own hut, or in a gently swaying hammock, visitors to the landing need only raise a signal and a fresh cold drink will appear. Now that's the way to run an island paradise!

Meal service is just as informal and will please even the most discriminating of tastes. Of course, there are fresh fruits and cooling tropical beverages to enjoy. Privacy seekers need only to pack up their selected items for a lunch ala fresco in their chosen piece of paradise.

On special evenings, a true island style feast is held on the island. This is one especially for lovers and honeymooners (no matter how long it's been). A sunset sail from the harbor complete with cocktails and champagne, arrives at the Lanai Landing just in time for the opening of the *imu* oven. Guests sit down to a dining experience to top them all. Of course, there's entertainment with the songs and dances of Hawaii performed in the authentic manner. Then there's just time to stroll along the beach, watching the lights of Lahaina, before it's time to return to civilization.

In fact, the hardest part of your day or evening at the Lanai Landing will be leaving . . . . . watching your own island slip away into memory as the green mountains of Maui grow closer. For years, voyagers to these beautiful islands have known that feeling of leaving a part of yourself on some forgotten beach. It's a feeling many of the Lanai Landing's visitors well understand.

87

offering the opportunity to view antelopes, giraffes, zebras, axis deer and more unusual animals living on the grounds of an 800 acre wildlife preserve.

Although Molokai does not have the best of visitor facilities, it is an island of back-to-basics charm, downhome friendliness and true aloha spirit. The beaches are not Molokai's best asset, but if you've been looking to get well off the beaten track, Molokai is the place to visit.

Lanai, the Pineapple Island, is a wonderful combination of flat pineapple fields and forested ravines and cliffs that drop steeply into the ocean. It is filled mostly with row after row of pineapple plants, more than 16,000 acres. Lanai is privately owned by the Castle & Cooke/Dole Pineapple Company, and boasts only 20 miles of paved road, but over 100 miles of rough tracks (each an excellent source of the rich red dust that chokes and discolors your body and your clothing).

The main center of Lanai is Lanai City. It consists of the very well kept, and recently renovated, Hotel Lanai with only ten rooms, and a patchwork of smaller homes with yards blooming in a variety of bright colored flowers.

All of Lanai's roads seem to radiate from Lanai City. To the north, Shipwreck Beach and Keomoku Village, one a graveyard for ships and other vessels blown ashore by the brisk tradewinds in the channel, the other a quaint ghost town from when a local sugar company failed in 1901.

To the southwest, you'll find the Kaumalapau Harbor, the main pineapple shipping point. To the south, off the paved road lie the remains of Kaunolu Village, the summer home of Kamehameha I. The area is now completely deserted, except for the remnants of a few rocks and trails.

Hulopoe Beach, to the southeast, is as unspoiled a beach as you can find in the state of Hawaii. Beachcombing, sunbathing, snorkeling, scuba diving, sailing and fishing are available on and off this gorgeous beach.

Northwest, the road will lead you to the "Garden of the Gods," an unusual view site strewn with large and small boulders. It's unlike anything else you'll see, and if you spend any time on Lanai, a site not to be missed.

Unusual for Hawaii, there are many Norfolk Pine trees carefully imported and planted by George C. Munro back in 1910. The effect of their planting has been to draw more moisture from the breezes and keep certain areas a little cooler than they would otherwise have been. They also add a unique scenic touch to the beautiful tropical island.

It won't take long to visit these places on the little Pineapple Island of Lanai. It's truly a down to earth adventure for the traveller who wants to see sites that are still untainted by modern civilization.

Lumahai Beach, Kauai

Kauai - The Garden Isle

The most northern of the Hawaiian Islands, Kauai is a tropical paradise with lush green vegetation, sparkling waterfalls and graceful rivers. The name "Garden Isle" stems from the fact that, as the wettest of the islands, the plants and foliage are always very lush and green. The earth is so fertile that utility poles have reputedly begun to grow again when placed back in the soil! The 33 mile by 25 mile island is also the oldest island in the Hawaiian chain.

The only volcanic evidence remaining is the ancient volcano Waialeale. Its' summit has eroded and the crater is now mostly swamp which collects water from the moist trade winds. However, you can seldom see it's peak because of the low-hanging cloud cover. Mount Waialeale is also the wettest spot on earth, with up to 700 inches of rain in a single year. Waterfalls spill over the edges of the crater, sourcing several large rivers, including the only navigable river in the Hawaiian islands.

Kauai was settled by Polynesian explorers more than 1,300 years ago, and was also the first island visited by Captain Cook in 1778. Along with Niihau, Kauai was never physically conquered by Kamehameha I. King Kaumualii, recognizing the likelihood of invasion, ceded to the all-island rule in 1810.

The island's history is filled with legends attributing mysterious events to the Menehunes, the leprechauns of the Pacific. These little people supposedly labored like giants to build huge structures which, to this day, amaze archaeologists. Mysterious ruins, like the Menehune Fish Pond located outside Lihue (reputedly built in one night), are unlike anything found on the other islands. Super strong, stocky and industrious people, the tales say they worked only at night, and required only a nominal payment such as one shrimp per worker for a night's work.

Wherever you stay, this is a wonderful island for sightseeing by car or by air. In fact, many of Kauai's most spectacular scenes can only be seen from the air. However, driving in Kauai can also be an exciting adventure. The roads are still narrow and interesting and there are many dramatic changes in scenery and terrain. Whether by air or car, you'll experience some of the most romantic scenery in the world. However, it is not possible to drive all the way around Kauai, as the road ends on either side of the spectacular Na Pali cliffs on the Northwest coast.

Waimea is situated on the Southern shore of Kauai. It is here that the beaches provide excellent opportunities for walking, searching for shells

Sinbad Charters

P.O. Box 3214
Lihue, Kauai 96766
(808) 245-3441

The breathtaking views of Kauai's shoreline and warm Hawaiian waters create the ultimate tropical experience. Luxury accommodations and personalized service from their highly qualified and fully licensed crew, and a selection of custom cruises, make for an unforgettable adventure aboard the 90 ft. motorsailing yacht, K'an tsui.

Sinbad Charters offers sunset sails, half and full day sails, overnight sails and custom cruises, even to "the forbidden island" of Niihau. K'an tsui comfortably accommodates up to 6 passengers on sailing adventures with all food and beverages provided. Snorkel and scuba outings can be arranged with a group of 6 people.

The unique atmosphere of the K'an tsui provides a new and exciting place for your group gatherings such as wedding, anniversary, birthday and cocktail parties, as well as conferences or any other events you might have. These functions are provided at anchor in various harbors around the island. Food and beverage service is included, decorations and any other special requests can be arranged.

Whether you stay on-anchor or under sail, Sinbad Charters offer a memorable experience for your special time on Kauai.

KAUAI

Haena Point
Haena
Haena
Hanalei Bay
Hanalei
Kalihiwai Bay
Kilauea
Kilauea Bay
KUHIO
56
HIGHWAY
Moloaa Bay
Moloaa

Makaha Point
Kalalau Lookout
Kokee State Park

Anahola Bay
Anahola

Kealia

550
KOKEE RD

Mt Waialeale
5,243 feet

OLOHENA RD
KUAMOO RD
580
Kapaa

Waimea Canyon

Wailua
Wailua Bay

56

Barking Sands
Mana
MANA RD
KOKEE RD
WAIMEA CANYON DRIVE
550
50

HAALO RD
583

Hanamaulu

LIHUE
57
51
Hanamaulu Bay

Kekaha

Waimea
KAUMUALII HWY
50
58
Lihue Airport

Nawiliwili
Ninini Point
Nawiliwili Harbor

Kalaheo
Lawai

Kaumakani
MALUHIA RD
KOLOA RD
Waita Reservoir

Hanapepe Port Allen Airport
Eleele
541
HALEWILI
540
POIPU RD
Koloa

Port Allen
Hanapepe Bay
LAWAI RD

Kukuiula Harbor

Makahuena Point

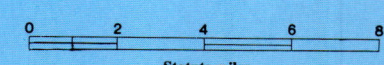

| 0 | 2 | 4 | 6 | 8 |
Statute miles

90

Menehune Helicopter Tours

3222 Kuhio Hwy. Suite #2
Lihue, Kauai 96766
(808) 245-7705

Many of the most beautiful sights on Kauai are only accessible by air. So, if you want the experience of a lifetime, looking into the depths of the incredible pink and brown Waimea Canyon, the majestic lush purple and green Na Pali cliffs, and visiting the very heart of Hawaii's oldest island (and the rainiest place on earth!) take a helicopter sky tour with Menehune Helicopters.

Although Menehune is the new kid on the block, they specialize in truly personalized tours, setting and maintaining meticulous maintenance and safety standards for their aircraft. Above all, they're one of the few helicopter companies where the owner is also a pilot, ensuring great care and attention, and maximum dedication to provide you with the unforgettable experience of an aerial ballet through the serene and majestic wonders of Kauai.

They specialize in two excellent and fully narrated tours of Kauai beginning at Lihue airport, from a 50 minute scenic tour to the 65 minute photographers delight! See Kauai's splendor with Menehune as your guide and experience the grandeur and beauty of Hawaii's Garden Island.

Fantasy Island Boat Tours

P.O. Box 639
Koloa, Kauai 96756
(808) 742-6636

Rafting the far reaches of Kauai in complete comfort and safety will be an experience you'll want to remember. Departing from Poipu Beach, Fantasy Island Boat Tours will take you on a 28′ Tropical Raft expedition to the far reaches of Kauai. You will see the famous Spouting Horn, and journey past the unforgettable spot used in the filming of well-known Fantasy Island. There your captain will fill you in on fun filled anecdotes about the actors and ever popular television show.

Your qualified guide will be happy to take you to watch the dolphins and whales frolic in the waves. Have your camera ready because chances are great you'll see one or both of these tame and delightful creatures up close!

Bluewater Sailing

P.O. Box 1261
Hanalei, Kauai 96714
(808) 826-9231 or
(808) 335-6440

Sailing along Kauai's breathtaking shores in the "Lady Leanne II," a new Pearson 424, could be your most memorable experience while on Kauai. Your captain, Rick Marvin, and his crew cater to sailing enthusiasts and novices alike. Established in 1980, Bluewater Sailing offers inter-island sailing or private parties with that extra touch to personalize your day of adventure.

You can take part in the sailing or just lay back and enjoy a variety of trips which include: Whale Watching, Niihau Sunset Sails, Sports Fishing, Snorkel Trips, Full Day and Half Day Cruises. Call for more information.

91

and driftwood, swimming and many other water sports. As the site of Kauai's first mission over 150 years ago, it offers the 1853 Waimea Foreign Church built from coral and sandstone, as well as the islands oldest home, the Gulick-Rowell House with it's New England architecture. Nearby stand the well preserved remains of Fort Elizabeth from which the Russian flag flew briefly, around 1817.

Mark Twain called Waimea Canyon the "Grand Canyon of the Pacific." Almost 3,000 feet deep, the canyon has many unexpected and dramatic vistas for such a relatively small tropical island. Complete with crisp air, spectacular colors and million year-old rock formations, the constantly moving clouds create a fascinating kaleidoscope of shadows on the canyon walls. Reachable by tour bus or rental car, it is a spectacular destination for a full day of scenic contrasts. Nearer to the top of the canyon, the Kalalau Valley Lookout provides one of the world's most outstanding views, especially when the day is clear.

Many people choose the better developed Poipu Beach area, on the southern shore as their vacation base. This southern side of the island is drier and usually sunnier than the windward shores, making this area ideal for water activities. There is a full range of golf courses, modern hotels, excellent condominiums and inviting vistas.

As you move toward the East and North coasts, you'll pass the center of business and government activity and the island's major airport at Lihue. Further up the eastern coastline is Wailua, on the Wailua river, home to the Fern Grotto and several excellent hotels. Rainfall keeps the Wailua River full year round as it flows through the Wailua River State Park, and the best way to explore this fresh water paradise is to take the short trip up-river to the Fern Grotto.

Cool and damp, this natural amphitheatre is often the setting for modern Hawaiian weddings accompanied by ancient Hawaiian love songs. Prehistoric ferns and trickling waterfalls, lush by day and eerie by night, hide the little known fact that the caves nearby were Royal burial grounds. Don't miss the ethnic villages and gardens by the river, and a walk through the grounds of the 100 year old coconut grove at the Coco Palms Hotel, sight of many movies and television shows.

Continuing North, you'll reach the turn-off to Kilauea Lighthouse. An interesting side trip, the state's northernmost point, contains a unique wildlife refuge for endangered sea birds and the largest clam shell lighthouse lens in the world. It's also a must-see spot for spectacular views in every direction of ocean, surf and mountains.

Just before the picturesque Hanalei Bay lies a community called Princeville where no building is taller than a coconut palm. Home to the Hanalei Bay Resort, you will find a world class golf course, excellent tennis facilities and secluded beaches inviting picnickers, photographers, lovers and those who enjoy water activities such as snorkeling and swimming.

On towards Hanalei Bay, there are several excellent viewpoints of the island's central peaks

Pacific Paradise Cruises

3222 Kuhio Hwy, Suite #2
Lihue, Kauai 96766
(808) 245-7705 or 822-1993

Pacific Paradise Cruises has magnificent cruises year round in Kauai. During the months May through September explore the Na Pali Coast on their 25' fiberglass ocean cruiser. Massive and magical, these cliffs rise 2,000 to 3,000 feet from the sea on the rugged Na Pali Coast. Travelling through ancient lava tubes you'll experience the cruise of a lifetime in this mythical area, and swim or snorkel while anchored on a reef at the Valley of the Lost Tribes.

When the water is too rough for cruising up north, Pacific Paradise Cruises journeys down to the serene South Shore, during the months of November through May. Leaving from Nawiliwili Harbor, you'll anchor near the secluded Kipu Kai Beach for swimming, snorkeling, fishing and, of course, whale watching. The cruise hosts a maximum of 6 passengers for the utmost in comfort, safety, and a truly personalized tour, with snacks, beverages and fishing and snorkel gear provided.

Aquatics Kauai Ltd.

733 Kuhio Highway
Kapaa, Kauai 96746
(808) 822-9213

Aquatics Kauai is the most complete dive store on Kauai. Their helpful staff will offer you exciting tour packages that allow you to discover the beauty of this island paradise from the sea. They can tailor a custom diving package to your individual needs that accommodates groups of all sizes, but please book in advance. These professionals will easily arrange a package to include any of the great marine activities available on the Garden Isle.

Dive package options include: condominium or hotel, car rental, a helicopter tour, air fare from the continental West and East Coasts and, of course, diving with Aquatics Kauai.

Kauai is the oldest and most tropical of the lush Hawaiian Islands, famous for an abundance of snorkeling and untouched diving areas along its pristine shores. Prepare yourself to encounter an undersea paradise of waters teeming with brightly colored trumpet and beautiful yellow butterfly fish. The richly colored coral reefs, and the unique lava tubes, all await you beneath the warm Pacific waters surrounding Kauai. Begin your adventure!

93

Lady Ann Cruises

P. O. Box 3422
Lihue, Kauai 96766
(808) 245-8538

View the spectacular sea cliffs of the Na Pali Coast from the decks of the stylish and comfortable "Lady Ann" or "Island Voyager". Lady Ann Cruises delivers a world of enchantment as you cruise past luscious valleys and cascading waterfalls, rugged mountain pinnacles and awesome rock walls that rise straight up out of the ocean. Then journey into magnificent sea caves or discover the beautiful, deserted, white sand beaches that invite you to snorkel and swim at fabulous reefs, alive with fish and fantastic underwater gardens. Truly an unforgettable experience!

clothed in foliage, often overhung with clouds and ribboned with white waterfalls. The Hanalei Valley and Bay lookouts provide excellent photographic opportunities.

Beyond the qaint township of Hanalei Bay to the Bali Hai outcropping are many caves and streams that you will see in and around the Haena region. There are several excellent snorkeling and diving areas along this northern stretch of coast, although visitors should carefully check conditions before entering the water.

When you reach the end of the road, at Haena, challenge the Na Pali Cliffs, where trail hiking here is an adventurous, but serious business. Trips of up to five days, with proper permits, offer a challenging, once-in-a-lifetime glimpse of an untouched environment. The cliffs rise 2,000 to 3,000 feet from the sea, with ridges forming a series of deep, lush, jungled valleys, and the trail winding its way for several miles along the cliffs, offering some of the most spectacular cliff views to be found anywhere in the world.

Kauai, although not yet very commercialized, offers a selection of excellent visitor related activities including breathtaking air tours, and exciting, scenic sunset cruises. With some of the best, easily accessible beaches of all the islands, Kauai can offer you a truly tropical, island vacation par excellence.

Captain Zodiac

Chin Young Village Shopping Center
Hanalei, Kauai 96714
(808) 826-9371
Lahaina, Maui
(808) 667-5351

Captain Zodiac Raft Expeditions are exciting and unique daily adventures to the remote coastlines of Kauai and Maui. With exclusive landing privileges, these thrilling expeditions take in the spectacular Na Pali Coast of Kauai with scenic waterfalls, sea caves, remote beaches and reefs for swimming, snorkeling, hiking and picnics. From Maui you can explore the island of Lanai for isolated bays to swim, sun, beachcomb, take a short walk or snorkle along coral reefs with exotic marine life.

All tours give you an excellent opportunity to view Hawaii's varied sealife, including dolphin, flying fish, sea turtles and sea birds. The winter months feature whale watching tours on both islands, complete with underwater sound equipment to hear the mystical songs of the whales. Beverages and snorkel equipment are provided. Call Captain Zodiac for reservations, and experience the beauty of Hawaii's remote beaches and wildlife.

Charo's

Hanalei Colony Resort
Haena, Kauai
(808) 826-6422

Lunch: 11:30 a.m.–3:00 p.m.
Dinner: 5:30 p.m.–10 00 p.m.

Charo! The name itself excites. Now there is a beautiful restaurant and bar called Charo's on the beach in Haena, at the Hanalei Colony Resort, owned and operated by the famous T.V. and stage entertainer. The restaurant has a casual, come-as-you-are, tropical atmosphere with plants and palms overlooking a picturesque beach and ocean setting. Specializing in fresh fish of the islands, the restaurant carries a full and varied menu including filets, veal, tenderloin steaks, chicken and Paella.

Dinner entrees such as medallions of veal francais, teriyaki filet, BBQ baby back pork ribs, fresh island fish, scampi, shrimp macadamia, lobster, scallops saute are all served with tossed salad, hot bread and choice of vegetable du jour. Charo's own favorite is Paella, a Spanish dish from a family recipe that contains fresh fish, crab claws, scallops, shrimps, clams and chicken served on a bed of saffron rice.

For a quick lunch and lighter fare choose from the shellfish macadamia, French dip, stuffed papaya, Polish sausage, mushroom cheeseburger or the good old American hamburger or cheeseburger prepared in Charo's own special way. Finger food and pupus (hors d' oeuvres) such as sashimi, escargot, chicken fingers, calamari fritas and fresh sauteed mushrooms are served from 3:00 p.m. to 5:30 p.m.

Beverages are specially concocted here as well. Wet your whistle with drinks like Papaya Colada, Margarita Magnifico, Banana Daiquiri, Tropical Fruit Fantastico as well as many old favorites like a Bloody Mary, Pina Colada, Chi Chi, or Mai Tai.

Families with children under 12 will appreciate the Keiki Fare (child's menu) with selections such as chicken Hawaiian and the special Charo's burger plate.

Why would an internationally acclaimed entertainer open a restaurant on the relatively secluded north shore of Kauai? In Charo's own words, "I discovered the Garden Island, especially the north shore, some years ago on my honeymoon. I fell madly in love with the beauty of this place and the people of the island, so I decided to reside here with my family on the north shore of Kauai, which I call my Fantasy Island. After

building our home and moving there I thought what better way to share this beauty with people than to provide an excellent dining experience in an intimate tropical setting. That's why I decided to open Charo's restaurant with excellent food and a friendly and casual atmosphere. I hope you will enjoy the atmosphere and the food as much as I do, and if you see me walk by, please let me know what you think of my place."

95

Bali Hai Realty, Inc.

P.O. Box 930
Hanalei, Kauai 96714
(808) 826-7244

Kauai, the oldest and most lush of all the islands is known as the magical Garden Isle. It's aura of remoteness with hidden valleys, secluded waterfalls, white sand beaches and perfect tropical weather make it one of the most beautiful places in the world to live and vacation. The friendly professionals at Bali Hai Realty can help you find your piece of paradise. They offer a wide range of excellent properties ranging from the mountains to the seashore, in some of the same locations that have been immortalized in movies such as "South Pacific" and the "Thornbirds."

One of the most beautiful places to call your own would be Kilauea Farms. Here you can build the home of your dreams upon gentle slopes, in the midst of breathtaking tranquil surroundings. At Kilauea Farms you can enjoy the satisfaction and pleasure of working the soil, keeping horses or raising livestock in your own fields. And yet, be close enough for shopping and resort living with nearby golf, tennis and many fine restaurants. Nowhere else in the world will you find land that offers the splendor of Kauai. A few 10 acre ocean bluff homesites are still available and include your own private trail to a secluded sandy beach. Let the specialists at Bali Hai Realty show you how.

*Taro fields in
Hanapepe, Kauai*

Hawaii - The Big Island

Hawaii is the southern-most island in the Hawaiian chain. It is almost twice the size of all the other Hawaiian islands put together, hence its' alternative name, the Big Island. It hosts several volcanoes; among them is Mauna Kea at 13,796 feet, the largest island-based mountain in the world; Mauna Loa at 13,680 feet, the world's largest active volcano; and Kilauea, which has been erupting frequently in recent years, and is the world's most active volcano. Little wonder that the Big Island is also known as the Volcano Isle!

Industry on the Big Island, is also measured in superlatives. This one island produces the most sugar, papaya, vegetables, antheriums, macadamia nuts and cattle in the state. The orchid industry, centered around Hilo on the northeast coast, is the world's largest, with over 22,000 varieties grown and a large proportion exported internationally.

On the other side of the island, in sunny Kona, you'll find the center of the only commercial coffee production in the United States. Just off this west facing coast lie some of the best deep-sea fishing grounds in the world. And, between Hilo and Kona is the privately owned Parker Ranch, covering 250,000 acres, one of the world's largest.

This island of superlatives also has a special place in history. King Kamehemeha I, the unifying king, was born and died here; Captain James Cook, the first westerner to officially discover the islands was killed here in 1779; and, the first group of missionaries from Boston landed here in 1820. The legendary goddess Pele, the Hawaiian goddess of fire, is believed to reside in the Halemaumau crater, near the Kilauea Volcano.

Despite the immense size of the Big Island, the resident population is less than 110,000. The Big Island has one major city, Hilo, the capital. It is Hilo's seaport through which raw sugar and cattle are exported to the other islands and onwards. Most areas on this northeast coast receive an yearly average of 132 inches of rain, called liquid sunshine by the locals. As a result, flowers and other plants grow abundantly, giving rise to a flourishing tropical plant industry.

Although the Hilo area has a lot to offer the visitor, the sunnier and drier west-facing coast of the Kona and Kohala districts seem to be the preferred vacation base. An infrastructure of visitor related facilities is growing in those areas. They already offer some of the world's most luxurious resort hotels, most of the Big Island's best beaches, and a large number of ocean activity options ranging from scuba diving to deep sea fishing.

For sightseeing, the Big Island has an interesting problem – size. By car, there is by far too much to see and appreciate in one day. By air, you can be guaranteed some exceptional aerial sightseeing, mainly from Hilo's airport. As in all of the Hawaiian islands, aerial sightseeing provides an outstanding once-in-a-lifetime experience of viewing the island in ways that cannot be duplicated by surface viewpoints. Once you've seen the island by air, then you'll undoubtedly want to get close to many of those beautiful sights by land.

From Hilo, you can travel 30 miles south, on Highway 11, to the Hawaii Volcanoes National Park. It is the home of Kilauea, Halemaumau and several other active volcanic sites. Visiting this area today can be more exciting than ever. There have been spectacular and frequent eruptions in the past few years with lava fountains shooting over 1,000 feet in the air! Call the Park Rangers at 967-7311 for information on the latest eruptions and viewing conditions.

Once at the Park, you'll be at 4,000 feet, and despite the hot lava, it can feel very cool. Also, you may want to wear covered shoes for walking on the lava rock. To find out where the most recent eruption site is, just ask the Park Rangers. You will either have to hike or drive through the park. In either case, be aware of the sulfurous fumes; if you have respiratory problems, it may be recommended that you do not go. The sights are incredible so make sure you have plenty of film. Even if there isn't an eruption, you'll get up close to a volcano and be as close as you could be to the process of creation.

Driving maps are available along with hiking information, at the Volcano Visitor Center. Color films of the latest eruptions and a brief history of vulcanology are worth the stop; especially the lava rock bad luck display with its letters from woeful tourists who "borrowed" rocks from the volcano despite warnings never to do so!

HAWAII

Upolu Point
UPOLU AIRPORT
Upolu Point
HAWI
Keokea Bay
NIULII
Haena Pt
HAWI. NIULII
NIULII
MAHUKONA
KOHALA MTS
Waimanu Bay
Waipio Bay
KUKUIHAELE
HAINA
HONOKAA
PAAHAU
Malae Point
25
WAIPIO
240
KUKAIAU
KOHALA
KAWAIHAE-MAHUKONA RD
270
Hawaii Belt Road
MAMALAHOA HIGHWAY
OOKALA
WAIAKA
KAWAIHAE
KAWAIHAE RD
WAIMEA
MAMALAHOA HWY
LAUPAHOEHOE
PAPALOA
Maulua Bay
KAMUELA AIRPORT
HONOHINA
PUAKO
HAKALAU
WAILEA
KAAHUMANU HWY
Mauna Kea 13796
220
PEPEEKEO
HONOMU
QUEEN
19
KEAMUKU
KAWAINIU
Onomea Bay
Mokihana Bay
190
ONOMEA
PAPAKOU
PAUKAA
Keahole Point
KEAHOLE AIRPORT
KALAOA
HILO
Hilo Bay
Honokohau Bay
Honokohau
SADDLE ROAD
200
Hilo Airport
KAILUA
Kailua Bay
KEAAU
Kahaluu Bay
Keauhou Bay
KEAUHOU
HOLUALOA
MOUNTAIN VIEW
KEAAU PAHOA ROAD
HONOLULU LANDING
130
PAHOA
KAINALIU
11
PAHOA-KAPOHO
WAIAKEA
Cape Kumakahi
CAPTAIN COOK
Mauna Loa 13680
KAPOHO
HONAUNAU
Kealakekua Bay
HAWAII VOLCANOES NATIONAL PARK
GLENWOOD
POHOIKI
Kiilae Bay
180
BELT ROAD
PAHOA KALAPANA ROAD
OPIHIKAO
KEALIA
Crater
HAWAII BELT ROAD
KAIMU
HOOKENA
Kauhako Bay
Black Sand Beach
KALAPANA
KAIMU-KAPOHO
PAPA
Milolii
11
Kaena Point
Hanamalo Point
WOOD VALLEY ROAD
11
Kapaoo Point
Mahuka Bay
Waiapele Bay
PAHALA
Kauna Point
WAIOHINU
HONUAPO
Honuapo Bay
NAALEHU
Pohue Bay
Waikapuna Bay
KAALUALU
Paiahaa Bay
WAIAHUKINI

Ka Lae (South Cape)

0 5 10 15 20
Statute miles

Nearby is the famous Volcano House, perched on the rim of the crater, a great spot for watching sunsets or just taking in the spectacular view. For adventurous souls, a six mile, round-trip hike through the forest to the heart of the volcano is recommended. There are several nature trails to take you into the lush forests of vegetation and flowering trees surrounding the park. The silver-colored trees with red blossom flowers are sacred to the goddess Pele, and are the flower of the Big Island, called Lehua.

Before leaving the spectacular sights of desolation, smoke, steam and ash, be sure to visit the Thurston Lava Tube. A magnificent fern forest surrounds the area and provides a graphic contrast of natural environments and forces at work.

Continuing southward past the black sand beaches of Punaluu, you will pass through Naalehu, a quaint village and welcome resting point prior to reaching the lava flows. Black sand beaches are created from the rapid cooling of lava flows by the ocean. Most of these beaches in Hawaii are in constant movement, disappearing as the ocean swells and currents sweep away the new land to broaden the islands base. In fact, most of the black sand beaches are not suitable for swimming because of the usually strong current and wave action.

Hildgund Jewelers

Mauna Lani Bay Hotel
Kawaihae, Hawaii 96743
(808) 885-6617

You'll discover the finest, authentic Hawaiian Heirloom jewelry at Hildgund Jewelers' dream store, located in the Mauna Lani Bay Hotel on the Big Island. For over a century, Hildgund designers and craftsmen have created custom jewelry with carefully selected, one-of-a-kind gemstones and settings. The "Hildgund Touch" is elegant simplicity with a European flair and the mark of excellence in custom designed jewels world-wide, supported by second-to-none personal service.

Hilo Bay Air

P.O. Box 4278
Hilo, Hawaii 96720
(808) 969-1545

If you really want to experience the scenic beauty of The Big Island, Hawaii, come try Hilo Bay Air's customized tours. Their local knowledge and expertise will assure you a truly exciting experience as you safely fly to Pu'u O'o vent, the present source of the Big Island's fantastic volcanic activity. When an eruption occurs, local television stations depend on Hilo Bay Air for on-the-scene report coverage, so Hilo Bay Air pilots can surely guide you to the right places.

Other attractions you won't want to miss are the views of the hidden valleys, sparkling waterfalls and the majestic coastline. There's the lush, green cane fields of the Hamakua Coast, the gorgeous black sand beaches at Kalapana, or just enjoy a local flight to Hilo's nearby falls which includes a panoramic view of old Hilo town.

Hilo Bay Air helicopters are equipped with two-way internal communications so your pilot can point out each spectacular sight and allow you to communicate with him or to enjoy the background music. "Up, up and away—the modern way!"

99

The well paved road continues past ancient and modern flows from the Mauna Loa volcano, around the southernmost point, toward Honaunau and the City of Refuge. This 400 year old, partially restored sanctuary, gives a true feel for the customs and lifestyle of the ancient Hawaiians. Macadamia nut farms abound here and tours are frequently available that offer bargains right from the orchards. Small boat harbors, magnificent hotels, beautiful beaches and spectacular hedges of bougainvillea will vie for your attention as you head toward Kailua-Kona.

Passing Kealakekua Bay, you'll be passing a site of strong historical significance. This is the bay in which Captain Cook made his original landing, to be welcomed as the god Lono, prior to his unfortunate, violent death in 1779.

The town of Kona conveniently offers every indulgence a visitor could imagine. Fishing? Some of the world's biggest marlin cruise offshore. Boating? Charter boats of every size ply the turquoise and azure waters daily. Diving? Snorkeling and scuba are offered by many local companies including certification courses. Shopping? Many smaller arcades compete with centers and hotel complexes. Entertainment? Combine dining, sightseeing and a show by enjoying a sunset dinner cruise or a luau at one of

the stylish local hotels; nightlife always goes with the hang-loose atmosphere here. Sightseeing? Every street has a different story, a different view and a different fragrance. Before driving onward visit the local farms growing Kona coffee and stop for a close-up look at the clusters of red berries at harvest time.

Further north up this coast, you'll pass by several of the classic hotels and resorts on the island. With superb beaches, resort facilities and every conceivable extra, many of these hotels will pamper the visitor in a way that is unbelievably luxurious.

Driving back toward Hilo, either by the saddle road (off limits to rental cars) or the Hamakua Coast is best done in daylight and at a leisurely pace. A stop at Waimea should include some up-country shopping at both old and new versions of shopping centers, art and book stores, antique and handicraft booths. The nearby Parker Ranch Visitor Center will give you a glimpse into the past and present day workings of this 250,000 acre cattle ranch.

From Honokaa, on the northeast facing coast, a short drive will take you to one of the ten best lookouts in the islands, Waipio Lookout. The views from this lookout provide an outstanding panorama of valleys and cliffs falling to the sea.

Once inhabited by nearly 50,000 Hawaiians, the Waipio Valley is a distinctly out-of-the-way scenic treasure. Approachable only by four wheel drive vehicles, the 2,000 foot gorge provides a fascinating glimpse of an older way of life.

Before reaching Hilo, sugar cane fields invite you to give up modern rewards and just enjoy nature's treasures; coastline on one side, gorges, waterfalls and streams on the other. Akaka Falls is just 10 miles before Hilo and worth a drive through verdant ferns and forest to the 420 foot landmark. Surrounded by tropical trees, sweet smelling ginger and a myriad of other flowers, it's a delightful stop to rest awhile and admire the ancient waterfall.

The Big Island also claims another first. The only tropical snow skiing center in the world. Mauna Kea collects snow on its peak each winter, and from December through March at its topmost elevations, provides the thrill of a lifetime for many ardent skiers. Lacking the sophisticated facilities you'll find back on the mainland, the only way to the top is by four wheel drive vehicle or helicopter. Once there, the views are stupendous, and the skiing a close second.

The Big Island - new, relatively uninhabited, historical and with a natural beauty all of its own, makes for an ideal vacation center if you don't mind the distance from the nightlife of Waikiki. Try it. You won't be disappointed.

Black sand beach - Kalapana, Hawaii

Hawaiian Holiday Macadamia Nut Company

P.O. Box 707
Honokaa, Hawaii 96727
(808) 775-7255
(800) 367-5150 (outside Hawaii)

The Hawaiian Holiday Macadamia Nut Company is the world's foremost processor of macadamia nuts. They have three Macadamia Nut Factory retail outlets to serve their customers directly. The factory is located in the "Macadamia Nut capital of the world," Honokaa Town on the scenic Hamakua Coast of the Big Island of Hawaii; about 40 miles north of Hilo, off Route 19. This facility offers free viewing of Hawaiian Holiday's factory where over 200 different macademia nut products are processed.

Hawaiian Holiday also has outlets conveniently located in Waikiki at 2430 Kalakaua, 2200 Kalakaua, and in the MacNuttery at 2098 Kalakaua Avenue. Each store offers free sampling of a selection of macadamia nut items, and you will also find Hawaii's favorite macadamia nut cookies, DeDomenico's Cookies, available in several varieties such as Volcanos, erupting with fresh-roasted macadamia nuts and pure chocolate chips. One of the most popular gift items are the famous Diamond Head chocolates; choice whole macadamia nuts especially chosen, then dipped in Ghiradelli pure chocolate. Go to Honokaa or one of Hawaiian Holiday's other Macadamia Nut Factory stores and indulge yourself in the realm of the worlds most "perfect nut."

All Hawaiian Holiday gift items are perfect to bring home to friends and family, and are packaged attractively and protectively for travel or mailing. For mail order call toll free (800) 367-5150

101

Accommodations In Hawaii

Whether you stay in one of the many luxury or moderate hotels, either fixed or floating; condominiums or bed and breakfasts available throughout the islands, there is little doubt that you will find yourself exceptionally pleased with the experience. Nowhere else will you find the aloha spirit so alive and eager to please.

Hotels in Hawaii, regardless of category, absolutely shine. You will notice how the "cleanliness is next to godliness" rule really seems to apply here. And the service is so friendly; smiling faces are everywhere. However, bear in mind that, although friendly and smiling, the service may not always be as prompt as you may be used to back home. Remember, the pace is a little slower here. And that's why you've come—to unwind, relax and enjoy "Hawaiian time."

If you're looking for accommodations that provide you with cooking facilities, you'll find that some of the hotels offer these options, as do the many condominium rentals available. And there are some well known large chains that are operated with hotel efficiency. Invariably, condominium units have kitchen facilities, and many include such amenities as restaurants, bars, tennis and swimming pools.

Private home and condominium rentals are also available on all islands, ranging from superbly luxurious beach properties to smaller, yet very comfortable studios. Depending on the number of people in your party, both options can be a very effective and economical alternative to conventional forms of accommodation.

There are other unusual, yet interesting and exciting possibilities. The bed-and-breakfast concept is relatively new to Hawaii, and could be an alternative you may wish to try. These may not be the kind of country farmhouses or inns you might find in other areas, but they can be very comfortable indeed. Those that are available away from the busy side of the island can offer homes right on your own private beach; a superb way to experience your personal paradise.

Another unusual alternative is the floating hotel, better known as a cruise ship. There are many advantages to staying in a luxury hotel that transports you through the islands in luxurious comfort with all the amenities and service of a shore based hotel at a cost that's easily comparable.

No matter what your choice for accommodations, you'll have no trouble fitting right into the island lifestyle, with its relaxed, comfortable pace. So come, share Hawaii's aloha spirit and experience a great tropical vacation.

Pacific Island Adventures

4218 Waialae Avenue, Suite 203A
Honolulu 96816
(808) 735-9000
(800) 522-3030 (outside Hawaii)

At last, visitors in Hawaii can escape the crowds and still enjoy pampered comfort in beachfront living! Owner, Rick Lewis, brings a decade of experience and an insistence upon excellence to this Hawaii based, private vacation beach home operation, insuring a special quality of homes and services worthy of the discriminating traveler.

Pacific Island Adventures specializes in unique, custom vacations catered to the VIP or professional couple in search of a "home away from home" atmosphere. Here they will find familiar privacy and the comfort of reliable local services while enjoying a picture-perfect, island-paradise setting.

The secret is in pre-planning and personalized follow-through. From the moment an island vacation is planned until it's happy memory, a representative will be there to make travel arrangements, recommend homes, housekeeping, even enticing extras such as babysitting, limousine service or a gourmet chef, if desired. And, since it's an island based operation an agent is always there, on hand, to insure all goes well during your stay in Hawaii. That way, the only surprises a guest may encounter will be pleasant ones, compliments of Pacific Island Adventures!

Guests select from a list of fine, privately owned homes and villas, each with a clear ocean view and charming beachfront personality of its own. Each client is personally greeted at the airport and escorted to their island paradise setting. Most homes are immaculately furnished; many with enticing extras to add to that special vacation ambiance. Prices on homes vary from $100 to $1,000 per night, leaving room for many comfortable options.

Pacific Island Adventures also makes it possible to create a vacation package which includes several days on a private yacht enjoying some of Hawaii's fabulous island cruising, fishing and diving areas off Oahu, Maui and the Big Island. The same attention to quality and fine service found in their island homes and villas also extends to the crafts and crews at sea. Only the best private charter sailing and motor yachts have been selected to service clientele of Pacific Island Adventures.

Whatever your pleasure, Pacific Island Adventures will arrange it with a personal attention to detail that has earned them a VIP service status among travelers of distinction throughout the world. Another reason they unabashedly suggest: "Millions vacation in Hawaii, a handful do it right," by calling Pacific Island Adventures.

103

Located across the street from the Waikiki Trade Center, you're able to walk to an abundant potpourri of nearby restaurants offering the widest choices of cuisine including International, French, Oriental, German, Italian and traditional American. For example, one of the finest and most popular Italian restaurants, featuring classic Italian cuisine, Matteo's, is located on the lobby level of the hotel.

You'll be within easy reach of entertainment selections which range from strictly Hawaiian music and hula, to contemporary jazz as well as the more contemporary discos. And for extra convenience, there is also a travel desk to assist you with any travel and tour arrangements you might want to make. Even though you're surrounded by the most popular dining, shopping and entertainment in Waikiki, you're just a short stroll away from world famous Waikiki Beach. As an alternative to the beach, there is a fresh water swimming pool and sun deck for your relaxation.

Each apartment is fully furnished with two double extra-length beds, color television, air-conditioning, complete kitchen and lanai. The best news of all is that the Marine Surf will satisfy your whims while complimenting your budget with excellent, competitive rates for both single or double occupancy depending on availability and season. For further information or reservations call the toll free number above.

The Marine Surf Hotel

364 Seaside Avenue
Waikiki 96815
(808) 923-0277
(800) 367-5176

The Marine Surf Hotel is known as the "extra special, extra friendly" hotel with spacious studio condominiums beautifully and comfortably furnished, offering the very best of Waikiki at your doorstep with the most affordable rates. It can also be your home away from home, with a complete kitchen. Enjoy the convenience of fixing coffee and breakfast at your leisure, or preparing your own meals while having the opportunity to intersperse your favorite home cooked meals with the wide variety of dining experiences that Waikiki has to offer.

American Hawaii Cruises

550 Kearny Street
San Francisco, CA 94108
(800) 227-3666

A special version of the aloha spirit makes American Hawaii Cruises extraordinary. *"Aloha,"* Hawaii's all-purpose greeting of hospitality, warmth and friendliness, characterizes the attitude you'll find on both the SS Independence and the SS Constitution. They are American vessels, recently refurbished, and both have American crews. Both ships were originally designed to accommodate 1000 passengers each on lengthy transatlantic cruises. They now carry 798 guests in comfortable staterooms; some even have king size beds, a rarity on most luxury liners.

The ships sail on Saturdays from Honolulu for seven-day cruises around the Islands. If you've arranged an air/sea package, you'll be greeted at Honolulu International Airport, and will be transported to the ship, where you'll be welcomed with a traditional lei greeting. The fun begins now that you're onboard and from then on, you'll be traveling through a paradise of palm trees, tradewinds, warmth and beauty. There's no place on Earth quite like Hawaii for scenic wonders and friendly people.

From a traditional *luau* (feast) to the seasonal whale watching off the coast of Maui, passengers find an exciting array of optional excursions to enjoy at their own pace.

There are numerous activities aboard ship, as well, that include pool parties, dancing, and singalongs. Classes in lei-making, ukulele-playing and hula-dancing are also available. You can play bridge or backgammon, lie in the sun, or best of all make new friends among people who enjoy cruising as much as you do.

The cuisine on American Hawaii cruises is American and continental, with a generous sprinkling of Hawaiian specialties. Feast on delectable mahi mahi and other fresh seafoods, savor pork baked in taro leaves, chilled papaya and kiwi fruits. Wines served are imports and selected California labels. Late evening snacks are served every night, and once a week there's a late-night Grand Buffet complete with fanciful ice sculptures. While you dine, you'll be serenaded by a trio of Hawaiian musicians.

What to wear? You won't go wrong with aloha attire. That means comfortable sportswear and, on the one or two dress up evenings, a lightweight suit or sportscoat and tie for men and evening dress for women.

Though the American Hawaii vessels are identical sister ships, each has her own individual character. The Independence caters more to family travel; it has a Youth Recreation Center, a video arcade and a fitness center with weight equipment. The Constitution offers entertainment in the "Starlight Lounge" with piano bar. That's not to say the youngsters wouldn't enjoy either

ship, especially during the summer and holiday seasons, since there are Youth Recreation Directors to guide special activities and teen disco nights, treasure hunts, crafts and classes to choose from. The Sports Director on board gives tips on snorkeling, sailing and windsurfing. He can also arrange for a deepsea fishing expedition or golf and tennis on shore.

Entertainment, not surprisingly, focuses on the lovely songs and dances of Polynesia, complete with grass skirts and feathery plumage. The programs don't stop there, however. You can also see live Broadway-style revues and major motion pictures. And if you're in the mood to perform you can participate in Passenger Night, a chance for you and your fellow passengers to display your talents on stage.

An American Hawaii cruise presents a unique opportunity to see all the contrasts in the natural beauty of the islands, not just a portion of them. Many visitors travel to only one island and think they've seen Hawaii, not realizing how different each island is from the others. On these cruises you can see their diversity, from the jagged lava rock and barren volcanoes on the Big Island to the lush tropical foliage of Kauai's rain forests.

You'll stop at five ports of call: Oahu, Maui, Kauai, and Hilo and Kona on the island of Hawaii. Each port has a unique character and definite mood of its own. Such variety provides an uncommon perspective that others often miss and is part of the reason why American Hawaii feels their inter-island cruises are so special.

By the end of your journey, you will have discovered the difference between just "visiting" the islands and becoming a part of them forever.

105

Hyatt Regency Waikiki

2424 Kalakaua Avenue
Waikiki 96815
(808) 922-9292

The Hyatt Regency Waikiki, world-renowned as the most prestigious hotel in Waikiki, offers elegant accommodations as well as a wide variety of dining, entertainment and shopping pleasures. Located in the heart of Waikiki, this hotel provides you with easy access to Waikiki Beach for suntanning and watersport activities.

A beautiful focal point between the twin towers that comprise this masterpiece is the spectacular open air atrium with three cascading waterfalls, extensive tropical foliage and a spectacular custom-designed 45,000 pound sculptured chandelier suspended from a height of six floors. Surrounding the three levels of the Great Hall are seven restaurants, six cocktail lounges and more than 70 shops and boutiques that bring exquisite goods from around the world. Cuisine choices reflect the finest of world class foods served in both casual as well as the most elegant surroundings. In the cocktail lounges, music choices vary from classical performances, ukulele artistry, to live Dixieland and contemporary jazz. Famous performers frequent these lounges for their own entertainment and are booked regularly for special shows.

Guest rooms at The Hyatt Regency Waikiki are elegantly designed, fully air conditioned with private lanai, plush wall-to-wall carpeting, twin mirrors, ample closets and color television. All rooms are bathed in warm earth tones and original art prints decorate the walls. Other special choices include: parlour suites, with all the amenities the guest can imagine, with an adjoining spacious living room; penthouse suites; the Ambassador Suite encompassing 1500 square feet of luxury, and the Presidential Suite with 2,000 square feet of elegance and six lanais offering panoramic views of the Pacific Ocean and Diamond Head. The Regency Club offers exclusive amenities which include a concierge to assist with dinner and tour arrangements as well as business needs; complimentary continental breakfast and hors d'oeuvres and cocktails in the afternoon, complimentary use of the Hyatt limousine for city travel and utilization of Honolulu's best social and recreational club with fitness and spa facilities. Regency Club guests also enjoy the use of the sundecks and jacuzzis, located on the hotel rooftops with spectacular 360 degree views of ocean, mountains and Diamond Head.

Within the $100 million Hyatt Regency, the discriminating guest will find Bagwell's Wine Bar which offers distinctive wines by the glass in an enjoyable atmosphere. In the elegance of Bagwells 2424, (see the Cosmopolitan section), where the emphasis is on excellence in cuisine and service, diners select from a menu of fine French creations, utilizing fresh island ingredients. A few samples from the menu include red snapper soup baked in puff pastry, lobster and scallop casserole with truffles and artichokes, opakapaka (pink snapper) with watercress and ginger, as well as tantalizing, freshly prepared desserts. The Bagwells wine list is one of the premiere lists in America.

The Colony Seafood and Steak House offers steaks, chops, prawns, lobsters, scallops and two choices of fresh catch of the day broiled over kiawe coals. Spats Restaurant and discotheque, with its stylish "Prohibition Era" Italian decor, is known for its "pasta with passion." All of the pasta is homemade and served with a variety of delectable sauces. Seafood, poultry and veal entrees are also offered. From 10:00 p.m. until 3:00 a.m., a popular Pasta Bar offers mini-versions of the Spats menu for hungry disco dancers. The Terrace Grille provides casual dining indoors and outdoors overlooking Waikiki Beach. The Hyatt's newest restaurant addition is Musashi, an innovative Japanese restaurant which treats the experience and fun of Oriental dining with as much attention as the food itself.

Harry's Bar is a charming sidewalk cafe setting with quaint umbrellas sheltering tables near the Hyatt's magnificent waterfalls. Featured on the menu are rich pastries, sandwiches and a full American bar. A Pasta Bar appears at lunch, and breakfasts are cooked and served al fresco. Harry's Cafe, located in a nook under the waterfall, is a charming French cafe where French onion soup, quiche and delicious salads accompany dark, French-roasted coffee. Ice creams are a specialty here—all homemade, of course.

The New Otani Kaimana Beach Hotel

2863 Kalakaua Avenue
Waikiki 96815
(808) 923-1555

The New Otani Kaimana Beach Hotel, built in 1964, is a 138 room hotel conveniently situated on the beach not far from the foot of Diamond Head. A relatively small hotel with over half its rooms overlooking the ocean, the New Otani Kaimana Beach Hotel has exclusive views that are practically unobtainable elsewhere in Waikiki. Surrounded by the 500-acre Kapiolani State Park, the "Kaimana" is located on one of the loveliest beaches in Waikiki, one that is shared with only a few luxury residential condominiums. All this away from the hustle and bustle of downtown Waikiki. Yet in a moment's caprice, all of this happy activity is only a short and pleasant walk away.

The New Otani Kaimana Beach Hotel offers all the conveniences of a larger hotel but in a pleasant, relaxed atmosphere. New services including a concierge, club privileges for frequent travelers, valet parking, an honor bar and other amenities in all guest rooms have recently been added. Completion of 19 deluxe one bedroom suites in December 1984 increased the number of suites in the hotel to 23. Also available are studio and one bedroom Garden Apartments with fully equipped kitchens for longer staying guests.

Should dining out be your fancy, the "Kaimana" features two excellent restaurants. The Hau Tree Lanai is fast becoming a landmark as one of the few remaining beachfront, outdoor restaurants in Hawaii. A remarkable fact when one considers how precious space is, on the beach at Waikiki. But it's on the food and friendly Hawaiian service that this restaurant's fame is founded. The Hau Tree Lanai features several unique delicacies made from locally grown ingredients, made all the more tantilizing by the use of fresh island grown spices. The flavor of entrees prepared this way is undeniably enhanced, as many a happy gourmet will boast. After dinner, listen to the waves breaking gently just beyond the restaurant's rail, amid the soft guitar music; that's how close you are to the beach. Cast your sight toward the horizon and keep a lookout for the Hawaiian sunset's legendary green flash at the instant day turns into night. Come back for a breakfast of continental cuisine at 7:00 a.m. or even later for lunch, served between 11:30 a.m. to 1:30 p.m. Dinner is served once again at 6:00 p.m. until 9:00 p.m.

A floor above is the Miyako Restaurant, considered one of Hawaii's finest Japanese restaurants. Open for dining from 6:00 p.m. to 10:00 p.m., the Miyako Restaurant offers a wide array of authentic Japanese cuisine. Traditional tatami style rooms seating a total of nearly 100 people are available for private parties and the adventurous diner. Western style seatings are also available in the Miyako dining room with a lovely view of Diamond Head in the background.

This cozy, small hotel atmosphere and hand-picked staff brings guests back year after year. These special people pride themselves in greeting everyone by name, and anticipate your every wish, to make your vacation in Hawaii truly memorable.

Pacific Hawaii Bed & Breakfast

19 Kai Nani Place
Kailua 96734
(808) 262-6026
(808) 263-4848

Japanese representative:
720 Ala Moana Blvd., Suite B-3B
Honolulu 96815
(808) 955-4701
Japan at: (03) 437-9821

Get away from the noise and bustle of the city, and customize your time in the beautiful Hawaiian Islands by enjoying the warmth and hospitality of Pacific Hawaii Bed and Breakfast. Choose a quiet cottage on a secluded beach or a private studio in a residential home. There are households available where fluent French, German and Spanish are spoken. You'll relish your "hide-away in Hawaii" through Pacific Hawaii Bed and Breakfast and still be close enough to enjoy Waikiki's exciting night life. Luxuriate in this unique experience.

Hyatt Regency Maui

200 Nohea Kai Drive
Lahaina, Maui 96761
(808) 667-7474

The Hyatt Regency Maui offers a rare blend of stylish elegance with the best that is Hawaii; breathtaking beauty, balmy breezes, and aloha-spirited people.

Throughout this magnificent resort the views are panoramic and unparalleled. The islands of Molokai and Lanai frame the horizon across the blue Pacific. A network of streams weaves its way through tropical and oriental gardens. Roaring waterfalls cascade into lakes and pools. Rich decor and over $2 million worth of Asian and Pacific art grace the lobbies and promenades.

Guest Rooms at the Hyatt Regency Maui have magnificent views of either the ocean, verdant West Maui mountains, golf course or lush gardens. Over three-quarters of the rooms have an ocean front or partial ocean view. They are fully air-conditioned with in-room controls, thick wall-to-wall carpeting, color television, private lanai, separate sitting area, king or double beds and airy interiors with an oriental influence. Hyatt Regency Maui offers a variety of suites providing additional rooms and amenities, like the Regency, deluxe, ocean and golf suites. The ultimate in accommodations is the Presidential Suite.

For a Polynesian dinner and show, what better spot than under the stars, steps away from the rolling surf and in the cool evening air of the Sunset Terrace. This outdoor entertainment center is the location of the Valley Isle's most spectacular *luau* and Polynesian show, the Drums of the Pacific. It's a superb dinner touched by the exotic flavors of a Hawaiian *luau*. Enjoy an authentic *imu* ceremony nightly. There are four fire dancers who twirl flaming three-foot knives, a Fijian spear dance performed by a Fijian Chief, and other songs and dances from the South Pacific.

Hyatt Regency Maui also offers several restaurants and lounges. Swan Court and Spats are recipients of the coveted Travel-Holiday award for fine dining. Swan Court, their fine dining room, is open to the peaceful influence of Japanese gardens, the sound of waterfalls and the ever present beauty of swans gliding gracefully as you dine. Spats is a restaurant and dance club, famous for its intimate atmosphere and exceptional Northern Italian cuisine. Breakfasts, snacks and beverages can be found at other restaurants and cafes in the hotel complex.

During the daytime, the Maui sun invites a variety of pleasures: tennis, golf, sailing, snorkeling, walking along sandy beaches or enjoying the great pool with its 130-foot lava slide, Grotto Bar and picturesque, swinging bridge.

To suit your entire family's needs, Hyatt Regency Maui's 18.5 acre "playground" is filled with excitement for children of all ages. With the many recreational and social activities planned throughout the year, children are a welcome addition to any vacation. They can choose from water sports, Hawaiiana arts and crafts, video game room, "Hyatt Theatre," or Kamp Kaanapali adventures in season. With all of the above facilities, it is not surprising that the Hyatt Regency Maui has become an attraction in itself and one of Maui's greatest treasures.

Kauai Vacation Rentals

P.O. Box 3194
Lihue, Kauai 96766
(808) 245-8841
(800) 367-5025 (outside Hawaii)

Do uncrowded sandy beaches, privacy and a holiday on a tropical island excite you? You can be a honeymooner looking for complete seclusion, an executive looking for a restful and relaxing setting, or a family wanting relaxation and space; renting a private home or condominium is the ideal way to enjoy your vacation on Kauai, the beautiful Garden Isle. Kauai Vacation Rentals offers you a selection of these opportunities, from Poipu to Haena, from comfortable economy to complete luxury.

Most of the accommodations access the beautiful white sand beaches that make Kauai famous. In addition, the island offers a wide range of outdoor activities to fill your days; from snorkeling the clear warm waters, to golf, horseback riding, hiking, touring, helicopter rides, water skiing, diving, or sailing. Kauai has it all.

If you choose to stay in a condominium, most complexes have swimming pools and tennis courts. Some offer saunas, jacuzzis and paddle tennis. All accommodations have complete kitchens and are totally furnished. Call for detailed information to get started on the best vacation of your life.

Kona Surf Resort

78-128 Ehukai Street
Kailua-Kona, Hawaii 96740
(808) 322-3411
Toll Free (800) 367-8011
(outside Hawaii)

One of the Big Island's many charms is the beautiful Kona Surf Resort at Keauhou Bay. Arriving at the Kona Surf Resort, you'll be greeted with a fresh and colorful orchid lei. You'll be wonderfully delighted to find an array of orchids decorating your room, as well as on dining tables and room service trays; the special touch of the Kona Surf Orchid Service offers you complimentary coffee every morning, and champagne and punch served in the lobby each afternoon.

The Kona Surf hosts 535 finely appointed rooms and suites, all boasting unparalled views of the ocean or garden, and featuring a private lanai, color TV, radio, courtesy coffee maker and luxurious bath amenities.

Throughout the day, a variety of activities are offered for your enjoyment; golfing on the 18-hole Keauhou Championship Course, tennis, fitness programs, complete ocean activities including snorkeling, diving, deep sea fishing, jogging and hiking trails, Hawaiian arts and crafts, and much more! You'll enjoy beautiful sunsets and great Hawaiian entertainment on the Nalu Terrace each afternoon, as you sip an exotic tropical drink. After sundown, three restaurants offer casual to fine dining, while at one of four cocktail spots you should be ready for a fantastic Polynesian show, compliments of the Kona Surf!

Hanalei Bay Resort

P.O. Box 220
Hanalei, Kauai 96714
(808) 826-6522
(800) 367-7052 (outside Hawaii)

Imagine luxury in a setting as unspoiled as old Hawaii. Where the natural beauty of the land renews the spirits of all who pass through. Hanalei Valley is such a place; and, the Hanalei Bay Resort captures this beauty in an elegant resort with all the comforts of home.

Located in the well known Princeville Resort area, where it overlooks the perfect beach setting in paradise, Hanalei Bay Resort is a cluster of 16 low-rise buildings, none more than three stories high. Relax in a luxury one, two or three bedroom, condominium units. Want to dine in? Your fully equipped kitchen awaits you. Spend the evening at "home" if you choose, enjoying cable color TV, or just relax on your private lanai cooled by the tropical breezes of Kauai's north shore.

You'll be happy to know there are eleven, plexi-paved championship tennis courts, three of which are lighted for night play. For the tennis enthusiast, a resident international tennis pro is always available for lessons at all levels of play, including video tape playback.

For the golfer in your family, the challenging 27-hole Princeville "Makai Course," site of the 1978 World Cup, surrounds the resort with the clubhouse just a mile away. Designed by Robert Trent Jones, it is ranked as one of the best in the United States.

If relaxation is what you seek, lose yourself on the secluded white sand beaches, or choose between two swimming pools, or sauna. Swimmers and surfers will appreciate the beautiful, private beach which is just a short, ten minute

stroll from the rooms. Guests with a busy schedule can ride to and from the sand and surf, and save time by using the year-round shuttle service. Snorkeling gear, boogie boards and children's life vests may be rented, while beach mats and coolers are complimentary. Nearby, windsurfing equipment may also be rented. Sea shell hunts, nature walks and other organized outings are also available through the activities desk, located in the main lobby next to registration; while the Aikani Lounge offers Hawaiian films, games, classes in Hawaiiana, and parties for the youngsters.

A superb dining experience awaits you at the Bali Hai restaurant and cocktail terrace, overlooking a seascape of legendary beauty. Named for the famous Na Pali peaks known as Bali Hai, the view is a scene of daytime blues and greens against the white sand; with the scarlet, orange and gold sky against the black silhouettes of the Na Pali coastline at sunset; a most spectacular sight indeed. The dining area is beautifully decorated with tie-dyed, batik banners and open to the air on three sides, with two levels of tables to allow everyone a breathtaking view.

The cuisine, continental with a touch of Polynesia, is superb. Dinner is a special adventure in dining that features steak, fresh local fish, scampi and a delicious seafood salad, all served with friendly and attentive service to make your sunset celebration an unforgettable experience.

The Hanalei Bay Resort is ideally situated for that sophisticated vacation in one of the most beautiful corners of the world. It's not surprising that "South Pacific" was filmed closeby; Hanalei Bay is a scenic dream, and sits at the doorstep of the Hanalei Bay Resort, waiting just for you.

111

Cosmopolitan Dining

The flavor and fun of the Islands are enhanced by a wide variety of dining out experiences that the first time and repeat visitor will encounter during their stay. The original local cuisine, typified by the traditional Hawaiian luau, has changed radically from what it once was in old Hawaii. The tender poi dog, raised carefully for the luau; the sweet potato, and the bland, somewhat fibrous, breadfruit are no longer part of the present day luau.

The original form and menu of the luau has changed to cater to modern tastes. Fortunately, some of the best dishes remain the same, though many of the textures of the foods may seem a bit strange. So, overcome your inhibitions, you'll be delightfully surprised!

Pau Hana & Pupus

You'll hear many references to "pau hana" time and "pupus." Pau hana is literally translated as "end work," and is usually the cause for celebration. Just before the weekend, "Aloha Friday" is the cause for even more celebration!

As with many other places, Hawaii has its version of "happy hour," where the drinks are discounted, or half-price. And, because things run a little slower here, most happy hours are longer as well. One of the nicest things, is that happy hour comes with the local custom of pupus; finger foods which can be hot or cold, anything from peanuts to stuffed crab claws and everything in between. So be sure to take advantage of a quiet, lazy afternoon with a good happy hour; and the pupus are usually free!

Paradise Pedicabs
Waikiki 96815
(808) 922-8161

Whether it's one of Waikiki's many shows, great restaurants, or an evening of nightclubbing, let Paradise Pedicab complement your evening on the town and get you there in style! Knowledgeable and qualified guides. Call Paradise Pedicab at 922-8161 for information and dispatch.

Many restaurants make good use of the quality, and abundant quantity, of the fresh island produce. Among the favorites are the sweet Kahuku watermelon, mango, papaya, banana, coconut, and of course, the pineapple. Local farmers and backyard growers also take great pride in providing some of the island's wonderful fresh vegetables such as crisp manoa lettuce, sweet maui onions, fresh corn and a variety of avocados.

While you are out discovering Hawaii on your own, be sure to keep your eyes open to see where the local residents eat. One need only to stop in any shopping center at lunchtime in Hawaii to catch the magical atmosphere of oriental cuisine. Whether it's saimin, a simple noodle soup; or hot manapua, a hot steamed doughy roll served with meat or beans inside, it can be lots of fun to try some of the local favorites for lunch. The surprises are endless. You may discover Chinese, Korean, Japanese, Vietnamese, Thai, or down-home Hawaiian food; these beautiful islands not only combine many ethnic groups but provide a truly epicurian melting pot.

For those who have discovered the delight of oriental food, Hawaii holds many captivating choices. Whether it's tempura vegetables, crisp wok cooking, won tons or peking duck, or the fun of the sushi bar, all your oriental appetite can be satisfied in a variety of ways, from casual to elegant. So, now is the time to leave the traditional and experience culinary adventure!

Evening dining in Hawaii is generally a casual affair. Many fine establishments have a dress code, rarely requiring a jacket or tie. Although it's often fun to dress for that elegant dinner, most visitors will find the relaxed island atmosphere very much in tune with their vacation needs. Where else, but in Hawaii, could you sit enjoying an excellent and delightful meal, with warm tropical breezes, while an island beauty visits your table offers you fragrant flowers and leis, or just her radiant Aloha smile. Bon appetite!

113

The captivating desserts include three fresh fruit sherbets with crushed raspberries, profiteroles served with melted chocolate, fresh fruit tart with kiwi and strawberries, or assorted fresh baked pastries and cakes from the dessert tray. A coffee menu offers teas and fine coffees, freshly ground, from around the world.

Bagwells Wine Bar is an excellent adjunct to the restaurant, with premium wines served by the glass as well as by the bottle. Wine tastings are often featured at the wine bar, with good reason— the wine list is, without doubt, one of the best in the world and has received the coveted Wine Spectators' "Top 100 Wine Lists of America" award. Some of the most extraordinary vintages of California and Europe are offered. Enjoy complimentary hors d'oeuvres including Bagwells' own freshly made pates, fruits and fine cheeses. The director of wines will be happy to discuss and assist you with wine tasting from their prestigious selection of over 100 varieties.

For your pleasure while dining, a classical guitarist is featured nightly, except Sundays. After five attire is required and jackets are suggested. Bagwells Wine Bar is open every night from 6:00 p.m. to 12:00 midnight. Once you've dined at Bagwells it's easy to understand why it was rated one of the top 75 restaurants in America by over 100,000 United Airlines frequent flyers. For the best ambiance and the finest in French-Continental cuisine, Bagwells 2424 should not be missed.

Bagwells

Hyatt Regency
Waikiki
(808) 922-9292

The ultimate in French-Continental cuisine is elegantly served in the luxurious surroundings of Bagwells 2424 located at the Hyatt Regency Waikiki. Dining at Bagwells is your opportunity to be pampered with their exquisitely attentive service. Expect the very finest from Bagwells, the recipient of six Travel Holiday awards for fine dining as well as the Carte Blanche award for excellence in service and cuisine. Every course is served with the style, skill and extraordinary attention to detail that is their trademark.

The menu selection at Bagwells is designed to provide a superb dining adventure to either the new dining enthusiast or the connoisseur. Choose from specialties including exquisitely prepared appetizers, salads, and soups such as red snapper baked in a light puff pastry, or lobster and scallop casserole with truffles and artichokes. Gourmets will be pleased to savor the entrees of opakapaka with watercress and ginger, breast of duckling with orange and black currants, medallions of veal with morrels and heavy cream, and broiled sirlion steak or filet mignon with herb butter.

Dinner: 6:00 p.m. to 10:00 p.m.
Valet Parking

Canlis

2100 Kalakaua Avenue
Waikiki
(808) 923-2324
Valet Parking

Lunch: 11:00 a.m. to 2:00 p.m.
Dinner: 6:00 p.m. to 1:00 a.m.

Romance is alive and well in Waikiki, thank you. Forget the concrete canyons that border Hawaii's most famous beach. There is a treasure of a place and, perhaps only one, where an extraordinary union of architecture, art and epicurean cuisine continues to create an atmosphere at once reassuringly timeless and refreshingly a la mode. This is Kalakaua Avenue's Canlis restaurant.

What makes Canlis so special is the excellence of its fare, combined with a visual feast of waterfalls cascading down massive, orchid-laden volcanic walls that together have, with an ease, elegance and graciousness of style, masterfully resisted, outlasted and overcome all the trendiness inherent in a resort community.

Luncheon in Canlis' main dining room, cooled by Hawaii's tradewinds that flow gently through the vertically louvered walls, offers a tantalizing array of delectables from fresh island seafood to delicious specials including duck a l'orange, roast lamb, and fettucini Jean-Pierre, plus a marvelous selection of salads and desserts. Remarkably, luncheons are very reasonably priced.

Dinners in Canlis are served every evening in the main dining room or "downstairs" in the Lotus Room surrounded by orchids and ponds. Among dinner delights are world famous Canlis Special Salad, fresh island opakapaka, mahimahi and prime American beef. Not to be missed is Canlis' wine list, with fine vintages to complement any meal.

Two years ago, when the restaurant celebrated its 30th anniversary, Canlis added two elements to its presentation that have produced little short of a renaissance in late night dining and entertainment in Waikiki.

Beginning at 9:30 p.m. each evening, Canlis offers a delicious, affordably priced late supper menu, from Canlis' succulent steak sandwich to Grand Marnier souffle, to delight the palate and, Wednesdays through Saturdays, the music of three-time Na Hoku Honohano Award-winner Jay Larrin to delight the soul. A native of Tennessee, Larrin's deep love and respect of Hawaii is strikingly evident in the lyricism and poetry of his music. "The Ko'olaus Are Sleeping Now," "Moloka'i Lullaby," and "The Snows of Mauna Kea," are but three of his many compositions which have rightly woven themselves into the rich tapestry of Hawaii's musical heritage.

Larrin's wit, whimsy, easy humor and lush music create a very special magic at Canlis, and *kamaainas,* visitors and celebrities have followed him there. They've become regulars.

Now, in its 32nd year, the restaurant that's captured the Travel Holiday dining award each year since its founding in 1954 by Peter Canlis, offers yet another superlative dining option: The Theatre Supper. Nightly, from 6:00 to 7:00 p.m. and again after 10:00 p.m., Canlis' specially priced theatre supper includes soup, salad and entree. The theatre supper menu is changed every six weeks so patrons can delight in sampling the artistry of Canlis' chefs.

Truly, the superb cuisine and service, the serene *kamaaina* elegance, that made Canlis one of Waikiki's most popular restaurants in 1954, continues to make Canlis one of the best and most respected dining adventures in Honolulu 32 years later. There is no cover charge or minimum for entertainment and jackets are not required.

Casablanca
1855 Kalakaua Avenue
Honolulu
(808) 942-2151

Casablanca—the city, the movie and now, in Waikiki, the restaurant and lounge. The romance of yesteryear is returning and nowhere is it more evident than in these lovely surroundings. In the restaurant you will dine in casual elegance in an airy, terraced dining area enhanced by a cascading waterfall, lush tropical flowers and melodious notes from the nearby grand piano. To compliment this charming room, sample the light, Continental cuisine, artfully presented with a true French flair.

The choice of exciting appetizers, including such delicacies as bay scallop pate in a tangy red pepper sauce, escargots in a light pastry shell spiced with a creamy garlic and tomato sauce, fresh Island fish marinated in dill, broccoli mousse with a refreshing lemon sauce or gelled rabbit pate in an onion compote, will delight the senses.

The myriad of exquisitely prepared entrees, such as the perfectly roasted breast of duck served on a bed of black current jelly, succulent lamb chops with fresh herbs, tender filet mignon laced with a touch of green pepper sauce, or the veal steak smothered with morel mushrooms, will tempt every palate. And, seafood lovers will particularly enjoy the unique red snapper sausage with a rich, cream sauce, the mahimahi sauteed in a delicate red wine and mushroom sauce, or the fresh ahi, carefully grilled and served with an excellent sauce Bernaise.

Food this impressive has its just desserts in the form of the nostalgic "Floating Island" (whipped egg whites floating in creamy custard), frozen chocolate mousse with chocolate sauce (a chocolate lover's dream!), delicious tartin tarts or creme brulee with fresh fruit. Discerning diners who value imagination and insist on performance will return time and time again to Casablanca, a true haven for the sophisticated palate.

Stepping into the adjoining lounge, Casablanca brings new meaning to the word "entertainment." State-of-the-art sound equipment reproduces with acoustic excellence a wide variety of music, ranging from classical to contemporary to jazz (appeasing every music lover's taste), while film classics and animated videos are projected throughout the room (for Humphrey Bogart fans this is a must!). Or, for more intimate and secluded seating slip upstairs to the balcony where one can overlook the constantly changing activity of the main lounge below, rather than participate in it.

An oasis for epicures and fun-lovers alike, Casablanca is rapidly becoming the most popular place in town, famous for its creativity in both dining and entertainment. "Play it again, Sam!"

Chez Michel

444 Hobron Lane
Waikiki
(808) 955-7866
Lunch: 11:30 a.m.–2:30 p.m.
Dinner: 6:00 p.m.–10:00 p.m.
Valet Parking

With it's chic, smartly decorated intimate rooms and lovely lattice work touches, the charming ambiance of Chez Michel invites you to relax and thoroughly enjoy your dining adventure. Centrally located in picturesque Eaton Square, and just a short walk from the Ilikai Hotel or Hilton Hawaiian Village, awaits a superior experience few can match. This restaurant is well known for its culinary delights and has been providing the islands with the best in French cuisine for many years. The attractive atmosphere and high quality of both food and service assure that Chez Michel is the perfect place for lunch or dinner, and an ideal place to experience a delightful sampling of truly authentic French Cuisine.

At lunch, Michel's salads will delight you. Select from his excellent chicken salad with apples and walnuts, cold artichoke salad with a tasty vinigarette dressing, or a great pasta salad. Then, try the quiche of the day, scampi provencale, Michel's fettucine aux fruits de mer, or braised short ribs, all excellent choices for lunch. There is also a great selection of soups and sandwiches to complement the extensive a la carte menu.

Dinner at Chez Michel will be a memory you'll long cherish. The ultimate in service, combined with the superior menu and relaxed atmosphere, create a memorable dining experience. The roast breast of duck in a sweet fruit sauce is an excellent way to sample Michel's fine cuisine. Perhaps the most tender veal dishes will be your choice; chopped veal served in lemon butter sauce and lightly flavored with Noilly Prat vermouth, or the medallions de veau, a veal tenderloin sauteed with a sauce of fresh mushrooms, sherry wine and cream. Your selection of the best in French cuisine also includes rack of lamb smothered with sauteed bread crumbs and fresh herbs, filet mignon served with Bernaise sauce, or fresh mussels steamed in white wine and flavored with shallots and parsley in a thick butter and cream sauce. Chez Michel has everything to truly captivate your senses.

The wide variety of desserts will entice you; crepes, chocolate mousse (from an old family recipe), chilled Grand Marnier souffle, creme caramel and fresh strawberries a la Romanoff, just to name a few. No one in Hawaii creates desserts quite like Michel. Each dessert is captivatingly delicate and typically French, a perfect way to complete your meal.

Naturally, to complement such magnificent French cuisine, a comprehensive selection of French and other fine wines is available. The intimate atmosphere of Chez Michel is the perfect setting for an enchanting evening. So, if you're looking for that rare and special evening with excellent cuisine and the best in attentive service, visit Chez Michel in Eaton Square.

Chef-Poi-Ardee?

Most tourists automatically wrinkle their noses and say an emphatic "Ugh!" before they even taste it. We're talking about poi of course, that much misunderstood and maligned staple of the Hawaiians.

Poi was originally made from taro root by the ancient Hawaiians. It's a mashed vegetable dish, beaten to a somewhat pasty consistency with a poi pounder, with water added to give it a liquid consistency. It was then cooked in an earthen Imu (oven) and served as a vegetable, to be scooped up with the fingers.

Usually the vegetable used was taro, but sometimes breadfruit or even sweet potato was substituted. It was,

and still is, considered impolite to serve thin poi. Correct poi should be able to be scooped up with the fingers in one delicious swoop.

So before you make a face, think about what you serve back home.

If you're from the American South—it's grits.

If you're from the Northeast—it's oatmeal.

If you're from the West—it's guacamole.

And if you're from the Midwest—it's cream of wheat.

So give our local version of these creamy dishes a taste. Who knows, you might just become one of poi's biggest fans!

Traditionally, the somewhat salty Hawaiian pig, known as kalua pig, is wrapped in taro leaves, then placed in an earthen pit called an imu along with the yams, breadfruits, and available fish. The imu adds a taste to the pig that can't be duplicated.

And how the Hawaiians love a luau! It's much more than a feast and partaking of food. The family, or families, work together to prepare the imu with feelings of aloha and warmth extending throughout the day, or days, as all work together in harmony. Today, although an authentic Hawaiian luau may be difficult to find, that's not the case for the aloha spirit that goes with it.

Many of the new luau dishes such as sushi or lomi-lomi salmon are welcome additions. Of course, every good luau offers poi (the substance resembling brown paste) and we encourage you to try it; but be sure you do so with the salty kalua pig because it's the combination of the two that make it so delicious. And don't miss haupia, or coconut pudding. This plain looking, jello-type white cake is an island favorite and proves that good things definitely come in small packages.

These beautiful islands, because of their location in the middle of the sparkling seas, offer an exciting variety of seafood. Some may seem strange to the newcomer, such as the opihi, a shell attached to the surfaces of the rocks and coral which the local residents eat raw. You may not want to brave it, understandably. Others such as the fresh mahi mahi, opakapaka, ahi, or ono just to name a few are all worth trying more than once, as the different cultures prepare them in a wide variety of ways.

Get a Shave Ice Lickity-Split!

Shave Ice is like nothing else you'll find on the Mainland. You might compare it to "Snow Cones" or "Snow Balls" that you're familiar with, but Shave Ice has a flavor and a history all its own.

It first arrived back in the early 1900's with the Japanese plantation workers. At that time, Shave Ice was reserved for very special occasions and created by scraping a block of ice and flavoring it with a simple sweet syrup.

Today, the tradition of Shave Ice continues, but the ice is now efficiently scraped by machine, and enjoyed anytime, not just on special occasions. It's different from its Mainland counterparts because the

ice is so fine and packed so compactly, not like the much coarser versions you'll find back home. Also, you'll find an amazing variety of flavors ranging from the familiar strawberry and cherry to the more exotic guava, lilikoi and coconut.

You'll find Shave Ice stands all across the islands. They might range in appearance from a rickity-slapped-together shed to a real "uptown" slick stand, complete with Shave Ice hats, t-shirts and other matching accessories.

So, wherever you decide to purchase your Shave Ice, you'll find the same sweet, unmistakable Hawaiian flavor and texture that'll have you craving for more... and more than likely, you'll be scoffing at their "country cousin" versions back home.

Chuck's Steak House

Kahala Mall
4211 Waialae Avenue
Honolulu
(808) 732-2861

Lunch: 11:30 a.m. to 2:00 p.m.
Dinner: 6:00 p.m. to 10:00 p.m.

The warm and cozy atmosphere at Chuck's is just what you'd expect in paradise. With gorgeous island touches in decor, it's comfortable booths, earth tones and soft lighting make you feel right at home. Chuck's is conveniently located at the Kahala Mall, yet off the beaten tourist track. Owner, Denis McNulty, prides himself in selecting the freshest quality seafood, together with prime and tender juicy meats. The finest food served by a friendly staff. And, with Denis' particular attention to freshness, your palate will undoubtedly enjoy a special treat and you'll know that you just can't beat the value or quality.

Lunch offers a complete assortment of salads like stuffed artichoke, chef's salad, crab Louie and garden quiche. Gourmet burgers include bacon, mushroom, avocado, BBQ, chili and teriyaki burgers for starters. You can make a selection from over 15 sandwiches, like the delicious crabmeat and bacon, or the succulent mahimahi. Whichever you choose, it's bound to be great.

Of course, for dinner, there's a whole range of tantalizing appetizers, including deep fried or sauteed zucchini, mushrooms or asparagus spears; escargot, and a local favorite, potato skins. There is also an excellent salad bar and a choice of soups to delight you while you sit back and truly relax in the cozy atmosphere of Chuck's. They also offer a wide variety of meats: tender filet mignon, New York steak, kalbi ribs and teriyaki sirloin, just to name a few. Seafood choices include succulent lobster, king crab, delicious scampi or the local favorite, fresh mahimahi almondine; each delectable and enticing! For those of you who have a difficult time choosing between steak and seafood, don't worry, you can have both with a combination dish such as steak and scampi, or steak and king crab. And, when your entree has succeeded in pleasing your palate, let a simple yet tantilizing dessert complete your evening or lunch, with a choice of several ice creams, cheesecake or the "calorie buster" Mud Pie!

Chuck's at Kahala is the place to call on during one of your out of Waikiki shopping or sightseeing tours, or just for something different. Only ten minutes from the center of Waikiki, follow the H-1 freeway toward Koko-Head (East), take the Waialae offramp and turn right at the

second traffic signal. About 200 yards to the first opening on the left will lead you to the door of a dining experience you'll love. Call for directions or check for reservation requirements. Chuck's at the Kahala Mall is excellent quality at a great price, and also very popular with the local people!

119

Matteo's

364 Seaside Avenue at Kuhio
Waikiki
(808) 922-5551

Dinner: 6:00 to 11:30 p.m.
Valet Parking

Matteo's, centrally located in the heart of Waikiki, is the ideal place to savor the finest in classic Italian cuisine. Completely renovated with lush earth tones, Matteo's will delight and charm you with its atmosphere. For that special celebration, for those private intimate dinner parties, or for the perfect evening, Matteo's will fill the need wonderfully. Easily accessible and with your comfort in mind, Matteo's offers the most complete Italian menu in Hawaii.

From its classic standards such as shrimp scampi or veal cutlet parmigiana to such tasty specialties as chicken alla Matteo's, a tasty chicken stuffed with mozzarella cheese, prosciutto ham and asparagus. Other delicious entrees include pork chops pizzatola, chops in a tangy marinara sauce with mushrooms; or veal rollatini, rolled veal stuffed with bell peppers, mushrooms, onions, spinach, prosciutto ham, mozzarella cheese and topped with marsala and mushroom sauce. All served with the freshest ingredients. Bella!

Try one of their many tempting selections from the complete dinner selection, such as shrimp marinara, grenadine of beef tenderloin, or a delicious piccata di vitella saute, delicate slices of veal lightly sauted in lemon and butter.

Matteo's has a wide variety of your favorite antipasto, hot or cold. The seafood combination platter consisting of calamari, shrimp, baked clams and stuffed mushrooms is wonderful. The shrimp cocktail served with a zesty sauce will delight you. Or, try the deep fried calamari which is absolutely the best around.

For those dessert lovers, Matteo's features the classic freshly made spumoni and tortoni. They have recently brought in their own pastry chef who makes various cakes and pastries daily, depending on what's in season. All of which will tantalize your taste buds!

A wide choice of wines is available to compliment your dinner. Matteo's has one of the most complete selections from Germany, France, Italy, California and Washington states. The finest of wines are now available "by the glass."

Compliments of Matteo's: if you mention the HawaiiGuide to your waiter, you will receive a free Souvenir coin of Hawaii, (minted in Hawaii), when you dine at Matteo's.

Musashi

Hyatt Regency
Waikiki
(808) 922-9292

Dinner: 6:00 to 11:00 p.m.
Valet Parking

In the usual Hyatt tradition, Musashi is an exceptional, traditional Japanese restaurant. Named after Miyamoto Musashi, the most famous of all Japanese samurai and a legendary symbol of strength and discipline, Musashi is more than just a restaurant, it is an imaginative attempt to create an entire experience, a treat for the senses. The fine cuisine is accompanied by a taste of drama and theatre, with elaborate and colorful replicas of the clothing of old Japan, over 50 types of dinnerware hand-selected from Japan and careful presentation utilizing bamboo, tropical flowers and other unusual accompaniments as part of the evening.

As the guest is seated in Musashi, a complimentary cup of sake is offered from a large, straw-wrapped taru, the traditional keg for storage of sake. If the guest is having teppan-yaki, he will be dressed in a Japanese hapi coat. A kago, modeled after the palanquins of samurai Japan, will carry the appetizer selection. The uniforms are colorful: hostesses and waitresses wear kimono-like gowns, while the waiters are in hakama. The teppan-yaki cooks wear samurai-like garb and the bus help is dressed in the manner of traditional street acrobats. The entire effect is one of brilliant color, originality and fun!

The menu is an imaginative offering of traditional Japanese as well as contemporary creations, utilizing many ingredients from the Orient. There are three separate dining experiences in Musashi: the sushi bar, the teppan grill and the dining room. The sushi bar offers a discriminating variety of only the freshest seafood the ocean has to offer, presented with eye catching, artistic skill.

For the teppan-yaki experience, guests sit around the teppan grill, while the cook prepares the food. The choices range from huge tiger prawns; succulent young island chicken; scallops; or the vegetarian platter, an elegant collection of fresh seasonal vegetables accompanied by ponzu sauce. Also offered are tender filet mignon and the Musashi grille, which includes filet mignon, succulent lobster and scallops. All entrees include the traditional miso soup, salad, rice, shrimp, stir-fried vegetables, pickled vegetables and green tea.

Anything the restaurant has to offer can be ordered from the dining room, including a wonderful collection of soups and salads like chawan mushi, chicken, crab, scallops and vegetables steamed in a creamy egg custard; sunomo, thinly sliced cucumber and shellfish marinated in a light vinegar sauce with a touch of ginger; or the ocean vegetable salad, a selection of king crab and fresh abalone accompanied by

Musashi's special plum dressing.

Entrees are most enticing and an entertainment in themselves. They include the Dream of Kyoto, beautifully presented in a lacquer box with 7 varieties of fish, beef and vegetable delicacies; an assorted seafood tempura moriawase, which consists of selected seafood, shellfish and vegetables dipped in batter, then deep fried and served with tempura sauce. Or, you might wish to try the very special Musashi Shokado, local shrimp onigarayaki, tender filet mignon, or the chef's personal selection of three daily specials, served with kobachi, sashimi, miso, rice, pickled vegetables, Japanese green tea and sherbet.

The dessert offerings are just as spectacular. The house favorite is a delicate tempura batter surrounding ice cream, then deep fried. Musashi's Jewel Box consists of five sherbets presented in a delicate wafer box served in a kiwi sauce. Also offered is the fruit cream crepe, which is fresh fruit-flavored cream folded in a dessert creme and served with kiwi fruit and berries.

Whatever your choice, your dining experience at Musashi is carefully designed to thoroughly please your palate and delight all of your senses!

The Luau - An Ancient and Modern Feast

In ancient times, Hawaiians drank a narcotic drink at luaus called "awa," and made from the roots of the piper methysticum plant, ate dogs that were fed only vegetables, chicken wings which were boiled in blood, and fish served raw with head and eyes intact. It may not sound tasty, but to the ancient Hawaiians these were considered great delicacies.

The menu has been substantially updated since then, and today, for excitement in eating and entertainment, the Hawaiian luau is the perfect place to be.

Luau means feast, and if you are fortunate enough to attend an authentic luau you are in for quite an adventure. For a luau to be authentic, the pig must be roasted in the ground, in an imu. An imu is a pit dug in the ground and lined with kiawe wood and lava rocks that will eventually steam and smoke the meat like no other oven can. At a traditional luau for celebrations such as weddings, birthdays and new babies, all the family members join in the preparation of the imu. After the pit has been dug, banana stumps are cut and used to line the inside. The moisture from these stumps prevents burning and creates the steam for cooking. The pig is then stuffed with rocks, wrapped in leaves, bound with wire, and placed inside the imu, along with yams, taro roots and sometimes chicken or fish. The imu is then covered completely with large thick leaves and soil. When removed, the result is called kalua pig.

Today, the luau menu consists of a variety of widely accepted tastes, brought together from various ethnic backgrounds. The laulau is pork, beef, salted fish and taro root tops wrapped in green ti leaves and cooked until very tender. A raw shellfish called opihi is served, as well as opae, baby shrimp. Lomilomi salmon is salmon marinated with onions and tomatoes. Poi, used as a staple in many Hawaiian families, is made from the taro root, baked in the imu and pounded into a thick brownish purple paste-like substance. As an island favorite, it is usually mixed with a stronger flavor to make an excellent taste combination. A very popular side dish is the delicious breadfruit called ulu. For dessert there is always coconut cake or haupia, coconut pudding of a white jello-like consistency.

It is appropriate to dress in Hawaiian attire for the luau, with men wearing flowered, bright print, aloha shirts and women in colorful muumuus. The haku lei, or floral headband, is a special crown for such an occasion, and most people generally wear leis.

See a local travel agent for information regarding the commercial luaus closest to where you're staying. Most offer open bars, and polynesian songs, dances and other entertainment as well as a menu consisting of many traditional Hawaiian foods. They may also have an imu ceremony if it's held outdoors. If you want a real authentic luau, you'll have to be more creative, by asking the local people working at the hotel, checking the newspaper or calling a church. Either way, don't miss out on the opportunity. The luau is a part of Hawaiian culture, old and new, and an experience that you'll remember for a long time!

Nick's Fishmarket

Waikiki Gateway Hotel
2070 Kalakaua Avenue
Waikiki
(808) 955-6333

Dinner: 6:00 to 10:30 p.m.
Valet Parking

Mention Nick's Fishmarket to residents and visitors alike in Hawaii and the unanimous response is overwhelming praise for this restaurant whose menu features the finest in seafood. The acclaim continues with the media, including food and wine critic, Robert Lawrence Balzer, who bestowed his prestigious Travel-Holiday Award on Nick's Fishmarket again in 1986.

Step into Nick's Fishmarket and immediately be impressed with the fine dining atmosphere and professional staff, led by general manager Randy Schoch. The decor is modern, accompanied by a collection of paintings by famed artists Leroy Neiman and Hawaii's own John Young, and offers privacy in its booths and tables, as well as the option of a private dining room called the "Wine Rack," which can accommodate up to 26 patrons.

As with all award-winning restaurants, it is the cuisine that entices people to visit, and it is Nick's exceptional food that brings in repeat reservations from VIPs, Hollywood celebrities, visitors to Waikiki, and local residents who continue to proclaim Nick's as their favorite dining spot.

A look at the menu at Nick's Fishmarket reveals that seafood is in abundance. Specialties of the house include live Maine lobster, flown in from the beds of New England every day. The array of fresh seafood is the largest in Waikiki, with the pick of the catch delivered daily to serve Nick's patrons. Onaga, opakapaka, mahimahi, swordfish, and ono are menu favorites, served in a variety of preparations ranging from being baked in parchment or topped with a lemon butter dill sauce, to a delightful Chicago style presentation with tomatoes, mushrooms and onions. Mainland markets provide fresh filet lemon sole, rainbow trout, catfish, broiled salmon, frog legs, and for shell fish lovers, Nick's offers an extensive selection of abalone, soft shell crabs, scallops, prawns and king crab legs, as well as oysters, clams and mussels.

As diners at Nick's know, the outstanding menu includes such house specialties as chicken oregano a la Sammy Davis Jr., the best calamari in town, an enticing sampling of seafood pastas, and even roasted fresh Mainland rack of lamb, flambe peppercorn filet mignon, and a selection of steak and veal dishes for the landlubbers.

The restaurant also features the full complement of appetizers, including the ever-popular Fishmarket chowder and unbeatable salads. Of course, Nick's Fishmarket has one of the most extensive wine lists in Hawaii, perfect after dinner drinks and desserts, and post-dining

entertainment in the Music Room for listening and dancing pleasure. Dolly Parton's protege, Norm Compton with the band Nueva Vida, performs regularly, until the wee hours of the morning.

Nick's Fishmarket is open nightly, with "Aloha" attire always appropriate and chicness always in vogue. There is convenient valet parking from the Kuhio Avenue entrance to the restaurant. All major credit cards are accepted, and for Japanese-speaking patrons, a special bilingual host is available to make menu suggestions and arrange for special parties. Reservations are recommended on weeknights, required on weekends.

Nick's Fishmarket: It wouldn't be a trip to Hawaii without dinner at Nick's!!

123

The Ancient Lei - A Modern Welcome

The traditional lei greeting, long familiar to Hawaii's visitors is actually part of an ancient ritual, an offering to the Gods. Beginning with the attitude, a spirit of love and thankfulness, each blossom is picked with a silent prayer, then strung so as to show its truest beauty. Each lei is conceived and crafted with love and affection.

In ancient times leis worn in a dance were never given away; they belonged to the goddess of the dance and the type of flower or fern used had a special significance. Even now, the fragrant Maile leaf is only used in ceremonies and special events. Today's leis also use today's flowers, and carnations take their place alongside ginger, pikake and orchid.

Decorating with leis is most evident in the attention given to costumes for parades. Even the horses are elaborately festooned, often the leis and vines hang to the ground and are braided into their manes and tails. Ancient birthdays, modern holidays and individual island commemorations are all wonderful excuses for a parade and celebration. And, of course, weddings and baby luaus keep lei makers busy year round.

It takes many thousands of flower petals or leaves to make some kinds of leis. The spiritual attitude when picking these delicate blossoms is as important as the symbolic welcome when the lei is given away. A strong ethic survives in the picking of these flowers; an area is never stripped, but preciously conserved and allowed to continually regenerate. If necessary, flowers and leaves are cut, not pulled out by the stalk or branch.

Each island has its own special lei made up of flowers indigenous to that island; the island of Niihau is the one exception, its leis are constructed of small pearly shells found only on its beaches and valued for their incredible lustre and delicate shape. Some leis made of feathers are more popularly used for headbands. Certain feathered leis have been long forbidden because of the rarity of certain birds; however other common feathers serve quite well, including peacock, duck and pheasant.

Leis of today are less structured than ever before, although the five basic techniques are still used. Whether braided, wound or strung, tied or knotted, today's leis are produced in much greater numbers though still using the same eye for color and form as in ancient Hawaii. No detail is too small; even the length is considered before the lei is begun. Hung above the bed at night, the fragrance will intertwine with the visions of the dreamer and add a new dimension to sleeping in the tropics.

There are contemporary leis made of candy, nuts and even small trinkets. Less traditional but more durable are the plastic leis that often welcome visitors with tour groups. After all, it's the spirit that remains; a symbol of beauty and true aloha, with every leaf, petal or feather supporting the welcome.

Nicholas Nickolas,
The Restaurant

Atop the Ala Moana Americana Hotel
410 Atkinson Drive
Honolulu
(808) 955-4466

Dinner: 5:30 to 11:30 p.m.
Valet Parking

Take the express elevator direct from the lobby of the Ala Moana Americana Hotel to the 36th floor penthouse, and you've arrived at Honolulu's most attractive restaurant. There is a sense of mystery and anticipation as you enter Nicholas Nickolas, The Restaurant, and move past the curved, sculptured walls into the lounge area and main dining room. A spectacular wrap-a-round view of Honolulu awaits you from every table.

The restaurant is opulent and regal; yet, the soft lighting and the textured, tufted and carpeted surfaces create a warm, relaxed, Hawaiiana mood that complements the city lights far below. The restaurant's color scheme, personally chosen by owner Nicholas Nickolas to "make every woman look more beautiful," consists of tones and shades of dusty rose, beige, deep mauve and a splash of powder blue.

Dinner at Nicholas Nickolas features a truly international mix of distinctive Continental cuisine. Shrimp, oyster, scampi and sashimi appetizers can be ordered as well as fettucini Alfredo prepared with cream sauce and ham, and Korean Ribs with a spicy Oriental sauce. The favorite among the salads is Nick's Classic Salad (patent pending), readying the palate for a main course which includes choices of fresh Island seafood, Greek lamb chops, Greek-style chicken, steak Hong Kong and a variety of steak cuts broiled over keawe (hardwood). A complete wine list complements all menu selections.

Nicholas Nickolas, The Restaurant, reflects Nicholas Nickolas, the owner, a self-made million-aire restaurateur who settles only for the best. "I will not operate a restaurant unless it is all gas," he demands. "Our style of cooking cannot be done on electric. I've turned down fantastic offers because they couldn't get me what I asked for." Nick opened his first restaurant in Honolulu in 1968, a second in Beverly Hills, Calif. in 1975 and a third in Chicago in 1977. Now comes his newest, and best yet.

After the dining hour has passed at Nicholas Nickolas, The Restaurant tablecloths are removed to expose polished black granite tabletops. A silver link curtain opens to reveal a stage that spotlights Hawaii's top entertainers. The travertine marble dance floor beckons and the restaurant is transformed into an exciting cabaret. The cocktail lounge is open from 5:30 p.m. to 4 a.m. every night of the week! All major credit cards are accepted. Free valet parking at the hotel entrance is available. Reservations are suggested. For parties and other special occasions, the restaurant offers a 35-seat glass-enclosed private dining area. The orchid-filled room is called "Nick's Lanai." For a truly outstanding dining experience, visit Nicholas Nickolas, The Restaurant.

Palffy

Pacific Grand Hotel
747 Amana Street
Honolulu
(808) 942-8181

Dinner: 6:00 p.m. to 11:00 p.m.
Valet Parking

The casual elegance and fine cuisine generated during the Austrian-Hungarian monarchy of the nineteenth century is brought alive at the Palffy Restaurant. Amid crystal chandliers, beautiful paintings, gyspy melodies and lilting Viennese waltzes, Palffy caters to your complete dining pleasure. The name of the restaurant is taken from a Hungarian count who,

in the mid 1800's, was the owner of the Viennese Opera House and a gourmet inventor of many great dishes and desserts. Owner Ben Smeisser and his partner, Bob Hall, have a background in European cuisine that assures you an authentic dining experience. Open for dinner and conveniently located just two short blocks from Ala Moana Shopping Center, Palffy is a fascinating dining opportunity you will want to experience.

Their hot and cold appetizers include, roasted bellpeppers with strips of smoked salmon, a prawn cocktail with classic brandy sauce, or escargots in mushroom caps, a Palffy favorite. Soups and salads include the magyar salad, a tomato, onion and avocado salad served with dill vinaigrette; and markklosschen soup, a delectable consomme with small marrow dumplings, just to name a few.

Or perhaps you would like to try the delicious hortobagyi-palacsinta, diced breast of chicken wrapped in a thin crepe laced with paprika sauce and garnished with fresh sour cream and parsley. An excellent seafood selection includes prawns, trout, flounder, scallops, or snapper all in their own individual gourmet sauces that make these dishes so delightful.

One of their entree specialties is medallion of milk-fed veal in paprika sauce with tasty mushrooms and sour cream sauce, called bakonyi borju szelet; or enjoy a Hungarian national dish, such as paprika chicken, called csirkepaprikas. In season, Palffy also serves two unique venison entrees, each prepared in a different, tantalizing way to tempt your palate.

There is an excellent dessert choice, but be sure to try delicious Hungarian crepes for dessert, filled with ground walnuts, rum and raisins, and glazed with chocolate sauce and fresh whipped cream.

Don't worry about being able to pronounce the menu at Palffy; the outstanding service and food will take you back to the old world from whence these dishes originated. Palffy is a truly unique dining experience. The cocktail lounge is open from 4:00 p.m. until the wee hours. There are also special cocktail hours from 4:00 to 7:00 p.m., Monday through Friday, with free hot pupus. Call for directions if you need them, it's well worth the effort!

Restaurant Suntory

Royal Hawaiian Shopping Center,
3rd Level - Waikiki
(808) 922-5511

Lunch: 11:30 a.m. to 2:00 p.m.
Dinner: 6:00 p.m. to 10:00 p.m.

Owned and operated by Suntory Ltd. of Japan, there is no better way to experience authentic Japanese dining than by a visit to Restaurant Suntory. Upon entering the restaurant you will immediately notice the large glass case, ceiling to floor, displaying the most beautiful array of crystal liquor bottles, each bearing the name of its owner. As is customary in Japan, when regular customers purchase a bottle of their favorite liquor, it is tagged with their name, and kept at the restaurant for use when they dine. Also, you will enjoy the attractive ikebana flower arrangements, traditionally Japanese, that decorate the entryway and every room of the restaurant.

The Sushi Bar is one that few can equal in quality and freshness. The choices include everything from raw tuna, yellow tail and red snapper to king clam, abalone and sea urchin, just to mention a few. And, of course, Japanese favorites like salmon roe, octopus and sea eel, all of which are available to order in any of the other dining rooms.

The Teppanyaki room is elegant in its simplicity with granite and wood tables where the chef creates special delights as you watch. Whether the taste be yakitori, broiled morsels of chicken and green onions, each skewer with a different marinade; delectably light shrimp and vegetable tempura, lightly dipped in batter and deep fried; to a fine cut of filet, fresh island chicken sauteed in a special sauce, succulent ocean shrimp sauteed with butter and wine, New Zealand lobster sauteed in garlic butter, Alaskan king crab or the chef's recommendation, live Pacific spiny lobster. You'll love the preparation show and adore the taste. You'll also want to try the chawanmushi, crab, chicken and vegetables steamed in a creamy egg custard and served chilled. What a sensation!

Then there's the Shabu Shabu room with an excellent menu of tasty appetizers including beef sashimi, smoked salmon or komochi konbu, traditional Japanese caviar. The entrees include beef and seafood shabu shabu, beef sukiyaki and sanpei nabe (lobster tails and salmon fillets accompanied by a selection of fresh vegetables and noodles in a flavored broth). For the taste experience of a lifetime, don't miss the outstanding tempura ice cream desert; rich vanilla ice cream encased in a delightfully sweet and crispy tempura batter, topped with strawberry sauce. The hot outer casing and cold ice cream inside will thrill your palate!

The wine list is extensive, consisting of over 50 different selections from California, France, Germany, Italy and Portugal as well as champagnes, sparkling wines and traditional sake. Anything served in the restaurant can be ordered from the Ozashiki Private Dining Room where you will be served in the traditional Japanese fashion by smiling, kimono clad hostesses who attend to your every need. So when your palate demands lobster, scallops, oysters, clams, salmon or beef, served with all the ceremony of formal Japanese dining and attention to detail, be sure to stop at Restaurant Suntory—an experience to truly remember!

The MacNuttery

2098 Kalakaua Avenue
Waikiki 96815
(808) 942-7798
(800) 367-5150 (outside Hawaii)

Irresistable is the word. So, indulge your taste buds at the largest and most extravagant ice cream store in the world. The MacNuttery is a unique combination of factory, store and restaurant; showcasing ice cream, cookies, macadamia nuts and chocolates. Mountainous ice cream sundaes are served in sparkling glass goblets with silver spoons. Directly above the counter, containers of melted pure chocolate, and hot creamy fudge are ready to pour generously over ice cream. And, of course, lots of crunchy Hawaiian macadamia nuts are sprinkled on top. The MacNuttery is not to be missed.

The MacNuttery, located conveniently in Waikiki on Kalakaua Avenue, seats more than 200 visitors in plush, comfortable indoor and outdoor settings. Be sure to savor a King Kamehameha Sundae served in a royal goblet filled with ice cold, fresh island fruits and crowned with a big scoop of rich vanilla ice cream. Or bite into one of Hawaii's favorite DeDomenico cookies, baked in several different varieties such as chewy cinnamon oatmeal plantations, lush in coconut and

raisins. At the same time you can view Waikiki's only full production chocolate factory where specially chosen whole macadamia nuts are dipped in creamy Ghiradelli chocolate to make the famous Diamond Head Chocolates.

The MacNuttery also features a selection of macadamia nut gift items that you can bring home to your friends and family, all attractively packed and protected for travel or mailing. For mail order call toll free (800) 367-5150.

The Liquor Collection

Ward Warehouse
1050 Ala Moana Blvd.
Honolulu 96814
(808) 524-8808

The Liquor Collection is no ordinary liquor store. Established to provide the most comprehensive collection of specialty beers, wines, and liquors, they also include what is probably the widest selection of miniature liquor bottles and unusual ceramic, decanter bottles in Hawaii.

Besides presenting all of the standard American liqeurs, there are special choices from Europe, the Middle and Far East, Asia and an extensive collection of Hawaiian products. You'll be sure to find that special and unusual gift at the Liquor Collection.

The staff also want to make your selections as easy and convenient as possible, and will gladly help you plan that special party; and even deliver larger requests to your door. So don't hesitate. Spend more of your time enjoying your selection from the convenience of the Liquor Collection.

128

A Shopper's Paradise

No matter how much time you spend in the islands, or what you do with the time you have, you'll undoubtedly make time to shop. Shopping is intrinsically a part of any vacation, as is seeing the sights. And, what Hawaii's visitors shop for could be anything, from souvenir items that rekindle fond memories to items for the folks back home; or even wonderful new island wear that help you fit right into Hawaii's scene.

Hawaii is truly a shopper's paradise; with everything from the well-known aloha shirt or muumuu, to jewelry made from artifacts found only in the islands, to footwear, bathing suits, beachwear, suntan lotion—all made in Hawaii. Don't forget that everyone loves the scents of Hawaii. Fragrances like pikake, ginger, orchid and plumeria, although worlds away from the sophistication of Paris, can be just as sweetly sensual. Then there are pineapples (packed for travel), macadamia nut products, a large variety of Hawaiian flowers and even seeds, specially inspected and packed for export from Hawaii. Many locally handcrafted items can be easily found, including fascinating bowls, platters and trays of monkeypod and koa wood; ceramic models and other interesting high tech artifacts; bambooware; everything imaginable made out of coconut shells and, of course, grass hula skirts (didn't someone ask for one?).

Paradise Pedicabs

Waikiki 96815
(808) 922-8161

Enjoy your shopping! Let us take you there. No walking, no packages to carry, no parking—no problems. Knowledgeable and qualified guides. Just call Paradise Pedicab at 922-8161 for information and dispatch.

Because of the islands' location, Hawaii has become a collector's dream with many exciting products from all over the Pacific, and throughout the Orient and Indonesia. You'll find many items often rare, or scarce, especially in the continental U.S.A. Jewelry abounds, with low prices on jade, coral, opal, olivine and many 14-karat gold items. An island jewelry favorite is real flowers and leaves dipped in 14 karat gold; or plumeria, delicately preserved in a clear plastic substance; it's so realistic that it looks natural.

The China Friendship Store, in Waikiki, offers a unique collection of oriental products, with over 21,000 different items ranging from jewelry to furniture; carvings, clothing, carpets, lacquerware, bamboo, hand-turned vases, Peking glass, hand-embroidered linens, and pure silk fabrics just to mention a few. Even more interesting; they also have frequent lectures, art and craft demonstrations by artists from the People's Republic, fashion shows, travel films and even cooking demontrations, all centered around the culture of the People's Republic of China.

Hawaii has a treasure trove of cultural shopping experiences. Although many are on Oahu, around Waikiki, the outer islands also have their share of interesting and exciting shopping experiences. And you also have one other alternative—books with information on Hawaii and Hawaiian history, with a great selection of color pictures, always make great souvenirs and gifts, and the HawaiiGuide is no exception, one that we hope you'll enjoy for many months and years after your visit to the islands! The stores that follow are a carefully chosen selection of interesting and easy to find shops, including several from two very interesting shopping centers—the Ala Moana Center and the Waikiki Trade Center. There are many other shops around, but we hope you'll visit those that follow—they enjoy serving the visitors and you'll find them very helpful in their own area of expertise.

C. June Shoes

Waikiki Trade Center
2255 Kuhio Avenue (at Seaside)
Waikiki 96815
(808) 926-1574

Located at the Waikiki Trade Center in the heart of Waikiki, C. June Shoes has one of the finest collection of designer shoes in the world within a single salon. Here you'll find shoes by designer artists such as Carlo Fiori, Charles Jordan, Stuart Weitzman, LaMarca, Xavier Danaud and Walter Steiger.

For those special needs from evening shoes to handbags, belts and jacket accessories, you'll find it all at C. June Shoes while you receive personalized service in an ambiance of elegance. The relaxed atmosphere of C. June Shoes makes it a pleasure to shop and coordinate your outfits, or simply enjoy the scenery of these graceful creations.

Melinda

Waikiki Trade Center
2255 Kuhio Avenue (at Seaside)
Waikiki 96815
(808) 924-6990

Melinda, at the Waikiki Trade Center, is the place to find extraordinary gift items for your friends, or yourself. You won't find Polynesian knicknacks, or monkeypod bowls here, but you will discover a remarkable selection of gift ideas ranging from one of a kind glassware and rare porcelain pieces, to exotic plastic sculptures and unusual clocks.

Visual effect, as well as function, describes many of the items available at Melinda. You'll find individually handcrafted items of Nourot glass, light sculptures and paperweights; the most exquisite collection of glass pieces, and one-of-a-kind vases with natural motifs of flora and fauna.

Art deco; Melinda carries an assortment of fine contemporary pieces. Also available are many beautiful porcelain Pierrots in a variety of sizes. Let's not forget the newest in high tech for adults and children alike, the Space Tubes! A big hit in Hawaii, and a great gift idea to take home.

One of the newest fragrances from Italy, Gianfranco Ferre, is carried exclusively by Melinda. An exotic floral blend of precious white Hawaiian flowers and fresh green leaves, strengthened by mosses and spices and enriched by a touch of musk, Gianfranco Ferre, is a rare blend of sophistication and mystery which make this fragrance persistant, sensual and long-lasting.

Fashions in Hawaii

Downtown Honolulu, at the peak of lunch-hour traffic, is alive and dazzling. Women pour forth from assorted buildings and various professions, dressed in an array of stylish fashions adapted for island living. The rage is the cool look of suits, lightweight jackets and silky dresses, adding that certain dash and polish to the staid business world.

The men of town carefully observe this parade of fashion passing by. They pick their favored vantage points on sidewalk seats and admire the color, the rush and the dress of Hawaii's working women. Most men prefer for themselves the Hawaiian casualness of aloha or polo-style shirts and, of course, the even cooler look of "shades" to hide those admiring eyes!

For what an eyeful goes up and down the busy downtown streets. Suits over silky blouses have become the rule for many women, especially those who have made their way to the upper echelons of management and business. Dressy leather shoes and bags, along with coordinated designer accessories, pull together a polished look that can be readly photographed for the pages of "Vogue."

The color and verve of the city lights and tropical landscapes reflect in the shades of silk and pretty patterns on flowing day dresses. Complete with a toss of shiny hair and flash of make-up, the look is as bright and happy as the island sunshine. Women of Hawaii grow up in surroundings of vibrant color and ocean movements, and the rhythm translates easily into the styles they wear.

There's also that cool, crisp linen combination of separates, shaded in island tones of bamboo, khaki and sandy white. Natural is the key, and fabrics that breathe and move with the often heady, humid air are the elements for this attire. It's a look that's matched up with cotton shirts, even playfully topped by a finely woven fiber hats and jazzed with jewelry; a look that's suited for work yet translates quickly into fun!

The traditional look of muumuus, the long, flowing gowns in which the early missionaries clothed the sensual bodies of the Hawaiian women, is still very popular today. In 1820, the missionaries came to the islands from the cold and virtuous climate of New England, intent on saving heathen souls. They prepared, during their long ocean voyage, by reminding themselves of the "depraved and uncivilized" sights awaiting them in the pagan, tropical lands. Still, their shock could not be contained upon their first glimpse of the Hawaiians.

Calvinist minister Hiram Bingham of Vermont wrote of that event, "The appearance of destitution, degradation, and barbarism, among the chattering, and almost naked savages, whose heads and feet, and much of their sunburnt skins, were bare, was appalling. Some of our number, with gushing tears, turned away from the spectacle."

The missionaries and their wives wasted no time in spreading the Gospel and clothing the Hawaiians. Their attempt to put the broad, fluid bodies of the Hawaiian women into the New England dress of tight bodices and long skirts met with little success. The Polynesian women were too accustomed to letting everything flow freely, and they discarded the close-fitting garments as often and as quickly as possible.

So, a compromise was struck. The fitted waistlines were let out and the cut of the dress was made looser in order to accommodate the comfort of the Hawaiian women. As the mission aries met with greater success in converting the people to Christianity, so did they find the islanders consenting to cover their bodies more and more.

Today, muumuus are still favored for their ease and simplicity, and are as easily accepted into the business atmosphere as they are at parties, nights-on-the-town or for casual lounge wear. The fabric and elaborateness of style can be matched to any occasion.

One of the dressier style muumuus, named for the woman who first created its fanciful look, features intricate pleats, stylish bodices and the perfect touches of lace and velvet trim over

Fabrications

Kahala Mall
Honolulu 96816
(808) 735-7622

"Fashion should refresh the senses and revive the spirits!"

At Fabrications in the Kahala Mall, you'll find a collection of exquisite fashions especially designed for tropical weather dressing and for your ultimate comfort. Created and produced in Hawaii, Fabrications' clothing is designed by Honolulu's leading fashion designer, Jeffrey Berman. His design is for graceful living when both business and social occasions require exquisite, but dependable classics. The silhouettes depict ease, comfort and fluidity. The look is that of resort wear, and international city dressing for year-round warm weather climates. You'll find particular emphasis on pure sunbelt dressing for international appeal, geared for women who demand the forward trend in fashion.

They also have a great upscale line of very unusual, limited edition garments available exclusively at Fabrications. Fabulous selections of jewelry and accessories to complement the fashions are another fare of Fabrications. See the special feature on the Bermans on page 33. The Kahala Mall is only 10 minutes from downtown Waikiki. Take the H-1 freeway East to the Waialae Avenue offramp.

Hilo Hattie's

700 N. Nimitz Highway
Honolulu 96817
(808) 537-2926

An exclusive collection of Hawaiian fashions. Available at over 50 stores throughout the islands. Call for the location nearest you.

132

flowing yards of delicately printed fabrics. The small, repetitive patterns of flowers on fine cotton fabrics are often called "missionary" prints, in tribute to the calico and conservative designs that the early clothiers often used.

The *holokuu* is another dressy muumuu style which features a fitted bodice and a short train at its hem. It's often made with beautiful lace and silk brocade, with dramatic curves to accentuate the fitting. The formal look of the *holokuu* makes it so appropriate for ceremonies and special occasions, and can be worn by brides, graduates and spotlighted hula dancers.

A few other local designers have built their reputations by creating trademark styles of muumuus. One uses block-printed fabrics that reflect Hawaiian motifs such as flowers, ferns and the ancient petroglyphs in oversize scale and in earthy tones of tan, green, white and black. The styles are loose and flowing in the traditional look or fitted and stately for a more elegant effect.

Many specialty shops are springing up around town, selling simple yet fashionable muumuus at prices to fit the working girl's budget. These shops offer a choice selection of styles and sizes, and have become very popular shopping stops for many local women.

Visitors who favor the brighter and flashier Hawaiian prints and styles can buy direct, if they choose, from manufacturers' outlets and garment factories. Many of these outlets combine a retail operation with a friendly tour through their factories. This has proven to be a winning combination for both the local manufacturers and the tourists, and is frequently scheduled into many travel itineraries. Hawaiian garment factories can be found in and around Waikiki and on the outskirts of downtown Honolulu.

While a lot of island men and women like to complete their wardrobes during vacation and shopping trips to the mainland, many are finding that the well known chains from the West Coast and other places are making the move to Hawaii. What's saved on travel expenses can now be spent on clothes, and more of it too! Shops like these offer an exciting selection of fashion-forward separates, suits, dresses and accessories. They're found in the larger shopping centers and malls, and can be easily recognized by their familiar trademark decor and windows.

Many clothing delights can also be found in small women's boutiques which have come up all over town. In these shops, the owner is often times the fashion buyer too. Honolulu's women are discovering great finds here and are especially grateful that most items are available only in limited quantities. The entrepreneurs who run these boutiques are generally young women who are very fashion-conscious themselves. Their buying trips take them to New York and the Orient, and their selections show a taste that's distinctly unique, interesting and so appropriate for the women of Hawaii.

Haute couture does have its own little niche

The Aloha Shirt: The Punk Rock Outfit of the 1930's

Hawaii had seen its very first Aloha shirt. The material for these shirts had come from colorful bolts of silk imported from Japan that eventually found their way to the hands and

Imagine for a moment the typical attire of the 1930's. The styles were conservative. The colors were neutral tones, consisting mainly of pin-stripes, starched-whites and off-whites. Then suddenly, around 1933, a real shocker appeared on the streets of Honolulu. It was a shirt of such wildly different colors, patterns and styling that it actually shocked the people of Honolulu viewing it for the very first time.

needles of some inventive young man who simply dared to be different.

Today, this fashion is enjoying a tremendous resurgence of popularity, with literally millions of Aloha shirts having been produced in the past 50 years or so. But it all started back in 1933 with an inventful young person who simply put a colorful idea to work and inadvertently started a fashion trend.

Looking back, if rock star Cyndi Lauper had been around back in the 1930's, you can rest assured her hair may not have been so colorful, but you can bet your last dollar that her Aloha shirt sure would have been.

in Hawaii with designer boutiques boasting exclusive labels from around the world. Much of this trade is geared to the wealthy visitors who travel from abroad, and the shops tend to be located around the Waikiki area or in the world-renowned, often visited, Ala Moana Shopping Center.

High fashion can also be found in colorful little shops with feminine names, such as those situated ideally in some of the town's most popular shopping arcades. Variety and pleasure can be found here, with almost every type of shop to delight the discriminating fashion taste. The purpose of shopping here is for fun; and interludes are provided by exciting restaurants, bookstores, gift shops and art galleries.

For men, aloha shirts are the accepted wear for virtually all occasions, business or pleasure. These shirts can be found in major department stores and specialty shops for men. Shirts range from the baggy, surfer-style "silkie" to the dressier, classic style complete with the button-down collar. There's always a wide variety available, with prints and fabrics for every man's taste.

The aloha shirt began its rise to popularity in the early 1930's. The first ones were made with the multi-colored, brightly patterned silk and cotton fabrics imported from Japan. Intended mainly for children's wear, the colorful prints began to catch the eye of the trendy young adults of that era, and a fad was born.

Tourists coming to the islands enjoyed seeing and wearing the brilliant shirts with their decorative designs in various combinations of coconut trees, hula girls, flowers leis, Matson ships and Hawaiian words. It seemed that the more garish the fabric, the more they could enjoy their vacation and get into the spirit of the tropical landscape. Through the years, the tourist business in aloha shirts and attire has proven to be a steady market greatly appreciated by the local garment industry.

Another boon to the aloha shirt fad was the start of Aloha Week in 1947. When this annual celebration first began, men and women considered it a delight to forgo the normal business attire and happily donned their muumuus and aloha shirts for the week of festivities.

Since the institution of Aloha Fridays, when the start of the weekend is signaled with the wearing of aloha attire, this style of dress has become quite common. Aloha shirts, muumuus and other garments with Hawaiian prints are seen around town on a year-round, daily basis. In fact, the accepted business attire for men in almost every occupation is the aloha shirt. Gentlemen wearing otherwise are often questioned as to whether they're appearing in court or attending a job interview.

Because of the wide acceptance of the aloha shirt, one of its greatest selling points for local men is how easily it can be adapted to different types of occasions. The basic style remains unchanged, but fabrics and prints can be selected to fit the degree of formality. Aloha shirts make their appearances at every type of celebration, from weddings to dates to picnics. Of course, for really dress-down, fun and sun occasions, there's the perennial T-shirt. The humorous little gags and oneliners sported on many of these shirts make liberal use of local humor and everyday sayings, all in a statement of fun.

A Stitch in Time from Hawaii

So you think the world's best quilts are found on America's Eastern seaboard? Well, think again, because some of the world's finest and most sought after quilts are found right here in Hawaii.

The first quilting bee in Hawaii occurred in 1820 with the organization of a sewing circle by the New England missionary wives.

The first quilts stitched were done in the customary New England style with pieces of calico and other cloth pieced together. But there was a definite lack of calico cloth in the Hawaiian Islands in those days, so, in the innovative manner of the islands, another, better way to decorate the quilts evolved.

As the story goes, a local woman one day put her pure white cloth quilt out to bleach in the sun. Upon returning later, she found the blossoming branches of a nearby Lehua tree casting flower shadows on the quilt. She ingeniously stitched the beautiful flower design on her quilt and, thus, started the first of many intricate and highly original Hawaiian quilt designs.

Today, the Hawaiian-style quilt is an artform unto itself. And if you ask around, you may be lucky enough to find one to spread on your bed back on the mainland. Just think, you could snuggle up under this quilt from a faraway tropical island. And best of all, you'd never have to worry about finding sand in your bed.

Hildgund Jewelers

119 Merchant Street
Honolulu 96813
(808) 536-8778

Windward Mall
Kaneohe 96744
(808) 235-5120

Hawaii's oldest and most prestigious jewelry store has been in business since 1873. The art of hand enameling has not been lost; and is intricately and traditionally preserved. You can see this precious work in the exquisite coat of arms and other fine jewelry available at Hildgund. The Hildgund stores cater to those looking for the quality of old style craftsmanship, and include some of the rich and famous in their worldwide clientele.

You'll treasure each piece of Hawaiian heirloom jewelry for its fine quality. Enticing multi-strand seed pearl necklaces with a safe diamond lock, or a rope of gold set with a diamond pendant of custom Italian design are only a few of their other truly outstanding pieces.

Over half of the beautiful Hildgund displays originate from their own master craftsmen. The fascinating Hildgund Bucky, obtained her master goldsmith and master designer qualifications at the Art and Fashion College in Vienna, Austria. A very talented artist, she is responsible for many of the store's custom designs.

Hildgund also specializes in the remounting and modernizing of older jewelry. For the interested client in Honolulu, they will graciously fly in for inspection their most extravagant pieces from the Mauna Lani Bay Hotel; or, for consultation on a custom piece, Hildgund would be happy to visit you at the Mauna Lani Bay store.

There are three Hildgund Jewelry boutiques: one in Kaneohe's Windward Mall, the dream store in the Mauna Lani Bay Hotel on the Big Island and the retail and manufacturing branch in downtown Honolulu. Although the Merchant Street, Honolulu store is the home base for their creative energy, each of the stores is an exquisite showcase for their works of art. Here, originals in Lapis Lazuli, Aquamarine, Tanzenite, Peridots, Sapphire, Rubies, Emerald, and precious Topaz are produced daily.

So, for that treasured piece that you would like to have as your own family heirloom, visit the Hildgund stores and enjoy "the Hildgund touch;" old-style quality combined with attentive and personal service.

Ala Moana—Hawaii's Center

Ala Moana is one of Hawaii's major attractions as the largest open mall shopping center in the United States. With the many repeat trips of both locals and visitors, there are over 42 million individual visits each year . . . that's over 3 times the visitor count for Disneyland!

Both visitor and residents alike are equally at home here. It's a meeting and shopping ground for Hawaii's modern-day, family-oriented people. And a golden opportunity for the visitor interested in the island way of life. You might meet last night's maitre d' at ease in polo shirt and shorts, hunting for a new snorkle and fins. It's quite possible that you'll see last night's stunning hula dancer shopping for a pareau or a fine Italian handbag; or, those amazing young men with their flying surfboards meeting friends for snacks after

Ala Moana is also an international center for more than 150 shops and restaurants that include several large department stores and many smaller specialty shops. East meets West in a thousand happy ways. Hula skirts and coral from Hawaii, chocolates from the Netherlands, lacquer chests from the Orient, baskets from the Philippines, elephant hair jewelry from India, designer fashions from France or just good old American jeans. Everything imaginable under the Hawaiian sun can be found within the center. Those described in the following pages are a selection of some of the most interesting and inviting among the 150 shops and restaurants comprising Ala Moana.

While shopping, rest under a giant fern beside the Waiola Fountain (living waters), or relax alongside the cascading mall pools alive with colorful Japanese carp. Awaken to the

school. And when he's not working, this is where your taxi driver takes his *tutu* (grandmother), family, or friends on Saturday afternoons.

When you visit Ala Moana, your appetite will have a rainbow of cuisines to choose from. Lunch on dim sum, Cantonese stuffed dumplings, steamed and plump with fresh shrimp, vegetable, char siu pork and more. Feast on sushi, the famed fingersize Japanese rice masterpieces. Order genuine Hawaiian luau dishes such as lomi lomi salmon, laulau, kalua pig and poi. Have anything American that you desire, from deli-counter to candlelight and linen. Mexican, Italian and Continental cuisines are available also. Ala Moana is truly Hawaii's Center of international *kaukau* (food).

rhythm of the islands at Ala Moana's Centerstage, where a free Young People's Hula Show is offered on Sunday mornings at 9:30. Here are the bright young talents of Hawaii in colorful costumes and flowers to entertain you on your visit. Ala Moana also frequently stages surprise events—from fashion shows and special sale events to free concerts. We know you'll thoroughly enjoy the experience of shopping in Ala Moana Center.

Take the #8 bus, leaving Waikiki every ten minutes. Ala Moana is less than a five minute ride from the heart of Waikiki. And it's on the bus route to every major visitor attraction on Oahu. Parking's no problem—there are over 7,000 free parking stalls. So come as you are to friendly Ala Moana, Hawaii's center.

Irene's Hawaiian Gifts

Ala Moana Center-Lower Level
Honolulu 96814
(808) 946-6818

At Irene's Hawaiian Gifts you can choose from hundreds of intriguing items featuring the best in local artistry and cultural heritage of the islands. For instance, Irene's traditional Hawaiian dolls come in a variety of native costumes and will impress you with their authenticity.

There are gorgeous carvings in beautiful Hawaiian woods depicting the state fish *(humu-humunukunukuapua'a)* and the state flower (red hibiscus). The Hawaiian "Lei of Love" is made from the beautifully polished *kukui* nut (the state tree). Hawaii's state bird, the nene, and the good luck owl, *pueo,* can be found in beautifully detailed ceramic pieces of lasting artistic value. So whether you're looking for fine Hawaiian jewelry or a unique Hawaiian gift, Irene's Hawaiian Gifts has a lot to offer.

T-shirt shops can be found all over Waikiki and at the regional shopping centers. Gaining a following once again are the hand-done, air-brushed designs of dreamy ocean scenes and lush tropical colors that were popular during the sixties. There's also the standard silk-screened shirts with every possible Hawaiian design emblazoned on them. Styles vary for men and women from the classic "T" to the tank or crop top.

What better place to shop for beachwear but Hawaii? Surf shops, which originally sold only surfboards, now display racks of clothing for beach and water fun. Most of these shops carry many internationally known brands. The crowd here is generally young, local and ready to hit the water on a second's notice. Surfshops are a great place to buy gifts and mementos of a Hawaiian vacation.

Clothing for fun and for evenings, designer wear and business wear; fashions for every occasion are found in Hawaii. When one doesn't have to wear layers of sweaters, coats and stockings, the imagination is free to run wild! Without doubt, the islands are an exciting and delightful place in which to live, visit and work, and the clothes we wear are really just a reflection of life in paradise.

Paniolo Trading

Ala Moana Center—Lower Level
1450 Ala Moana Boulevard
Honolulu 96814
(808) 941-0135

The tradition of the Hawaiian cowboy is alive at the Paniolo Trading Company. They feature elaborately embroidered boots, lizard skin and work boots. Lee shirts, Levi jeans, Stetson hats, buckles and belts are all in stock at Paniolo Trading. So, whether you're looking for that special gift, English / Western riding supplies or the largest selection of name brands, you'll find what you need at Paniolo Trading.

The Rainbow Collection

Ala Moana Center—Lower Level
Honolulu 96814
(808) 947-9092

The Rainbow Collection, located on the street level of the Ala Moana Center is an exciting, innovative and beautiful place to shop. There are magnificent displays of natural and sculpted mineral pieces, and shelves lined with a dazzling array of exquisitely colored gemstones like alexandrite, tanzanite, green garnet and the elusive fine quality pink tourmaline. And, the rarest tourmaline of all, the gorgeous red rubellite, will delight even the most particular collector.

Owners Bob and Karla Brom take great care of these beautiful stones from the moment they come out of the ground, to the finished product and beyond. They are truly a complete jewelry store. They mine, cut, design, manufacture, appraise, repair and maintain these exquisite pieces.

Carrying a full spectrum of colored gemstones, they work closely with local artists to design and manufacture custom original pieces in various price ranges. This is one of those special stores you don't want to miss!

Villa Roma

Ala Moana Center
Upper Level
Honolulu
(808) 949-8377
Waikiki Shopping Plaza
Waikiki
(808) 923-4447
Windward Mall
Kaneohe
(808) 235-5990

At Villa Roma you'll find all the excitement of what's new in fashion. European styling and design in sportswear, classic separates and stunning eveningwear, is available in all the well known brand names. This one store has it all!

Shirokiya

Ala Moana Center—Upper Level
Honolulu 96814
(808) 941-9111

"Where East Meets West" can surely describe Shirokiya, a most unique department store from Japan. This is one of those stores that can tell you a great deal about an important part of the culture and tastes of Hawaii. They are unusual in that 60% of their merchandise is imported from the different prefectures of Japan. They bring you famous and noted products with traditional and cultural aspects, as well as the highly technological advancements of today.

Once you enter Shirokiya, you will absolutely feel that you are in a different world. Your eyes will feast on many unusual and exotic items of the orient. They carry a wide variety of top brand Japanese audio and video equipment, often before these items are available in mainland USA

stores. Food, housewares, furniture, arts, toys and fashion...they also carry European designer lines such as Gucci, Loewe, Valentino and Givenchy.

You can see and enjoy a delicious selection of traditional Japanese foods served within the store. The famous Japanese "bento" is served daily with over 50 varieties to choose from. Their evening buffet is another service guaranteed to make your shopping experience at the store a most enjoyable one. Starting at 4:00 p.m., the sushi bar opens for the more challenging appetizers. An added extra would be a visit to the famous Saint Germain Bakery on the mall level to really make your shopping complete.

The Shirokiya store is in the Ala Moana Center, with branch stores in the Pearlridge and Kaahumanu Shopping Centers. You'll also find them in the Boutique at the Hawaiian Regent Hotel. Visit Shirokiya and experience an important feature of Hawaii's culture.

Chocolates for Breakfast

Waikiki Shopping Plaza
Ala Moana Center-Upper Level
Kalakaua Avenue
Honolulu 96814   (808) 923-4426
(808) 947-3434

Chocolates for Breakfast is an exceptional store on a par with the boutiques of the world's great resorts. A favorite with local and visiting celebrities, Chocolates for Breakfast carries a wide range of fashion from the casually elegant to the best of the world's top designers. Diane Freis, Jessica McClintock, Norma Kamali, and Jonathan Hitchcock are just a few of the design lines available at this unique store.

Nicole

Ala Moana Center-Upper Level
Honolulu 96814
(808) 955-2033

The first thing you'll notice when entering Nicole are the vibrant colors ranging up and over the rainbow. Bright red, green, yellow, pink or turquoise and the combining of those colors in bows, straps, and inlays add to the wide variety. Carrying a complete selection of quality shoes for the fashion conscious working girl, Nicole has them all. Caressa, Allure, Calvin Klein, Evan-Picone, John Higdon, Nickels, David Evans, Bernardo, and Famolare, just to name a few. Eye-catching mesh and leather inlays exude quality. Sleek shoes, set off with beautiful reptile skins on the heel, toe or straps put Nicole in a class by itself. So when you're thinking of those clean, intricate lines that do so much for your wardrobe, think Nicole. A truly exceptional shoe store, catering to every woman's accessory needs.

Sports and Recreation

With gorgeously warm weather, sunshine practically every day and the steady trade winds blowing lightly, the islands of Hawaii are perfectly made for a large variety of outdoor sports and recreation. Sunning at the beach, swimming, surfing, playing in the park or jogging with friends are a few of the activities that have become a way of life for both visitors and *kama-aina* alike. It's a lifestyle that's undeniably healthy, relaxing and just plain fun to be a part of!

The beach is only a few minutes' drive from wherever you may be standing, on any spot, on any island. Living in these islands, surrounded by the Pacific Ocean, it's only natural that ocean sports have become the most popular for the local residents. Almost every child in Hawaii is taught the basics of water safety at an early age ("Never turn your back on the incoming waves!") and is quick to enjoy playing in the surf and to appreciate the taste of salt water.

The world-renowned Hawaiian sport is that of surfing. It is practiced on almost every beach on every island, with certain spots attracting better surfers, bigger crowds and more recognition, because of the tremendous size of the waves and excellent surfing conditions. Many of the prominent surfing sites are on the island of Oahu, where the big waves roll in on the famed North Shore during the winter months. Waimea Bay, Haleiwa, Sunset, the Banzai Pipeline; these beaches are close to being a surfer's Mecca, as they travel from around the world to take on the challenge of the sea. Waves reach astounding heights of 30 to 40 feet, near storm conditions, during the winter. It's an awesome sight to witness these huge breakers, and even the most daring of surfers respects the power of the ocean enough to stay ashore at such times.

Surfing was practiced by the early Hawaiians as a favorite pastime and a competitive sport. Both men and women rode the waves. Some of the first boards were made from a wood called olo and even highly prized koa. The boards were especially heavy and sometimes up to sixteen feet long. Since the long planks of wood were somewhat difficult to find, the big boards were reserved for chiefs and other high ranking *alii*.

In 1907, author Jack London visited the islands for a lengthy stay and experienced the joy and exhilaration of riding the waves himself. He wrote about it in *Learning Hawaiian Surfing: A Royal Sport at Waikiki Beach*. "The whole method of surge-riding and surf-fighting, I learned, is one of non-resistance. Dodge the blow that is struck at you. Dive through the wave that is trying to slap you in the face. Sink down, feet first, deep under the surface, and let the big smoker that's trying to smash you go by, far overhead. Never be rigid. Relax. Yield yourself to the waters that are ripping

The Biggest Wave Ever Surfed

The year was 1868 on Kauai. As the story goes, a giant tidal wave hit the island that year taking everyone by surprise. One local resident was in his home built of wooden planks when the tidal wave struck, smashing his home to bits. He suddenly found himself being swept out to sea with the debris that was once his home.

Being an inventive man first, and a surfer second, he did what he considered the logical thing and grabbed a plank from the wall of his house, climbed aboard and surfed the next wave in to safety ... a giant 50-footer.

True or not, the sport of surfing actually originated in Hawaii with the first surfboards being massive instruments 16 feet long, two feet wide and weighing up to 150 pounds. One early visitor to the islands in 1823 wrote that there was a "mass reaction to good waves ... farming, fishing and tapa-making were all dropped as men, women and children all went surf playing."

Today, the surfboards and the sport of surfing has changed dramatically, but the Islanders love of surfing hasn't. Because on those days when the surf is especially good, you'll likely find quite a few empty desks in offices and classrooms and quite a few occupied surfboards all across the islands.

and tearing at you. When the undertow catches you and drags you seaward along the bottom, don't struggle against it. If you do, you are liable to be drowned, for it is stronger than you. Yield yourself to that undertow. Swim with it, not against it, and you will find the pressure removed. And, swimming with it, fooling it so that it does not hold you, swim upward at the same time. It will be no trouble at all to reach the surface." Obviously, Mr. London knew how to respect the power of the ocean. It's something that every smart surfer learns very quickly

Hawaii's most famous surfer is the legendary Duke Kahanamoku. His love of the ocean, swimming and surfing was apparent throughout his life, and it was this love that he took around the world as Hawaii's goodwill ambassador. Duke first gained fame during the 1912 Olympics in Stockholm, Sweden, where, representing the United States in the swimming competitions, he broke the 100 meter world record. Duke resided in his beloved islands until the end of his years, and is credited with promoting the sport of surfing to its presently recognized status.

Today, surfing is big business and very popular all over the world. Australia, California, Japan, France, Spain, and Peru are some of the international locations where the surf craze has hit hard. There is a professional surfer's association that holds surf meets annually in Hawaii, under the sponsorship of several well-known companies. Network television tries to cover these events, but being at the mercy of surf conditions and tide, which sometimes necessitates the cancellation of meets, doesn't make it easy for them.

Newer, lightweight types of boards of man-made materials are favored by today's younger surfers because of the way they can maneuver and fly faster on the waves. Surfing paraphenalia of all kinds is flooding the market with surf leashes, boogie boards, surfer magazines, jams and baggies, all big sellers to surfers and non-surfers alike. Wearing the right piece of clothing is important, as the "surfer look" has always been a serious study in the art of looking cool.

A first cousin to surfing and becoming very popular in recent years is the sport of windsurfing. Someone once came up with the ingenious idea of securing an upright sail to a surfboard, allowing surfers to ride the water on a waveless day. Lo and behold, the art of windsurfing was born. The sport has literally taken off since. On a day when the winds are blowing briskly off the coast of Diamond Head, or the shores of Kailua Bay on the windward side of Oahu, you'll see dozens of bright and colorful sails on boards being skillfully maneuvered in, and up out of the water, by enthusiastic windsurfers. The uninitiated observer may wonder how these sailing boards are ever navigated back to shore.

Another highly popular ocean sport, that doesn't require a board, is bodysurfing. Bodysurfers do exactly what that word implies; they use their bodies in a rigid, extended position, much like a board, and ride over the waves. Many skilled bodysurfers use swim fins to help them glide in and out of the waves. Popular bodysurfing

spots are Makapuu and Sandy Beach on Oahu's east shore, where the waves really churn and pound up right on shore. These are not the best places for a novice to learn, so when conditions look prohibiting, take heart in watching the exciting show from shore. The amount of abuse the waves can render is terrifying. Yet, at the same time, to experience a good ride is just exhilarating.

A variation on this sport is boogie-boarding. A small, compact board made of polyurethane foam, boogie boards are held under the body to give a smoother and faster ride. These boards often come with leashes the way that surfboards do, which means less chasing and more riding the board. Boogie boards come in various sizes to fit the bodies of all ages, and can make wave-riding a great deal of fun, even when the waves are small.

Plain old swimming is still lots of fun, too, enjoyed by locals and visitors alike. There's no hardship in finding a beach with one's favorite conditions: a little wave action, a warm sun, an ocean vista or other beachgoers to watch. The few problems that may occur, might be finding a little privacy and parking, especially on the weekends, when a gorgeous Hawaiian day attracts everyone!

Another water activity that a large number of people find enjoyable is scuba-diving and snorkeling. Throughout the islands, there are places where both the seasoned diver and the novice can find exciting times. For the inexperienced, diving means taking instruction and

Paradise Pedicabs
Waikiki 96815
(808) 922-8161

The most intimate way to discover paradise, in a Paradise Pedicab of course! Personalized tours. Sightsee exotic hideaways. A once in a lifetime experience. Knowledgeable and qualified guides. Call Paradise Pedicab at 922-8161 for information and dispatch.

143

The Scoop On Beaches

Your first glimpse of the world famous Waikiki Beach, with the spectacular view of Diamond Head in the background, will remind you of the postcards, calendars and films you've seen before. One of the most photographed beaches in the world, this two-mile stretch of white sand, hosts over 4 million visitors annually. Some come to swim, surf or canoe and others just to watch. The people are as diverse as the activities; so much so, that it's difficult to imagine this beach devoid of sun tanned bodies, bikinis and bright beach towels!

So that your visit will be as pleasant as possible, it's important to know the different types of beaches and what safety precautions are recommended. Hawaii has three kinds of beaches: County, public and private. The county run beachparks have bathroom facilities, public telephones and lifeguards on duty, equipped with emergency supplies. Public beaches are the most common around the islands, but do not, in general, have any lifeguards or bathroom facilities. There are only a few private beaches in Hawaii, restricted mainly because of their general inaccessibility preventing one from entering unless you're a resident or guest in a close beachfront home or hotel.

There are six safety rules to understand before you venture out with loved ones into Hawaii's waters. The first rule is to never go swimming by yourself. The ocean's waves are powerful and one could tire easily and need support getting ashore. If you see large waves, a rocky coast or a beach that drops sharply to the water, do not swim there. Your chances of enjoying yourself would be slim with these conditions. If you're in the water and sucked down with the undertow, don't fight against the current. In relationship to the beach, swim parallel or diagonally to it toward the white water until you're out of the current, then head back to the shore. If you are swimming in water where there are windsurfers, regular surfers or boogie board riders, stay clear of the surfers and their boards. Unintentional contact with those boards can be very dangerous. And, when you arrive at the beach obey warning signs, like red flags, cautioning you that there is a dangerous

undertow. Finally, it is a good idea to beware when swimming in fresh water. These attractive pools and rivers usually have sharp rocks on the bottom. Generally, always check the safety of a beach before entering the water. Don't be too alarmed, it's fortunate that there are plenty of beaches for everyone to find their favorite spot with the right conditions.

Calm waters, year round, make Waikiki Beach one of the safest in Hawaii for young and old alike. There are concessions selling beverages, snacks and beach supplies dotted along the beach, owned by the various hotels. There are also suntanning centers available to sell you the best in tanning and skin protection products. It's a good idea to have them recommend lotions or oils according to your skin type, as well as the best hours to tan given the length of your stay. Following these tips will give you the best chance of going home with a rich, dark and glowing tan you'll always remember.

Surf's up! Oahu claims it has some of the best surfing beaches in the world, and surfers worldwide agree: amateur and professional contests draw the best to Sunset Beach with winter waves regularly topping 30 feet. Generally calm in summer months, the North Shore, and especially Waimea Beach areas, are for spectators only when the big ones roll in. Often televised, professional surfers meet the challenge of winter waves for increasingly larger stakes and points towards world titles, almost every weekend in Winter.

Another winter surfing favorite is Maui's Honolua Bay, with perfect tubes; often up to 14 feet and one of the finest breaks in the state. Kauai's top surfing spot is Pakala Beach, 2 miles west of Waimea. The long walls provide seemingly endless rides and the local people have nicknamed it "infinity beach." Worthy of mention, too, is Major's Bay, near Barking Sands Naval Station with good winter and summer waves. Beaches state wide have surfboard rentals and instruction available at nearby surf shops or at the beaches themselves, especially Waikiki.

Windsurfing! Soon to be an Olympic event, this is the fastest growing water sports here and certainly one of the most exhilarating. Jumps from big waves can reach 50 feet or more, and speeds over 40 miles per hour can be reached on a tack. Maui boasts a world class windsurfing beach, called Hookipa, located on the road to Hana. Breezy days draw upwards of 50 enthusiasts. Beware: this is not a place for learners and swimming is definitely not advised due to the strong local currents. On Oahu, "Lighthouse" at Diamond Head near Waikiki, offers beginners and experts alike constant trade winds and every size wave imaginable. Although a lengthy walk down from the road, the scenery is marvelous and it's just a short drive from Waikiki. Stop at the Lighthouse turnout for a spectacular view almost any afternoon. At the

North end of the North Shore's Sunset Beach, trade winds carry windsurfers flying skyward, side by side with the regular surfers. Winds here often blow steadily at 25 miles per hour, making for ideal wave jumping action. Also on Oahu, on the West side, windsurfing is just catching on, and Makaha Beach Park is becoming popular year round.

Snorkeling! Hanauma Bay is unsurpassed anywhere in the state for both accessibility and an abundance of marine life. Dozens of species are tame enough to eat right from your hand and underwater pictures are often crowded with fish fins and face masks. Go early to enjoy uncrowded and calm morning waters, but the fish are hungry all day long. Stay in shore to safely enjoy the total environment and the large schools of fish. Mask, snorkel and fins are available for rent in Waikiki, as well as complete tours that include instruction and lunch. The tours are superb for first timers, but don't forget camera, film and especially sunscreen. Also, close to Waikiki, Diamond Head Beach Park has extensive shallow reefs that begin at the foot of the crater. Showers are available and a small grassy area invites frequent rests and picnicking. Within walking distance of most major hotels is the beautiful Kaimana Beach with a natural coral reef just off shore and calm waters that invite swimming and other more passive water activities.

Each island has many great beaches that are easily accessible and breathtaking to view. To list and describe them would take close to a hundred pages, so we recommend that when you're on the island you're going to visit, check local publications or travel desks to find the best beach for your particular activity. Whichever island, the beaches of Hawaii are a great place to spend your vacation time tanning, exercising and having fun. Enjoy them the way that the original Hawaiians have for centuries before you.

Kailua Beach, Oahu

maybe even receiving certification. Many organizations can provide safe instruction and the whole process can be accomplished easily and quickly in a short vacation. Snorkeling does not require certification, nor does it require expensive equipment and yet, in some areas the fun that it can give is truly outstanding. Floating leisurely, over bright coral reefs or rocks, the view of the undersea world is incredible. The coral reefs are filled with an abundance of marine life. Some of the fish are so tame and accustomed to human intrusion that you're treated to a show every time you visit this natural underwater attraction. Another favorite pastime in Hawaii is wading in the shallow water near the shoreline, feeding the fish with crumbs of bread (the island variation of feeding pigeons at the zoo!).

What's a cross between water-skiing and windsurfing and looks like a motor-cross on the ocean? Jet-skiing, of course! Jet-skis can provide an exhilarating ride, allowing you to race across the water for the fun of it. It's best on a relatively flat day when the waves don't drag down the horsepower of the motor-driven skis. It also allows the skier a lot more control than conventional water-skiing, although spills into the water are not completely unavoidable. Skilled jet-skiers can be seen doing "wheelies" and other fancy jumps over the water, just having fun and showing off.

Fishing is very popular in Hawaii and understandably so. The ocean has always been a generous provider of food from the days of the first Hawaiians. With the popularity of seafood at many local parties and in island homes, fishing is a convenient way to meet the demand and appetite for fresh ocean catches. On top of that, it's a source of recreation and relaxation enjoyed by many. There are many forms of fishing, including casting from shore or dock, shallow water fishing from a small boat, or deep sea fishing for the larger game fish. There are several boat operators who take small groups of people to their secret, favorite spots off-shore for deep sea fishing. The grand fishing event of the year is the Billfish Tournament held annually in Kona,

on the island of Hawaii. Fishing teams arrive from around the world to do battle with the marlin, vying for the winner's prize for landing the biggest. There's an exciting feeling of competitive tension at the end of each tournament day, when thousands of pounds of fish are weighed in at the Kona pier.

Making a popular comeback, with the Hawaiian cultural renaissance of the past few years, has been the sport of competitive paddling. Canoe clubs from throughout the islands practice regularly, in waterways and the open ocean, with their specially designed and crafted outrigger canoes. Every canoe has a Hawaiian name and receives a Hawaiian blessing. The clubs sponsor men's and women's teams, in different age

brackets, in various competitions. Paddling is also offered as a credit course in many high school curricula.

The big event of the year for paddlers is the annual Molokai-to-Oahu Canoe Race. Teams from Hawaii, California, Tahiti and even some of the inland states of the USA, compete to be the first to cross the grueling 40-mile channel between the islands of Molokai and Oahu. It is an exciting scene to watch from the Diamond Head look-out as the canoes near the finish line and at the end of the race when the winning team pulls their outrigger onto the sand.

Sailing is also a large recreational sector in the islands, either with the traditional hobie catamarans or the more orthodox single hull vessels. Several catamaran rental agenies exist, especially around Waikiki. Because of the native coral reefs and shallow areas, it's more difficult to find larger sailing craft for personal charter. Many other crewed charters do exist, and offer a very enjoyable recreational alternative, with a whole variety of options.

For the world class sailor and cruiser, Hawaii is well known. During 1986, several boats and teams are based in Hawaii in preparation for the America's Cup defense, to be held in Australia in 1987. These large, graceful sailing vessels are a beautiful sight, racing against each other on Honolulu Bay.

Every two years, the world's longest regularly scheduled race brings a large group of ocean sailing boats, and an even larger (party-minded) group of sailors to Honolulu. The Trans Pac race, from Los Angeles to Diamond Head, brings some of the world's best known long distance boats to Hawaii. That's a signal for a series of very competitive trophy races to be held around the islands, over a period of several weeks during the summer. The whole scene is highlighted by an almost continuous celebration amongst the boat crews.

While sailing is a very popular local activity on a year round basis, the one disadvantage for most residents is that boatslips are very difficult to obtain, with waiting lists up to 5 years at the municipal Ala Wai Yacht Harbor, just outside Waikiki.One exciting sport that doesn't take advantage of the ocean, except for its breathtaking view, is hang gliding. This is not a pastime for the faint hearted who suffer "high anxiety." Taking off into the strong tradewinds, from the cliffs behind Makapuu Bay, suspended from a "kite" in a cocoon-type bag, can only be a thrillseeker's delight. The view from the top, however, on a clear, sunny day is quite magnificent! The view from down below, from the safety of the beach is also quite a display, as you look up and see those large, colorful flying machines floating above.

Hiking is a popular form of recreation that goes high up into the mountains and away from the clutter of the city. There are many well traveled hiking trails, of varying difficulty, on each of the islands. The mountains of Hawaii provide lush, green landscapes and unique tropical flora and fauna for nature-lovers. Local hikers enjoy walking the trails and picking leaves and ferns that can be used to make *haku,* or braided, leis. Most of all, they appreciate the exercise, fresh air and tranquil peace of the mountains.

One of the other major visitor sports is golf. Hawaii has over 40 golf courses scattered throughout the islands. Although the majority of the courses are on Oahu, there are several world class courses on the neighbor islands. Each year, several international tournaments are held at various courses around the state of Hawaii, such as Kapalua Bay and Princeville. Nowhere in the world will you find a course in more scenic settings. So, if you're a member of a golf or country club back home, bring your membership card along and arrange for guest privileges at one of the private clubs in Hawaii.

In recent years, Hawaii has become one of the world's favorite tennis locales. There are some fantastic court complexes at a number of various hotels in the islands and a variety of good public courts are also available through the Parks and Recreation departments.

Skiing in Hawaii? Of course, and with a season from December through April (weather conditions permitting). However, one can only enjoy this sport on the Big Island at Mauna Kea, with an altitude of almost 14,000 feet. Although not as commercially developed and organized as most well known ski-resorts, the skiing can be excellent, often surrounded by absolutely breathtaking views. To reach these slopes, it's a several hour drive in a four wheel drive vehicle, or if you prefer, the ski shop where you rent your equipment will provide a shuttle service. Wouldn't you just love to tell your friends back home about this one!

Polo in Hawaii

POLO! In Hawaii? Very much so! This year, 1986, is the centennial celebration of the introduction of the sport of kings, princes, movie stars (and cowboys) to Hawaii. This exciting equine sport was first played in Hawaii during the heyday of the ranching and plantation era in the Islands in 1886.

On Oahu, the polo matches are very much a public event with teams coming to Hawaii from all over the world to test their skills against the Hawaii teams. British, Argentine, Chilean, Mexican, Australian, Kenyan and Irish teams, amongst others, journey to Mokuleia during the season from mid March through August.

Matches are every Sunday beginning at 2:00 p.m., with gates open to the public at 11:00 a.m. The Hawaii Polo Club is headquartered at Mokuleia on Oahu's scenic North Shore—only 45 minutes from Waikiki. The playing field, right on the beach, is one of the most picturesque spots in the Islands. Picnicking is ideal with restroom and picnic facilities available, along with food concessions and a bar, during the matches.

Admission is $5.00 for adults, and children are admitted free. Special events planned for the 1986 season are the British-Hawaii games (April 20th & 27th), the Celebrity Benefit Match (June 22nd), and the Centennial Celebration-Great Gatsby Day (a fundraiser for the Historic Hawaii Foundation, August 17th).

For further information, call the Hawaii Polo Club at 942-5210.

Snow skiing at Mauna Kea

football games—the NFL Pro Bowl and the Aloha Bowl. For resident Hawaiians it's one of the few occasions that they can see the big football names in person. That partly makes up for all those Monday Night Football games that often start in mid afternoon in Hawaii, because of the time difference!

With all of this fun and sun, it's no wonder that people have come to think of Hawaii as the playground of the Pacific. Those who live here, and the thousands more visiting each year, know a good thing when they see it. People who enjoy working up a sweat and actively seeking exercise and movement can choose from a wide variety of games and sports. Others, who would rather participate as spectators, also have their choice of events to watch. In Hawaii, the hard part is deciding which one to choose.

Naturally, residents of Hawaii indulge in many of the usual American pastimes, such as baseball, softball and volleyball. Various organizations provide structured competition, and many local, individual games are played. As you're driving around outside of Waikiki, you may be lucky enough to see a game being played at one of the numerous fields. Stop for a few minutes and share the experience of the locals. Once each year, Aloha Stadium, near the Honolulu airport, becomes the scene for two important American

At Your Service-
Information
for Visitors

From the early 19th century, Hawaii has been a service oriented community, and this is even more true now. A large selection of services are available to support both visitors (for pleasure or business) and residents alike. There are also a few important state regulations, that each and every visitor should be aware of; after all, running up against unknown rules can be inconvenient at best.

Whether it's business or personal, everything from beauty, medical, dental, office support, travel/tour, educational seminars, real estate, banking and almost any other "home away from home" service you can think of, can be found during your stay in Hawaii.

Agricultural Regulations

All incoming and outgoing baggage is inspected at the airport. Most fresh fruits, vegetables and plants may not be taken out, with the exception of pineapples and coconuts. Papayas, avocados and bananas can be taken from the islands if they are fumigated first at the Plant Quarantine Division, 701 Ilalo Street in Honolulu. Mangoes and lichees must be peeled and pitted before export to the Mainland. Fumigated fruits approved for export to foreign countries are available for purchase at the airport. In some stores you can also find fumigated seeds/seedlings of various Hawaiian plants, which may also be

taken home as the start of your tropical garden (if your home climate supports it!).

Most of the flower leis sold at Hawaii's lei stands may be taken to the Mainland. Those which may not be taken out are the rose, gardenia, jade flower and maunaloa.

Animal Quarantine

Hawaii is rabies free. There are restrictions on the importation of all animals and birds, with some animals being quarantined at the station on Oahu for 120 days at the owner's expense. Call the animal quarantine station at (808) 488-8462 for further information.

Banks

Many banks in Hawaii are associated with Mainland U.S.A. or Japanese banks. Almost all banks have routine credit card and traveler's check cashing services, and many have currency exchange facilities. Normal banking hours are Monday through Thursday, 8:30 a.m. to 3:00 p.m., and Fridays, 8:30 a.m. to 6:00 p.m. Many banks have 24 hour automatic teller machines for certain credit card/cash card transactions.

Bus

Although bus transportation is more widely available on Oahu than on the outer-islands, where the buses mostly link the airport to other points, public transportation can still take you many places at the top of each visitor's list.

There are several routes that would be special to visitors staying in Waikiki. The #2 (School-Middle Street) starts at Kapiolani Park (near Diamond Head) traveling down Kuhio Avenue for such destinations as the Bishop

Museum, Mission Houses Museum, Honolulu Academy of Arts, and downtown area including Iolani Palace, State Capitol and the Civic Center. The #8 will take you to Ala Moana Shopping Center, the largest open shopping center in the world. The #20 (Airport) will take you to Pearl Harbor. And the #52 (departing from Ala Moana Center) will give you the circle island route; a four hour trip over the Pali to Kailua, along the coast to the northern tip, then down the interior of the island back to where you began.

The fare is 60 cents for adults and 25 cents for students and people over 65. Exact change is required. For more information on bus routes and schedules, call 531-1611.

Climate

Hawaii's tropical climate is superb. From April through October, temperatures range from 73 degrees F to 88 degrees F. It's a little cooler in the winter months, but the mercury rarely drops below 60 degrees F. Higher altitudes, such as Kula and Haleakala on Maui and Waimea/Kamuela on the Big Island, get much cooler. The tradewinds keep the islands from getting too muggy. Once in a while a southerly or westerly "Kona" wind creates a humid condition, but it never lasts more than a few days. Hurricanes rarely strike Hawaii. Civil Defense provides adequate warning in the event a hurricane does threaten the islands.

Each island has two main weather areas - the windward and leeward sides. The windward areas, facing North, are subject to the full tradewinds, and may occasionally receive light showers. For this reason, the windward areas have more lush tropical growth and although the temperature may feel a little cooler, it's deceiving. The occasional rain showers are also refreshing rather than a problem. The leeward areas are dryer and because they're sheltered from the full tradewinds by the mountains, they will feel warmer.

Currency

Foreign currency may be converted at one of several exchange offices at the International Airport terminal, and at some bank branches throughout the State.

Directions

The most common directions given in Hawaii are not North, South, East and West. Instead, islanders use mauka, which means towards the mountains; and makai, which means towards the sea. On Oahu, they also use Diamond Head or Koko Head, two famous landmarks to the east of Waikiki; and Ewa, a town west of Pearl Harbor. These directions are used in traffic reports as well as casual conversation, so it's useful to try and make some sense out of them.

For the Handicapped Traveler

Visitors who are not so spry, and require wheelchair or other special assistance, will find it relatively easy getting around in Hawaii. Many hotels have wheelchair ramps, rooms, baths, parking stalls and low phones to accommodate the handicapped traveler. The same goes for major points of interest, beach parks, shopping centers and most major show rooms. Honolulu and the outer-island airports all have the proper ramps or elevators; even the cruise ships are well equipped.

There are two tour companies, Why Not Travel at (808) 947-7044 and Handicabs of the Pacific at (808) 524-3866 that can handle tours for any individual or group with special needs. Also, a bus service is available in Honolulu for those requiring assistance to move around; call the Handi-Van Service at (808) 955-1717 for more details.

Immigration

Visitors to Hawaii arriving from foreign countries must show a valid passport with a USA visa and a health certificate with a current smallpox vaccination. On arrival from a country outside of the USA, visitors and residents alike will have to clear U.S. customs control.

153

Island Information and Assistance Centers.

OAHU

Police — Fire — Ambulance	911
Telephone Information	1-411
Life Guard—Waikiki	922-3888
Coast Guard Rescue	536-4336
Hawaii Visitors Bureau	923-1811
Oahu Weather Report	836-0121
Surf Report	839-1952
Hawaiian Waters Report	836-3921
Time	983-3211
24-Hour Prescription Service	737-1777
Suicide & Crisis Center	521-4555
Poison Center	941-4411
Honolulu County Medical Society	536-6988
Physicians Exchange	524-2575
Hawaii Dental Association	536-2135

MAUI

Police — Fire — Ambulance	911
Coast Guard Rescue	244-5256
HELP—24-hr. medical service	244-3748
Hawaii Visitors Bureau	244-9141
Maui Visitors Information Center	661-8340
Weather Report	877-5111
Hawaiian Waters Report	877-3477

KAUAI

Police — Fire — Ambulance	911
Coast Guard Rescue	245-8111
Hawaii Visitors Bureau	245-6761
State Visitor Information	245-3582
Aloha Bus	245-9232

BIG ISLAND

Police — Fire — Ambulance	911
Coast Guard Rescue	961-6181
Hawaii Visitors Bureau	935-5271
State Visitors Information—Kona	329-3423
State Visitors Information—Hilo	935-1018
Volcano Eruption News	967-7977
Weather Report—Big Isle	935-8965
Weather Report—Hilo	935-6360
Hawaiian Waters Report	935-6976

Mail

Current United States postal rates apply. For up-to-date information about rates and the amount of time it takes letters and postcards to reach their destinations, call or visit the nearest post office. The main post office is located on King Street across from Iolani Palace in downtown Honolulu (546-5625). There are branches at Ala Moana Shopping Center and on Saratoga Road in Waikiki, as well as in the major towns on Oahu and each of the Neighbor Islands. Hours are: Monday through Friday, 8 AM–4:30 PM, and Saturday 8 AM–12 noon.

Various office and business service companies exist in most large towns in the islands. The following service centered in Honolulu.

THE MAILBOX (808) 942-3785
1750 Kalakaua Avenue, Suite 103
Honolulu 96826

For yachtsmen, writers and travelers; be represented in the most professional way with your own reception desk at "Century Suites", including mail, telephone and a prestigious address.

Medical/Dental

Should you require medical or dental services during your stay in Hawaii, the good thing to remember is that you're still in the United States and any problem that might arise can be taken care of quickly and effectively.

Medical and dental services can be found in the yellow pages of the telephone directory. The following services specialize in providing visitor assistance. However, for ambulance service emergency, telephone 911.

ALA MOANA FAMILY & EMERGENCY MEDICINE (808) 943-1111
1860 Ala Moana (across Hilton Hawaiian Village)
1778 Ala Moana (across Ilikai Hotel)
Free Hotel Pick-Up
Affiliated with Queens Medical Center 24 hours—
7 days a week
Medical, surgical or emergency services.

DOCTORS ON CALL (808) 926-4777
Hyatt Regency Hotel (2424 Kalakaua, 4th floor)
Reef Towers Hotel (227 Lewers);
Hawaiian Regent Hotel (2552 Kalakaua)
Complete medical services; house calls to Waikiki Hotels.

Safety

When traveling in the islands, always lock room and car doors and use caution with strangers. Car break-ins and beachside burglaries and thefts of personal property do occur and can spoil anyone's vacation. Avoid hitchhiking at any time. If you have car problems in areas away from population centers, call (if possible) the car rental company or the police and wait for assistance.

The Sun

Practically everyone who comes to Hawaii visits a beach for sunbathing or water sports. In Hawaii, the sun's rays can be vicious. Too much

exposure to the sun without protection, will not only be very painful, but severe cases may require hospitalization that can certainly ruin your vacation! Visitors are advised to liberally apply a good sunscreen to the exposed portions of their skin prior to spending time in the sun. It's best to tan slowly, depending on your skin type, and to build a tolerance for Hawaii's intense rays.

There are many remedies available for minor sunburn, but the locals prefer the juice of a freshly cut aloe plant. Aloe plants are not sold at drug counters, but many remedies contain the juice. Ask a pharmacist for assistance.

Telephone

You can dial anywhere in the world from the Hawaiian Islands. Long-distance telehone call rates are listed in the various county telephone directories, or may be obtained by dialing "0" for operator assistance. Within each island, local calls from a pay telephone are 25 cents. Calls between islands are toll calls, and often can be more expensive than calling from Honolulu to the mainland USA. Most hotels have a minimum charge for each call from your room.

Operator Assistance	0
Directory Assistance	1-411
Military Information	471-7411
Calls to Continental USA 1-(Area Code) Number	

Time

Time differences are as follows:

Hawaii Standard Time	12 noon
Pacific Standard Time	2 PM*
Mountain Standard Time	3 PM*
Central Standard Time	4 PM*
Eastern Standard Time	5 PM*
Atlantic Standard Time	6 PM*
London	10 PM
Paris	11 PM
Japan	7 AM Tomorrow

*For Daylight Savings Time (usually May-October), add one hour.

Do not be frustrated by time schedules in Hawaii; they're often not as strict as those on the mainland or elsewhere. Islanders have a way of arriving for appointments about 10 minutes late. This is a local phenomenon known as "Hawaiian Time." To arrive at a party or an appointment about 10 minutes late is "being on Hawaiian time." For the correct time in Hawaii, call 983-3211.

Tipping

A 15 percent tip for good service is appropriate at most restaurants. Airport porter's fees run about 50 cents per bag. Taxi drivers usually receive 15 percent plus 25 cents a bag.

Final Word

All of you have traveled many miles over the ocean to visit Hawaii, and some of you do not even speak the language. We admire your willingness to travel this distance, and thank you for coming to Hawaii to share our slice of paradise. After all, if it wasn't for people with a sense of adventure - Hawaii would never have been discovered.

Credits

Cover Photos:
Tom Selleck - Courtesy of C.B.S.
Charo - Courtesy of Kjell Rasten

Feature Photos:
Magnum P.I. Cast - Courtesy of C.B.S.
Charo Feature Photo - Courtesy of Kjell Rasten

Photo/Art Credits

David Cornwell: Pages 3, 5, 6, 7, 10, 22–23, 26LO, 27T, 28, 30, 33T, 40T, 53, 54, 59B, 59C, 60T, 60C, 60B, 61T, 71B, 72, 88B, 108TL, 108B, 112B, 112C, 141, 146B, 149INSET, 157.

Jeff Helberg: Pages 21, 32T, 34, 38, 39T, 39B, 73, 79B, 118BC, 134, 144T, 148T, 153T.

Ric Noyle: Pages 9, 32B, 52T, 75T, 102, 112BR, 131, 133, 135, 143T, Back Cover

Douglas Peebles: Pages 1, 2, 4, 17, 26C, 26RI, 26RO, 27B, 58B, 62T, 78B, 85B, 86, 92, 96B, 100, 101T, 118R, 142, 145, 148B, 150TL, 155, Cover Background

Allan Seiden: Pages 13, 14, 15, 16, 29, 33B, 37, 43T, 52B, 61B, 97, 129TR, 144B, 146T, 151, 156B.

William Waterfall: Pages 18, 20, 24, 25, 26, 31, 35, 50, 58T, 62B, 80, 124, 147, 149, 152B, 154T, 154B.

Caree Waltz: Pages 78T, 119, 132B, 139.

Contributing Writers

Shannon Stewart, Ann Schwartz, Wayne Harada, Paula Mantel, Jeff Reiss, Deborah Greene, Tracy Bennett, Judy Frostega, June Kaneshiro, Sam Malvaney, Cathi Bell, David Huffman and Elissa Josephsohn.

Concept and text by Michael and Kathea Latham
Produced by Pacific Publishing
Personal Assistant: Teresa Garbe
Basic Design: Bill Fong and Leo Gonzalez
Layouts: The Other Type
Cover Design: Allen Hori
Production Design: Allen Hori
Typesetting: Unitype

Printed in Japan

Premier Edition - June, 1986

Pacific Publishing
1750 Kalakaua Avenue, Suite 3901
Honolulu, Hawaii 96826

Index